Dancing Thru Lye

On Toes of Gold

By Lucile Iverson South

Production under supervision of
Designers Eye Graphics
PO Box 381 - Cliff, New Mexico 88028
Cover Design by Cassandra Colley ~ Designers Eye Graphics
Artwork by Diane Iverson

Printed and Bound in the United States of America
International Standard Book Number: 1-57636-153-5

This book is dedicated to the memory
of my loving Mother,
Who made it possible
For my dreams to come true

and to

My wonderful husband, Rider South,
Who encouraged me to write my story
and has supported my journey thru its pages

ACKNOWLEDGEMENTS

My first book was made possible because of the help of many friends. They were willing listeners and gave me courage to continue through the years. I want to thank Janaloo Hill Hough, Diane Lindsey, La Vera Shoup, Annette Parent and Betty Martin. And last but not least thanks to my nephew Douglas Iverson and his wife Diane.

When it was decided to make a second printing of the book, it was Cassandra Colley of Designer's Eye Graphics who took my ideas and made them a reality, again. Thanks also to Margaret Loring for her expertise in editing the book.

Table of Contents

Bobby Burgess the well-known dancer in the Laurence Welk Television Show.

Here are his comments about Lucile and her book:

"Growing up in Long Beach, CA and following Lucile Iverson's dancing adventures paralleled mine almost to a tee, but Vaudeville vs. Television.

A very good writer, this book is a fast well written read, especially for those interested in the dancing and entertainment world.

It's fun, it's personal, and it's informative all at the same time.

It's a romantic story, first kiss & first love.

It's a vaudeville story, a peek at backstage, and life on the road. It tells the joys, the pains, the ups and downs of show biz. It's all there.

I highly recommend getting ready to be entertained, so find a comfortable chair because you won't be able to put this book down."... Bobby Burgess

The Russian Dance was One of My Favorite Dances

My Highland Fling Dance Costume

First Toe Dance

Introduction

"When the music starts, Lucile, you go to the center of the floor." As she spoke, Dorothy Baas, my first dance teacher put her hand on my shoulder. She was waiting for the orchestra to start the introduction to "Whispering," a popular Fox trot of the 1920's. The orchestra leader's baton descended, and the music started. Miss Dorothy's hand gave me a gentle nudge toward the center of the shining ballroom floor.

I was just eight years old, and this was my first solo ballet entrance, a tiny figure in a ballet costume. My little toe slippers went tap-tap-tapping on the slippery dance floor, and I was being careful not to fall. The spotlight followed my blonde head to the center of the ballroom floor. There it became a pool of light in an otherwise darkened world.

I remembered my dance. I remembered to smile. All too soon, the dance was over. I raised my arms over my head and pointed my toe to the side. I was ready for the two cartwheels and then my Grand Bow. Miss Baas probably held her breath. Cartwheels in toe slippers! She was breaking tradition by ending the ballet dance with an acrobatic trick, but she wanted to show off my cartwheels.

The first one was good. On the second one, oh no! My foot slipped when it came down, and suddenly I was on the floor! At least part of it was right, so I tucked one foot under me and pointed the other in the proper position for the Grand Bow. After lowering my head for a couple of seconds, I sprang to my feet and ran back to my teacher and my mother. My heart was beating so hard I hardly heard the applause.

Miss Baas again gave me a gentle push towards the spotlight waiting for me and said, "Go take your bow." I was embarrassed because I had fallen. Miss Bass was so proud of me and I had let her down. While running to the center of the ballroom floor I had an inspiration. I knew what I should do.

Again, I pointed my toe and repeated my two cartwheels, but this time I did not fall. Deliberately, I slid to the floor and went into my Grand Bow. The audience gasped, and then I heard the applause, louder than before. I ran back to mother. Her hug told me that I had done the right thing. Miss. Baas gave me a big smile and patted my shoulder.

"Did Lucile fall?" a friend asked mother.

"I don't think so," Mother answered. Then we exchanged secret, happy smiles.

Well, that first fall when I was eight turned out all right. I had learned a lesson. Even a fall isn't a disaster. There were to be many more falls in my future, but I had discovered that all I had to do was bounce up, smile and continue my dance. Then I'd have the joy of that wonderful new sound--applause.

This is my story, the story of my career as a dancer. Fame was never to be my lot, but certainly my love for dance gave me a life that was unusual. It was full of many hours of practicing, lessons, auditions, disappointments, and achievements, but it was never dull. Though I never became a ballerina in a ballet company, I was a teacher of ballet and other dances.

I will also tell about the many changes occurred in the years between 1912 and when we entered a new century. My story begins in 1928 when I came to one of the many turning points in my life.

In theaters across the United States, the newspaper advertisements said I was the dancer "On Toes of Gold."

Chapter 1

It was in the fall of 1928 when Mother and I rode the elevator to the rehearsal room in the Knickerbocker Building in Los Angeles, California. I was going to audition for the theatrical Producers Fanchon & Marco. Their "Ideas" were showing at theaters in states as far east as Utah. Mother had convinced Daddy that I should see if I had a future in show business instead of returning to high school for my junior year. Daddy did not want to take us to the audition, about an hour and a half from our home in Long Beach, so Mother and I traveled there by ourselves.

This night would decide what the future would hold for me. My heart was pounding so hard I could feel it pulsating at my throat. Mother told me I should just follow the others. Daddy had wanted me to continue with my schooling until I graduated from high school. But before the fall semester, Mother persuaded him to allow me to audition. So here I was, sixteen years old, about to embark on a professional career, if they accepted me.

Arriving at our floor, we could see the rehearsal room at the end of the hall. Mother was always fussy about what she wore. She had been too slender and the recent few pounds she had gained suited her. She adjusted the hat that completed her ensemble perfectly. The brown tones of the coat and dress complimented her chestnut brown hair, and the blue scarf at her throat enhanced her blue eyes. I was proud of my pretty mother.

I knew I looked good in my new dress. Girls envied the dresses Mother made for me in styles copied from magazines. She knew the colors which suited me best, choosing pastels because of my blonde hair and green eyes. Ready-made clothes did not allow for my broad shoulders and slim body, so she bought material and made my clothes instead. I wore the latest fashions while she saved money for dance lessons and new costumes.

When we went into the rehearsal hall, we came to a desk where a young woman introduced herself as Alice. She nodded her head towards the dressing room, where I could see girls emerging in their rehearsal clothes, and I went to change. Alice showed my mother a chair, placed against the wall, where she could see everything. She was the only mother in a room filled with girls, mostly older than I was. The bare room had only the desk, a few chairs, and a piano. Some of the girls were talking to the pianist who was lazily running his fingers over the piano keys.

Alice walked to one end of the room and told us to make lines and give ourselves enough space to dance. I went to stand beside a girl who looked close to my age. A lady dressed in a becoming suit came into the room. I knew at once that she would be the one who would decide my fate, because she was already looking us over. A younger woman dressed in a white blouse and black trunks came in and put some ballet slippers by a chair. I was glad I had followed Mother's advice and had put on tap shoes like the rest of the girls. The young woman, evidently the instructor, told us to follow her, and we began to do the standard single time-step. We went on to progressively more difficult steps that I was able to do easily. Some started to have trouble following the advanced steps. We then were told to change into ballet slippers.

Evidently some of the girls did not do ballet, and they sat down. The remaining girls did not seem to have much ballet experience. The instructor noticed I was familiar with the work, and she asked me to go in front. Alice, who had been making notes, told us to rest and, one at a time, go to the center of the room. We were to do right and left kicks and splits. Some girls were unable to do both splits. I was glad when it was my turn; mine were okay.

I hesitated instead of sitting down, and Alice asked if I could do more acrobatic work. I nodded my head. After I did front and back walk-overs, she said to stop. Next, we lined up according to our heights and, putting our arms around the girls next to us, tried to follow the teacher, who did waist-high kicks to the front. At first, a few could not coordinate, but finally we got together, and our instructor gave us a chorus of steps to do. I was not the only one who was relieved when Alice said, "Stay where you are and I will talk to each of you."

She consulted with the woman in the chair briefly. We were quiet when she went to each girl, telling some to stay and others to leave. A few were told to practice and come back again when they felt ready for another audition. To my relief, I was told to stay.

Alice introduced the remaining girls to Gae Foster, the person who had been observing us. I was the last one to be interviewed, and when I stood up, Miss Foster told me to bring my mother with me. Mother sat down where Alice had been sitting, and I sat on the floor facing them.

"I produce some of the 'Ideas' for Fanchon & Marco," Miss Foster said. "I like your daughter's work and would like to ask you some questions. How old is Lucile?"

My heart sank. Would I be too young? Mother told her I was sixteen. Then she asked, "Do you intend to travel with Lucile?" Mother said, "Yes."
Miss Foster wanted to know how long I had been dancing and did I have professional experience? Mother told her I had been dancing since I was eight years old, and when I was eleven, I had traveled southern California performing in theaters in a Kiddie Revue. I had been considered a professional since then.

"Well," said Miss Foster, "Could Lucile start rehearsing with my production, 'Up in the Air Idea'? I need another dancer. She is quick in learning steps and can catch up with the others. I would like her to start rehearsing tomorrow."

15

This was going faster than we had expected. Mother turned to me, worried. "Do you want to go into her show?"

"Yes," I said, my head in a whirl.

We were to go to the Westlake Theater the very next morning at nine o'clock for rehearsal. The show would open in two weeks at the Loews State Theater. I would be told when we were to come back to the Knickerbocker building to sign my contract and make the arrangements for Mother to travel with me. Miss Foster said, "I'll see you tomorrow at nine," and left the room.

Mother helped me change to street clothes in a hurry so we could go to the station where the big red cars were. They were larger than streetcars and went to many of the surrounding towns. We had traveled on them for years, so we knew if we didn't catch the ten-twenty car, we would have to wait until eleven o'clock. When we made the earlier car, we talked about how surprised we were about my being accepted and the fact I was to start rehearsing in the morning!

Aida Broadbent, one of my dance teachers, had sold her studio to Ernest Belcher, a Los Angeles teacher, and was now with Fanchon and Marco. We had been friends and had shared her excitement when told about her new adventure. Mother and I went to see her when the "Moonlight and Roses Idea" played at the West Coast Theater in Long Beach. She did a solo toe dance, and she was also line captain, which meant she was in charge of the chorus girls. They would travel the coast as far north as Vancouver and then go east to Salt Lake City where the unit would close.

When we arrived home, Daddy and my brother were waiting to hear what had happened. Alton, seven years older than me, could hardly believe that I had been accepted and would be going right into rehearsal. Daddy was quiet, and when I started to curl up beside him on the couch to talk, Mother shooed me off to bed. It was awhile before I went to sleep, I was so excited, and there was so much to think about. I could hear Mother and Daddy talking in their bedroom.

Next day, when we were on the red car again, Mother told me what they had talked about. Daddy had said he didn't approve, but if we wanted to travel, he would not stop us. Mother should travel with me, but we would have to live on my salary. He could not afford to send her any money. Of course, we would always have a home with him, but when we were away from home, we were on our own. Traveling had never been discussed before, and no one had imagined I would be in a show so quickly.

When Mother and I arrived in Los Angeles, a streetcar took us to the Westlake Park, which is now called Mac Arthur Park after the World War II hero. The Westlake was across the street and the theater was familiar because I had performed there doing adagio in a dance act the year before.

We entered the theater, and I reported to Miss Foster, who told me to work with the half of the girls doing a tap dance. The other half were learning to walk on stilts. So now I knew why it was named "Up in the Air Idea."
Later I was told to find my size stilts and practice walking on them. The stilts were in three different sizes, and I found a pair of the shortest. Some of the girls were on that height and the rest were on stilts that were twice as high. The tallest girl in the group was practicing on a pair that made her really tall. It didn't take long for me to know those stilts did not like me. Though the girls tried to help me, when they started practicing a military routine on the stilts, we all knew I was a disaster.

The dance instructor pulled me aside and pointed me in the direction of Miss Foster, who was watching us. I started thinking fast, planning how I would convince her that I could learn to walk on stilts. But that was not what she had in mind for me.

"Do you dance on your toes?" she asked.

"Yes, I do."

She pointed to a girl who was not on stilts. "Go learn her toe dance," she said. The toe dancer and I worked together the rest of the day.

We showed Miss Foster our dance, and she explained the tallest stilt performer would have a huge skirt in the finale. We would make our entrance from under it. Years later, when I saw the Nutcracker Ballet, I watched the tiny dancers come out from under

Mother Hubbard's skirt, and it brought back memories of the "Up in the Air Idea."

I practiced my acrobatic work back stage when the others were resting, and it was noticed. Miss Foster asked for me again. She said, "Do you have an acrobatic routine?" I showed it to her. She said she liked it, and it would be in the show. I would be in the opening tap dance; my acrobatic dance would be in the middle of the show, and the toe dance in the stilt finale. Mother had been shopping while I rehearsed, and I could hardly wait to tell her my good news. She was relieved when I told her I would not have to walk on stilts.

The next day Miss Fanchon came to the rehearsal. We were told to do all of our routines, including my acrobatic dance. Afterwards, I was told to see Miss Foster, who gave me an encouraging smile and said, "Miss Fanchon would like to talk with you." Without any hesitation Miss Fanchon told me abruptly, "Lucile, I would like you to be in my next production, the 'Orientale Idea.' Be at the Knickerbocker Building at nine in the morning to start rehearsing." I was dismissed. Evidently I didn't need to answer. If I did not like the change, it didn't matter.

I had been helping the instructor and Miss Foster called me back to work with the tap dancers. "I hope someday you will be in one of my shows," she said. I wished I would still be working for her. She was nice to me, and I was not at all certain I would be as comfortable with Miss Fanchon. When Alton, my brother, asked me what Miss Fanchon was like, all I could say was, "She has really dark eyes. I felt a little like a tiny bug under her eyes."

I wondered what I would be doing in the Orientale show. I did hope there would be an advantage for me to be with Miss Fanchon, who was such a different type of person than I had ever known. I was never comfortable with her, but I was to continue to be in her productions. I learned later she and her brother, Marco Wolf, had been a dance team. They had opened a dance studio, and after a few years had started to produce shows.

Next day, I met Mary Miles, an acrobatic dancer. We were the same height but were different in all other ways. She had dark hair and eyes, and her figure was more solid than mine, not plump, but rounded.

Miss Fanchon said, "I want you to compare your different acrobatic tricks and set a routine. Tell me when you have it done."

It was happening again. The toe dancer hadn't liked having a partner, and I felt the same resentment coming from Mary, who didn't know I was unhappy about losing the solo spot in the "Up in the Air Idea." Still, getting away from the stilts was worth it, and I would not be in the chorus.

Mary and I had different styles of acrobatics. Sliding into a split, she could remain there for a long time. While doing a handstand she would open her legs into a split and walk on her hands making a circle. She could do back flips across the room easily.

During the past summer, I had gone to a gymnastics teacher in Hollywood. Mother wanted to know if what I had developed by myself was all right. He said everything was fine, and suggested I join the class his son was teaching. When it came time for the leg stretch to make our splits and kicks better, he forced my right leg too far. I felt something in my leg seem to tear. When I cried out, he said, "Oh, do you have a pain in your fanny?" Well, I didn't know what a "fanny" was, but I certainly had a pain. (Nowadays, people have buns). Thereafter, when I did a split or a high kick with my right leg, it hurt.

Mother and I decided I should have private instruction with the owner/teacher. He said I was so limber, I could become a contortionist, but we did not care for that idea. We liked his suggestion that I should learn gymnastics.

He attached a leather harness around my waist, which was connected to a pulley, and by holding a rope coming down from the pulley, he had control. Until I learned the tricks, he prevented me from hitting the heavy mat. The belt never became comfortable, but I learned a back somersault in the air as well as back flips and front walkovers without hands. I never felt good about the back flips because my wrists hurt when I did them, but I did not have any difficulty doing the back somersaults without any hands. They were fine on a thick tumbling mat, but I never did feel secure doing them on the floor and never used them. Perhaps if I had lived near the studio and could have perfected them, I would have had more confidence doing them.

I always used my limber acrobatic work to help sell the ballet-type dances. Tumbling did not seem to fit, so after two months, we stopped the lessons. I could jump in the air, bend back and bring both feet to my head. Everyone called it double head kicks. I tried for years to find a better descriptive name, but they continued to be called double head kicks. One day, as an experiment, mother and I counted how many times I could do them in succession. I could have continued, but I stopped at a hundred. The unusual trick became my trademark. I also could kick the back of my head, one foot at a time many times. When I saw the popular comedian, Rene Riano, do side head kicks in a movie, I copied what she did. I put my backbend hippity hop trick in the dance, but won't even try to describe that one. I never saw anyone else do it.

The dance with Mary was a challenge, with each of us doing her specialty and then combining the tricks we did together. We finished with synchronized spotters. Miss Fanchon liked the results. To my relief, I would not have to do any splits, or so I thought.

We went to the costume department. After I undressed, two pieces of muslin were placed in front and back of me. A lady carefully started to outline my body with pins. Then using a big marking pencil, she drew lines under my breasts and around my body. After doing the same above my hips, she cut where she had marked until I was in a rough version of a bra and trunks. She nodded to the girl who had been holding the pins, then went to Mary. The girl opened the back of my bra. She cut it and cut the back of the trunks down so I could ease out. Ease out I did-those pins were sharp and were out to put a hole in me!

When Mary and I reported for our first fitting, I had three sets of bras and trunks. Two were of a scratchy metallic cloth, one gold, one silver. The other was black satin.

Mary was given a bright orange velvet leotard, with diamond shaped pieces of gold leather material sewn all over it. Her headdress was a fuzzy orange wig. My costume was of an Oriental type with a bra covered with faux gems and a full skirt of figured material, also covered with gems. A wig of black velvet with a bun in back had a pair of large golden hoop earrings attached, and placed by my ears.

The chorus girls danced in back of us to the "Song of India." They wore half-and-half costumes. One side was made like Mary's and the other side like mine. The "Song of India" was divided into classical and jazz rhythms. Tommy Dorsey later made an arrangement the same way that was wonderful. The girls faced toward me first, and we did a classical type of dance. When Mary started her dance in front of the girls, they turned toward her, and the music changed to a jazzy rhythm. The girls joined her in a jazz dance.

Every sixteen bars, they turned with the change in the music. It was classic versus jazz, and was to become a favorite in the show.

Miss Fanchon told me to do a slow split while holding my skirt, bending forward and billowing the skirt forward, then do a backbend with the skirt going in that direction. I did the split at the rehearsals, and I hurt from my earlier injury. But once I was on the stage during the performance, I didn't feel a thing! A wonderful thing was to happen by the end of the tour-I could do the split anytime without pain.

The two-piece silver costumes, trimmed with jewels, were for the finale. A helmet of the same silver material covered our hair completely. The chorus girls had been practicing on tom-tom drums, while Mary and I perfected our acrobatic routine. We were to perform in the semicircle they made. An adagio team would complete the production number. That afternoon we were introduced to them.

I whispered to Mary, "He was my adagio partner." I pointed to Ed. She wanted to know more. When we were having our lunch break, I told her about Ed and me. When I was studying with Ernest Belcher one evening, Ed asked me to try some adagio work with him. We worked so well together that we decided to become partners. Ed and his wife Rita also lived in Long Beach, so we practiced in a studio there. We worked hard and before long we started to dance for some of the clubs where I had performed. We formed an act for theaters, one of them being the Westlake Theater. One day, when we were practicing a new trick in the studio there, he dropped me. He had been holding me up in the air with one leg, and we were turning, when a girl suddenly opened the door. Startled, he dropped me onto my stomach with such force, I doubled up backwards, my head touching my hips. The doctor said I had injured my lower back and that I might have a problem with it in the future. I had to stop dancing for two weeks.

Upon my return Ed wanted me to audition for a Hollywood show that would travel if successful. Mother had not agreed. I was not sixteen yet, and I was to continue my current school year. While I had been under a doctor's care, Ed had started to work with the girl who had opened the door. They went into a show that folded after a week. Our little dance act was finished and I had lost track of Ed. Mary asked me if it would bother me to be in the same show with Ed. I didn't think so. We went back to the rehearsal to find out what we were going to do in the rest of the finale.

The set would occupy the back of the stage with several steps leading to a higher level. The girl's drum number was the start of the sequence; our acrobatic dance followed. Then Ruth ran onto the set with Ed swinging a whip, chasing her. She fell onto the steps, and Ed continued whirling and cracking the whip. The chorus girls left, and Mary and I had to stay on the steps in terror, but that was not an act. Sometimes on a small stage, we would get stung by the tip of the whip. After throwing the whip aside, he went to Ruth, who cowered from him. They started their adagio dance routine after a bit of pantomime.

The dance Ed and Ruth did was composed of tricks Ed and I had done. At the conclusion, Ruth fled to some stairs at the rear of the set to the second level. Facing up stage, she fell backwards off the platform into his arms. Ed and I had done this on the beach when we had found a pole several feet high left over from some activity. I had loved soaring through the air into his arms. It made an exciting climax to their dance, but I was glad she was doing it and not me.

Since I was under age, Mother came to the Knickerbocker to sign my contract. Each floor of the Knickerbocker building was involved in the production of "Ideas." Business offices on one floor and rehearsal rooms and costumes were on other floors.

Alice arranged the terms: my salary was $55.00 a week, less 5% agent's fees. My contract read, "Five percent [5%] of above salary is to be deducted by Fanchon & Marco Inc, for procuring artist for this engagement." If I had been older and wiser, I think I would have argued that point. Part of the cost of Mother's transportation would be held from my salary each week. She would have the lower berth, and I would have the upper berth in the Pullman coach.

If we rehearsed to a later hour, I had to wait in the station for the eleven o'clock red car. That did not bother me. I had more time to enjoy reading, especially since my discovery of a new publication, the Reader's Digest. My vocabulary improved because of their informative articles, and the size was convenient for me to carry. I started a lifelong habit. Not only did the Reader's Digest help me at this time but also the books I invested in when I started writing this book helped in many ways.

Mother was busy getting our clothing ready for traveling. We were limited in what we took, so our suitcases wouldn't be too heavy to carry. Everything we put in the suitcases had to be necessary. Our problem was solved when our friend Lester Fountain, the manager of the West Coast Theater in Long Beach, offered to lend us money for a trunk. He had become interested in my career several years before and was happy to lend us the money. We used that trunk for many years.

On November 3, 1928, the day before the "Idea" was to open at the Loews State Theater in uptown Los Angeles, the entire dress rehearsal was held in the Manchester Theater in the suburbs. It was larger than most of the neighborhood theaters and had all the necessary requirements for staging the productions. The audience came each week to see the latest "Idea" and they were very critical. There would not be any "walk throughs" at this dress rehearsal. Everything was supposed to be ready.

I had danced in many southern California theaters, old like the Manchester. In the future I would be dancing in cities with new, beautiful, large theaters, not at all like the theaters we have now. Those built before the Depression had to accommodate large audiences. Some were called "The Palace Theater," and they all earned that name.

After customers purchased their tickets at the box office, they entered a door that was twice as large as usual. The young man standing at this door was dressed in a uniform that would have been acceptable at any palace. The lobby was as large as an entire modern theater. Lush thick carpets covered the floors. The room, two stories high, would have an ornate staircase that led to a similar room, the mezzanine. The decor of the lobbies and mezzanines was most elaborate: grand mirrors in golden frames, statues in niches, brocade or velveteen lounge chairs and sofas, sparkling crystal chandeliers and sidelights. The uniformed ushers entered the auditorium through large gilded doors and took patrons to their seats with a discreet flashlight. If you had entered before the show had begun, you could see the immense chandelier in the high ceiling. In some theaters there would be exquisite statues in alcoves with subdued lights shining on them. The seats were as comfortable as an armchair at home. The organ would rise up from the area of the orchestra pit with the organist playing, and when the show started, it would sink down out of sight.

The organists were excellent musicians. During the silent picture era, they accompanied the picture, portraying the action with mood music. With talking pictures, they were no longer needed except for their lovely music.

Often the main curtain was velour in warm colors, many of them golden and heavily decorated. The curtain would open to the sides to reveal the movie screen and the stage. When the curtains were lifted, they went up to the loft in the back of the theater building.

Perhaps readers can remember watching films about the theater with a chase taking place backstage. Frequently, one of the actors would climb into the loft where there were catwalks going from one side to the other, with many ropes needed for the curtains. If the villain was being chased, he was the first to come down, the hard way!

The Metropolitan Theater in Boston, and the Fox Theaters in St. Louis and Detroit are a few of the old movie palaces. A few of these magnificent theaters have been restored, and traveling shows and operas use their large space.

Vaudeville started in the last part of the 1880s. By the Twenties, there were big theaters all over the country, which belonged to either the Pantages Circuit, the Orpheum Circuit, or to smaller local circuits. It was a wonderful time to be in show business.

Theaters started to show newsreels, short subjects, and travel films. They were similar to the films seen now on T.V. They would be about 20 minutes long and were followed by trailers showing what the next attractions would be. The vaudeville acts would follow, and after them the feature film. Most of the time, the whole show was continuous. People could go in at any time, seeing everything, and a family of four could see all of this for a dollar or two.

The vaudeville section usually started with an act that would take full stage. It would often be what was called a "flash" act, with a theme of some sort, composed of singers and dancers. They would usually use scenery for the act. When they had finished, the scene would be changed. A drop (curtain) would separate that area from the action going on in front on the apron, which was next to the footlights and had a hardwood floor. The act that performed at this point was in the number two spot. Whoever held the number two spot had to be good enough to keep up the momentum the first act had created. I recall seeing some wonderful tap dancers who danced in the number two spot. Instead of the hardwood floor on the apron, sometimes they used the floor behind, made of softer wood, which was not as good for some types of dancing. When I did acrobatic dancing on the soft wood floor, sometimes I'd get splinters in my hands and in other parts of my anatomy.

From there on, the acts would be of all types: trapeze performers, jugglers, and animal acts, to name a few. The next-to-closing act belonged to the headliner. Feature acts had movie stars, famous singers, comedians or magicians. They had their names on the marquee. The closing acts used the full stage.

Stage shows were different from Vaudeville. The Publix Circuit shows, produced in New York, were like the Fanchon & Marco productions. They had a theme. Instead of the flash acts, featuring a group of dancers, they had a chorus line that would do two or three dances during the show. The singers would sing throughout the show. The head-liners normally made just one appearance, but sometimes they would take part in the rest of the show. There were times in these shows when the orchestra would be on the stage instead of in the pit. If the show needed a Master of Ceremonies, the orchestra leader would take that part.

When we arrived at the Manchester after the morning rehearsal, electricians were choosing the colored gelatins for the stage lights. The footlights took time to set up because squares of colored gelatin had to be placed in each one. In modern theaters, foot-lights are already colored and set in a solid row. Colored lights shone from the wings, too. The lights were attached to connected pipe standards. Again, gelatin squares of different colors were fitted in front of them. In later years, these lights were permanently installed and made more compact. Single performers often were fussy because the wrong color gelatin could result in a very unflattering light, making a difference in their appearance. Amber was the favorite for awhile.

The big switchboard was on stage near the entrance of the first wing. The electrician controlled all the lights except the spotlight, which came from the projection room high above the balconies. Larger theaters usually had two spotlights. The movie was projected from the same place. The electricians controlled the "house lights." I was always interested in watching them gradually change from house lights to stage lights. These big men manipulated the switches in a groove with a great deal of sensitivity that did not match their size. They moved quickly in front of that large switchboard and they did not say "Please" when they wanted you out of their way. If you were going to be in the limited space backstage, you soon learned to anticipate what the men were going to do and would stay out of their way. This was their domain.

There were "Fly men" who worked the drops, or curtains. They were busiest when the shows opened and closed because they had to hang the drops for the acts. The drops were tied to long, heavy, metal bars that were lowered by ropes from the loft. The curtain spaces were numbered, and they were changed to make different sizes of the stage available. Men would work the corresponding ropes stationed along the wall, always on stage right.

Backstage, the theater has an aroma, different from any other, and if you have come back from an absence, it is like smelling a little bit of heaven. It is a magical place. A whiff of rosin, a bit of paint, dust from the curtains, the sweet smell of greasepaint, a tang of human sweat, all blended together in the heat of the lights. I fell in love with it when I was very young and I have never gotten over it. I would continue my career in many theaters, in many cities, but now we had a dress rehearsal for a large production, and I was both nervous and excited.

Mary and I were told what we were to do for the opening number. Setting up the opening of our show involved two scrims, something I was unfamiliar with. Our scrims were curtains or drops of lightweight material with scenes painted on them. These scrims were different because they had slits a few feet apart extending from a foot from the floor to waist high. The scrims parted in the middle so four of the sixteen chorus girls were seen in front of each side, and each girl put her upstage leg into the slit.

Mary and I were at the middle openings of the first scrim. All the costumes were brassieres and trunks made of either silver or gold material. Our scrims portrayed giant lanterns, and a design of an oriental type bridge. As the scrims parted, Mary and I slowly walked backwards with our sets of girls. Jue Fong, a tenor with a beautiful voice, was in front of the second scrim singing the "Kashmiri Song."

The second scrim had Chinese tigers painted on it, and the eight girls moved backward, leaving Jue Fong in the center of the stage to finish the song. Jue was dressed in a colorful Mandarin coat, heavily embroidered with metallic threads. His powerful voice filled the theater without any sound system. Besides the opening number, Jue Fong sang "On the Road to Mandalay" later in the show. Then he always had to do his encore, "When Irish Eyes are Smiling." Jue had been with several "Ideas" and was a favorite with audiences, and with us. We called him "Juee."

England Ong, a diminutive girl, followed the opening number singing, "Baby, I

Don't Mean Maybe," first in English and then in Chinese. Dressed in embroidered blue satin pajamas, she wore her jet black hair in a Dutch bob, a style Colleen Moore, a current movie star, had made popular. England was full of good humor and was always smiling.

Skeeter and Ray Hartwell's Spanish dance was humorous and later Skeeter entertained us with her Oriental dance comedy.

We rehearsed until it was time for the theater to open for the first evening show. Mother brought milk shakes for Mary and me to drink while we put on our makeup.

The whole production ran smoothly with only a few changes. After the last show, with Mary's experienced help, I covered my costumes with a large sheet and gave them to the wardrobe lady for her to hang in a large crate. Our makeup box and shoe bags went into other big crates.

It had been a long day, getting up early in Long Beach for the rehearsal at the Knickerbocker and then going to the Manchester for more rehearsing followed by the two shows. Daddy was waiting in the car to drive Mother and me home. Before I fell asleep in the back seat, I thought, "Tomorrow we will be at the Loews State Theater and by the end of the day, I will know for sure I am on my way to a new, exciting career."

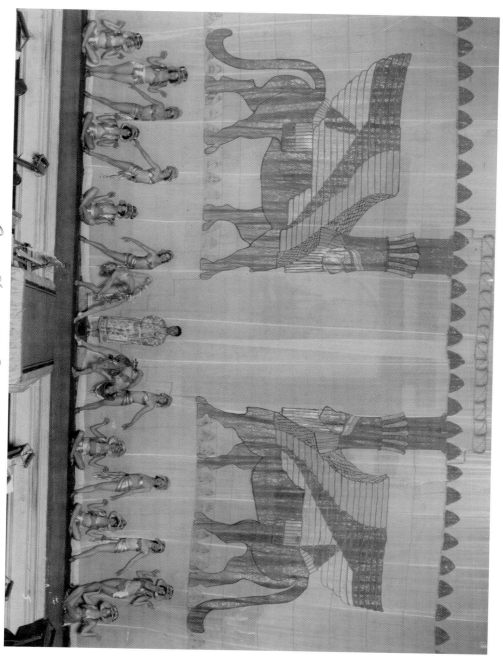

Opening Sequence of the Orientale Idea

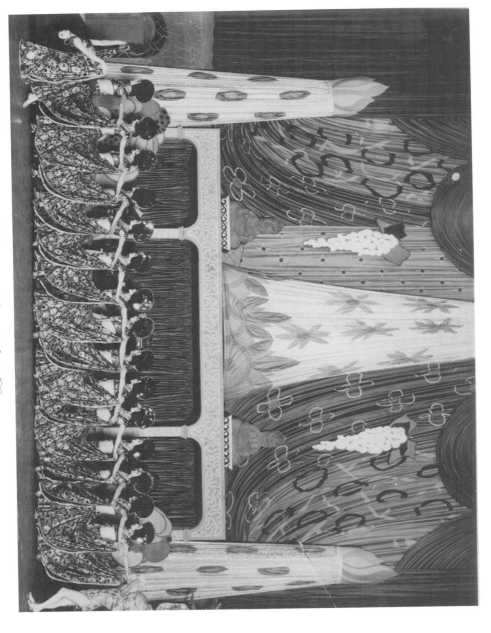

My side of the Song of India Dance

Mary's side of the Song of India Dance

Mary and Myself in Song of India Costumes

Publicity for Manhattan Idea, I am the one on Top

Ruth and Ed Kover, Adagio Dancers

Finale of the Orientale Idea was repeated in the Waltz Idea

Chorines in Finale of Waltz Idea

Entire Cast of Screenland Melodies Idea

Finale of Manhattan Idea

Monkey Antics, Two Men from the Bruno Weiss Trio

Monkey Antics, Two Men from the Bruno Weiss Trio

Charlie Chase, Appeared with Manhattan Idea in Chicago

Dorothy Mackaill, My Movie Star Friend

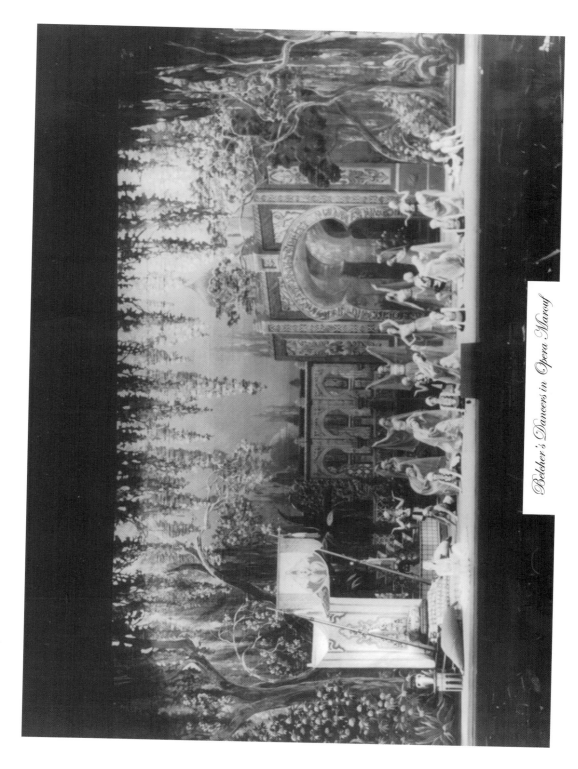

Belcher's Dancers in Opera Marouf

Belcher's Dancers in the First Ballet at the Hollywood Bowl

Chapter 2

The Orientale Idea opened at the Loews State Theater in Los Angeles on November 4, 1928. Mary's and my pictures were on display in the lobby, and I was a very proud girl. It was not the first time for me to dance at the Loews State Theater, but it was under different circumstances.

During the early days of the Depression, theater managers often would have amateur nights to lure people into their theaters. An opportunity was given for tiny tots to the aged, to perform for theater audiences.

In 1924 Mother had arranged for me to be on the amateur night program, doing my Russian Dance. A troupe of Russian singers and dancers, on the regular program, watched my dance from the wings. Afterwards, they enthusiastically complimented me on how well I had done their native Cossack dance. While I was getting dressed to go home, I wondered why Mother wasn't there to help me. After I had put on my street clothes, I found her in the dressing room of the Russian act. When I came in, Mother told me they had asked her if I could join their act on the Orpheum circuit. She thanked them for the honor, but said I was too young and explained I would have to finish school before I could travel.

The manager of the act, who was the only one speaking English, told her I would be well cared for and that they would love to have me join them. At the end of the tour I could return home. Evidently, he realized she was not going to change her mind, so he asked us to wait for a few minutes. They began to talk to each other in their own language, which was Russian. One of the young girl dancers left the room. She carried a pair of shiny black patent leather boots when she returned. They motioned for me to sit down and the manager put the boots on me. The soles were flexible, like a ballet slipper. They were a size too big for me and I was disappointed until he said I would grow into them and they wanted me to have them. We thanked them and left in a daze. I felt like I had been in a dream, but it was true, because I was carrying the boots. After they fit me, I wore them until I outgrew them. We looked and never could find another pair like them. Now, several years later, I was going to be on the same stage and would be traveling as a member of a troupe.

When Mother and I entered the theater, I saw Al Lyons, whom I had admired when he had led the orchestra at our own West Coast Theater. He was "tall, dark and handsome." I never thought I would ever be talking to him, and now I was to tell him how to play our music.

Jumi Kawahata had been added to the show. Although she was petite, she had long legs and could not only kick high, but could stand on one foot while holding the other leg straight up alongside her body. She traveled across the stage by turning the supporting foot in and out. Even Mary had to admit she could not do that.

We found our costumes and hung them in the dressing room we would be sharing. Dressing rooms were always the same, differing only in size. A long shelf ran the length of the room with a long mirror. This is the makeup table. It is illuminated with bare light bulbs. Hooks on one of the other walls would hold costumes and our personal clothing. A sink was available but the other facilities were down the hall. If there was a window, it was generally frosted but at least it made the room look less like a cell.

After the rehearsal was over, we put on our lightweight robes and started to apply our makeup. We were using the same type of makeup until Mary came to her eyelashes. She had an object that looked like a small can except it didn't have a bottom or top. She placed it into a small tin with a candle, which she lit. A tiny metal pan containing something black quickly melted. Mary dipped a round tooth pick into the black fluid and carefully put the drop on her eyelash. I had wondered why she had first put a small amount of Vaseline on her eyelashes and had separated them into individual clusters. I asked her what she was doing. She told me she was building a drop of wax on each group. It was called beading and was better than mascara. Then I could hardly wait for Mother to buy my beading set and I built my beaded lashes up to my eyebrows. Whenever a restaurant had round toothpicks, I would take several to use for my new eye makeup. I soon found I had a problem Mary did not have. On hot days I would become really limber and when I did my "double head kicks," my toes would touch my beaded eyelashes and smash them. The lashes had to be repaired between shows.

When false eyelashes came into style, they made eye makeup easier but were expensive. We trimmed the strip of eye lashes to fit the eyelids so they looked glamorous but still natural. Unfortunately, we would lose them on stage. The stage hands came to the rescue and found them when we told them how much they cost.

That day we did four shows, and we soon found out the costumes for the opening and closing numbers were not comfortable. Our skin became chafed where it came in contact with the metallic cloth. Mother covered the edges with a soft material, and it felt much better. Metallic cloth continued to be popular and Mother became an expert in shielding my skin from coming into contact with it.

Metro-Goldwyn Mayer's "Cardboard Lover," with Marion Davies and Niles Asther was showing. There was also a novelty advertised. To quote the poster out front, "The World's 8th Wonder. Fox Movietone TALKING NEWS. SEE! HEAR! WM. GREENE, Pres. A. F. of L....BILLY SUNDAY.... ELK'S OPERA CHORUS. SEE! HEAR! on FOX MOVIETONE. SHUBERT'S IMMORTAL SERENADE.

Before the last show, Mary and I slipped into the wings of the stage to watch this new wonder-movies with sound. People were soon saying, "It's just a new way to lure people to the theaters. Just a novelty. It won't last long." How wrong they were.

That night, after the last motion picture had been shown and the theater had emptied, the photographer came to take photos for future publicity. Automatic flash attachments were not around yet and all photos were black and white. The tripod was set up with a big camera on it. He would duck under a black cloth that was draped over the camera and peer through the lens. Coming out he would adjust us and go under again until he finally told us to hold still. One hand held a long slim tray of powder that made the flash. It was coordinated with the camera so it flashed with each picture and had to be refilled every time. Every pose had to be taken several times and after awhile, my muscles were complaining. Mary was having the same problem and when we finally had an opportunity to sit, we giggled when our legs trembled out of control. At last, when all the photos had been taken someone called out, "Look at the schedule changes. We do five shows tomorrow and the first one will be early."

After the first show the next day, I was so tired I cleared space on my makeup table, folded my arms and rested my head on them. I was planning to take a nap.

Mary had a different idea. She had discovered I was innocent and could not wait to wise me up! Mother was out of the room, so Mary started to talk about men and sex. I had learned many new things in recent weeks, but the next week, every chance she had, Mary gave me a different type of education.

Mother thought I was too young to date. She had never given me any advice about boys or told me anything about my body, sex or relationships. In the twenties this was not so unusual. "Sex," the word itself, was a naughty word.

One time I had talked to a girl about boys in junior high school. She only confused me when she told me that women gave birth when their stomach popped open and the baby was lying there to be removed. The husband had something to do with this and that was why it was so important to be married. When I asked Mother about babies, she said kisses made babies and respectable ladies didn't talk about it. My dancing kept me so busy I did not have time to think about things like that anyway.

One night when I had been rehearsing with Eddie, Mother asked him to take me home because she had other plans. He kissed me good night, my first kiss from a man. It was different than I thought a kiss would be. I worried for the next month. Maybe I was going to have a baby! I didn't think he should be kissing me since he was married.

Mary's mother came to the dressing room after one show and I never saw her again. Mary never talked about her. It was like she never existed. Her brother came to see Mary several times, and asked me for a date, but Mother told him I was not dating yet. Mary thought that was funny.

I went to the theater on my own because Mother was busy, and she and Daddy came for me at night. I had often gone to Los Angeles by myself for my lessons with Mr. Belcher, so going to the theater was not much different. All too soon the week was over and we would start to travel.

The next morning, we were up early and Daddy drove the three hours to the California Theater in San Diego. We rehearsed at nine with Al Berti and his Music Masters and I found out that Juni, the little dancer, was only with us for the Los Angeles show. "The River Pirate" with Victor Mc Laglen and Lois Moran was the picture showing. Daddy drove home after seeing it.

There were Navy ships in the harbor at the time, and I think all the sailors came to one matinee. They really liked the "Song of India" dance. They stood up and cheered and, in show business vernacular, we "stopped the show." One of the theater critics on the local newspaper seldom gave a good revue, but he gave us such a splendid one, Variety, the trade paper, copied it. For one brief week, we were IT.

One day, a rack of dresses appeared back stage for all the girls to model in a style show after the matinee. One dress I was given to model was of black satin, cut on the bias so it clung to my body, a change from my usual style. I wanted it and pleaded with Mother until she gave in and I had my first grown up dress. I probably resembled an exclamation point in the black dress, but I didn't care.

Daddy came to San Diego closing night and took us back to Long Beach. The next day, November 11th, we were up early to make the drive to the Glendale Theater, miles away. Each morning that week I took the Red Car to Los Angeles and then changed to one for Glendale. Alton or Daddy came to take me home after the show. We followed the same routine for Pasadena the next week.

The last night in Pasadena, we did not go home to Long Beach. Instead we were to take the night train to Fresno so Daddy and Alton drove us to the station after the show. The excitement of at last going on the road was dimmed when I had to say good-bye to them. I knew I was going to miss them and that made me sad. Daddy said it would be a good experience for me and gave me an extra hug.

Our coach was on a side track. Mother kept saying, "Watch where you are going." We had to cross over tracks and I always tripped over things. She had told me often, "You have your head in the clouds. You could trip over an eyelash." I seldom fell, but made spectacular recoveries.

This time I kept my mind on what I was doing and soon we found the night coach. The porter had made up the berths, and all we could see down the aisle were the green curtains hanging over each section. Mother found ours, undressed and retired into her berth quickly. All the worry of packing was over, so she could go to sleep right way, and she did.

After I changed into my pajamas and was on my way to our berth, I heard some of the girls of the chorus talking and laughing. A few years later, it was a fad to see how many people could pack into a telephone booth or a small car. Now the girls were not having a contest but they could have won one with ease there were so many in that berth. They managed to squeeze me in. They were taking turns telling stories. I had no idea what they were laughing about, but I would laugh when they did. They realized this quickly and would laugh at nothing at all, just to hear me laugh. Finally I caught on to their joke and left. When Mother heard the kind of stories they were telling, she suggested that next time I read until I got sleepy.

Instead I found something much more interesting to do when I heard and felt the coach moving. I went into the ladies room to a window where I could look out and I became fascinated by the maneuvering it took to position our coach for the train that would be picking us up later. Each time we were leaving a town I would either watch from the ladies room or try to see out of the window in my berth. Mother had most of the window in her lower berth but I managed to see some of the activity through my share.

In the morning, we saw the coach had been sidetracked at the Fresno station during the night. We caught a cab and went to the Wilson Theater where the marquee said our motion picture was "Lady Be Good" starring Dorothy Mackail and Jack Mulhall.

Jay Brower was the orchestra leader. We knew Jay from the West Coast Theater and he was surprised to see me in the show. I learned we would have what they called split weeks. This one was the three-day weekend in Fresno and four days in San Jose. San Francisco was our next stop, where we would be appearing all week at the Warfield. It was an older but famous theater on the equally famous Market Street. During the orchestra rehearsal, when Mary and I had a few minutes free, we went to look at the elaborate social room downstairs where, in the olden days before prohibition, people went during the intermission.

In my imagination, I could see ladies in dresses glittering with jewels, escorted by gentlemen in tall hats and black capes. I could even imagine the strong perfume in the air. I had read the stories about this flamboyant town during the Gold Rush era. I thought there must have been many real life dramas that occurred in this very room. Too soon, we heard the music of the act before ours and returned to the stage, back to reality. The Warfield is still operating but just for special performances.

Rube Wolf, Fanchon's brother, was the orchestra leader and the Master of Ceremonies. It was Rube Wolf week and he received all the publicity because it was his birthday. "Take Me Home," with a new star, Bebe Daniels, was the picture.

Rube's wife, the former Sunny Perry, had been a dancer with Fanchon & Marco "Ideas." She was dancing that week as part of the celebration. A costume change prevented me from watching her dance, but Mother told me she was lovely. On Saturday, Rube and Sunny's baby was brought to the theater by his nurse. Rube proudly showed him to the matinee audience. The baby must have been a real trouper because he did not cry when the audience applauded loudly.

Rube had given a little statuette of himself to a girl from the audience the previous night. No one had taken a publicity picture, so Rube asked me to pose with him between shows. I wore my new black dress for the occasion. Because I was not the real girl, my face was behind his in the photo of our embrace. All you can see of me, besides his holding me, is the statue in my hand which I held out in back of his head.

Sunny and Mother were watching and Rube made us laugh with his jokes. They rather adopted Mother and me, and the four of us went out after the last show for a night lunch. Our friendship was to last a long time.

One night after the show, I saw my first Chinatown with Mary and Mother. It was so different, as though we had traveled to China. The smell of incense and herbs filled the air and Mother had to pull me away from the shops because I loved everything I saw. I bought two small ivory figures after the polite sales clerk told me their story. They were Netsukes and first appeared in Japan during the Edo period 1615-1867. They were used as a toggle by the Japanese to fasten a small pouch or purse to a kimono sash. The carved miniature sculptures were made of wood or ivory. Less than two inches high, they portrayed religious figures, legends and the culture of Japan. They cannot be made of ivory anymore. The modern ones are nice, but just don't feel the same. My ivory figures were the start of a small collection of oriental art.

The next engagement was across the bay in Oakland. We had heard about the T and D Theater in advance. Theatrical people called it "Tough and Dirty," and we found the name was right. The backstage and the dressing rooms were neglected. A big machine occupied most of the downstairs floor space, and it rumbled constantly. Appropriately, the film was "Me, Gangster," a heavy melodrama. It starred June Collyer and Don Terry. Everyone was happy when the week was over.

The Senator Theater, in Sacramento, California's capital city, was a welcome change. We saw an apartment listed on the bulletin board and when Mother returned from looking at the place, she was all smiles. I was looking forward to the home cooked meals, thinking we could save money, too.

Then Mother had a suggestion that we ask one of the chorus girls to stay with us and share the expenses. I couldn't believe her choice. Nancy did not know the first thing about personal hygiene. She agreed and moved in with us. I washed my hair frequently, and the first night Mother said it would be fun for us to wash each other's hair. I asked if she wanted to take the first bath or should I? Mother offered to wash her clothes with ours. We followed the same routine all week. Mother's goal had been to help her, and it worked.

Her complexion improved after it had been cleansed regularly, and her hair became soft. The other girls became more friendly and would go shopping with her. She started to buy attractive dresses and soon you could hardly recognize her as the same person. She became more self confident and was included in the dates the girls would go on after the shows. A few years later, I heard she had married a millionaire!

"Owen Sweeten and the Super-Soloists," as advertised, made sweet music. Richard Dix starred in the picture "Moran of the Marines." The widely publicized Ruth Elder was the co-star. She had been one of the first women flyers.

Not all of our shows were in big cities. We played a split week with Medford and Salem, Oregon. In one of those two towns, a stage hand told us a church was having chicken dinners, and they welcomed people from the shows. We found the church, felt welcome and really enjoyed their delicious dinner. When we were leaving, they gave each of us a piece of mince pie to take back to the theater to enjoy later. We never found a church serving good chicken dinners in a small town again.

Mother and I often took walks between the two night shows. If there was a bright moon, we would walk after the last show. We preferred the small towns much more than walking in the cities. The streets had trees, and I confess we enjoyed taking a peak at the lit up windows as we passed by. Maybe we had a touch of home sickness. When we arrived in beautiful Portland, we again found a small apartment. This time it was just big enough for the two of us.

The Publix Theater was new and modern. There was an elevator to take us from the stage level to our dressing rooms. I would run down the winding stairs to the stage, but after my dances, I was grateful to take the elevator going up to my third floor dressing room.

An unusual feature was the overture before the stage show. The orchestra, plus the organist at the big Wurlitzer organ, played concert music. The organ music resounded through our dressing rooms. It reminded me of the time years earlier when I had danced with the Ernest Belcher dancers in the film the "Phantom of the Opera" starring Lon Chaney. Mother and I saw the picture but we could not find me in the ballet because that scene was really brief and the dancers were small.

The second morning, while Mother was shopping, and before the theater opened, I was practicing in the mezzanine in the front of the theater. A young man's voice came out of the darkness, "You are a good acrobat." I said, "Thank you." Evidently, he had been watching me practice while on his way to the dressing room for the ushers. He disappeared and I forgot the incident.

Later that day, the backstage doorman told me there was someone in the Green Room to see me. The Green Room in the theater is for the performers to entertain their visitors. My visitor was the mysterious young man with the deep voice. He had blond curly hair and blue eyes, and he introduced himself as Ronnie. We sat and talked until Mother came looking for me.

Ronnie was comfortable to talk with, and the way he looked at me made me feel special. We saw each other between shows and took walks in a square block park near the stage door. When it rained, I would bundle up and we would walk back and forth under the trees sharing an umbrella. The other girls on the show would have dates in many of the towns and perhaps Mother thought it was time for me to have some male companionship. She didn't say much about my seeing Ronnie until he asked if I could go out after the last show for a night lunch. Then she said, "No."

However, the night before our closing night Mother said I could ask him to the apartment to have a snack with us. Mother did allow us a moment alone for a goodbye, and when he kissed me, I was thrilled. Of course, I thought I was in love. For a time we wrote letters to each other, but when his letters stopped coming, I didn't write either.

We had a one-day engagement in Pendleton, Oregon, cowboy and Indian country. The theater was small and when we went backstage, I was reminded of the small stages in the towns where I had danced with the Kiddie Revue.

After we rehearsed with the orchestra, we had some time before the one matinee and decided to walk around the town. We saw Indians and some real cowboys, making it seem unreal, like a movie set. It did not take much time to walk through the town and, coming to a hill, we decided to climb it.

We were joined by several of the girls and Mother took some pictures of us while we ran around like liberated kids. A strong wind was was blowing that messed up our hair and no one would have believed we were the glamorous ladies they saw on the stage.

There was not enough room on the stage for the whole chorus line, so each show, four of the girls of the line didn't dance. There was so little room, Mary and I had to be careful to avoid running into each other when we did our acrobatic dance.

In some of the older theaters the curtain ropes had to be pulled up and down by hand. The heavy ropes would go down into a hole, go under the floor and come back up again. On this stage the hole for the front curtain was bigger than most, and was close to the side of the stage. During the "Song of India" routine I stepped back as usual when she made her entrance. My foot went into the hole. Mary saw me going down, down, down. I managed to get up without too much harm, but it was scary. We all had a good laugh after the dance was over.

The Indian men, never any women, sat in the front row. The blankets they wore almost covered them entirely. They enjoyed the show but they didn't applaud. They would just mutter, "Ugh." We were told this meant we were pleasing them.

We found a restaurant and had a good western meal. I remember it was on the hot side and not just from the stove! Most everyone in town must have come for the night show, the theater was so crowded. No Indians, though.

Our coach had been sidetracked and was waiting to take us to Tacoma, Washington. I slept better than usual that night because of the fresh air of the afternoon. It was a special day. In the morning, as we approached Tacoma, Washington, Mother and I watched the scenery from the window. It was different from southern California and I thought wistfully, Daddy would have liked to take us on a Sunday drive here, but he was back home in Long Beach, probably getting ready for work. We had to be ready to get off the train when it pulled into Tacoma. Having a coach at our disposal had spoiled us. Now, it was rush time again.

Exciting! When you are doing your act, and you are the center of attention (yes, it is exciting). When you are in the wings waiting for your entrance and the adrenalin hits you. It is an addiction from which few show people recover. Once a ham, always a ham. My friend Catherine, who had been in my dance act, once said, "It is a disease, but seldom fatal."

We were meeting many of the people we had known in Long Beach. Mother and I were happy to see Don and Iris Wilkins at the Broadway Theater. Don directed the orchestra, and both played the organ. They had come to Tacoma the previous week and it was good to see someone we knew. They were happy to see our familiar faces, too.

The picture here was "Outcast" with Edmond Lowe and Corrine Griffith. Miss Griffith was a popular movie star for several years. Louise Fazenda, a comedian I had always liked, was in the picture. Sometimes I would sit in the wings to see parts of the picture show. This is one I watched.

Mother and I were lucky to find an apartment just across from the theater. It was close enough for me to go to between shows. Reading a book in a soft chair was better than sitting on the hard dressing room chairs. It doesn't sound like a treat, but week after week on hard chairs made a soft seat special!

One late afternoon after the matinee, when we were preparing our dinner, we heard a terrible noise across the street. It was like steel being twisted then falling with a dreadful crash. We looked out and saw the marquee of the theater and twisted metal covering the sidewalk in front of the theater. No one had been hurt. Only a few brave people came to see the night shows. They entered through a side door which was normally an exit. We never found out what had made the marquee fall.

The Seattle Theater in Seattle, Washington, was one of the largest on the coast. I loved the big stage because Mary and I had plenty of room for our duo acrobatic routine, something which didn't occur too often. "Me Gangster" was the film here, but it didn't seem as sinister as it did at the dreary old T & D in Oakland.

Some of the girls had been here in previous shows and knew the stage hands. They would play cards, Pinochle or Bridge, between shows and Mother would join them. I played solitaire, read or embroidered. In some towns, the drugstores would have a few books to be loaned after a deposit was made. Mother and I would often make use of their small libraries.

One day England and the girls played a trick on the stage hands. After a show, the men would remove their protective overalls by sitting down in a chair, and, after pulling them down to the floor, they would leave them, ready to be stepped into again. The girls tacked the bottom of the overalls legs to the floor. When the fifteen minute signal was given, the men went to put on their overalls. It was funny to see their struggles until they realized what had been done.

In the mornings, Mother and I would go to Seattle's famous Pike's Wharf, where articles were displayed from all over the world. There were fish that I hadn't even heard of before, and we watched the live lobsters in the big tanks before we had shrimp cocktails for lunch.

The merchandise was arranged attractively and, as usual, I lingered at the Oriental displays. Mother would tempt me away, mentioning it was time we bought our

43

candy before we left. We looked at all the different candies displayed and each would buy a sack of our own preference. Love of candy was one thing we had in common.

Next, we had a one-day stand at Bremerton. Juee, having been there before, knew the theater owner also owned a hotel. It was probably the best one in Bremerton at that time. The manager scheduled the last show so no one could catch the last ferry to Seattle, so everyone would have to stay at his hotel.

Juee and the manager of our show chartered a small fishing boat for the cast to make the trip to Bremerton. It smelled of fish. Oh, how it smelled of fish, and of the fuel used to run the boat. It was anything but a smooth ride. I was glad Mother had decided not to make the trip. After the last of four shows, we went to our small, smelly boat. It was rather exciting, but I was glad when we reached the pier in Seattle. When I joined Mother, she said I smelled of fish, and I stayed under the shower in the bathtub a long time.

It was one of the first showers we were to see in a hotel. The shower was in the tub with the water coming from the faucets via an attached pipe that went toward the ceiling. The pipe went into a circle of pipe with the curtain hanging on it and the water came down from an inner circle. It was better when they designed the curtain to go across the front of the tub. Then it would not cling to my wet body.

Mary and I were fined in Bellingham, Washington. We had gone out front to see the picture, between the two evening shows. Usually, after the feature picture was shown, it was followed by the newsreel, but no one told us the schedule had been changed. The picture over, we dashed to our dressing room to dress for the opening number. We did not know we had missed the fifteen minute buzzer or the five minute warning. We heard the overture for our show! I had one foot into my trunks for my costume and Mary was in the same position. The scrims opened without us. Almost immediately the manager of the show knocked on the door. After a brief lecture he said, "You will be fined five dollars." I never missed an entrance again.

We were looking forward to the week's engagement in Vancouver, Canada. We were surprised how different everything was. Jackie Souders, the orchestra leader at the

Strand Theater, tried to make us feel at home. Mother and he became friends and they visited between shows. I think Mother missed Alton.

One show, during the half and half dance with Mary, I fell down. In one part of my routine, I walked backwards across the stage in a semi-backbend. My full skirt was trimmed with all kinds of decorations. I held it out to the sides with both hands but still I had to be careful not to step on it. One matinee I did step on it. I slipped, and went down on my seat, my legs flying up in the air. Jackie came to me and with an elaborate bow, he helped me up. He said, "Lucile Fa down." This was a laugh line a comedian had made popular. The audience laughed in relief. I wasn't hurt and went on with the dance.

I had promised myself one thing after going to the theater with a group of Mr. Belcher's students to see one of his former students-I would always laugh if I fell. The dancer had met with some success in New York and was making an appearance at Loews State. In the middle of her dance, she fell. Just sat down. It was embarrassing I know, but she made it worse when she stomped off the stage, not hurt, but angry. I always remembered how startled the audience was. They sat in silence for a moment, then there was a murmur amongst them I would never forget, and never wanted to hear again. I vowed I would always laugh if I ever fell during a dance.

Jackie introduced us to one of his friends who came to visit us in the Green Room. When Mother learned he owned a clothing store for men, she said, "Lucile might like a fur coat. Do you know a good furrier?" This surprised me. When Mother had said I needed a warmer coat, she hadn't mentioned a fur coat. Our new acquaintance said, "One of my friends sells furs. Why don't we go see what he has?"

The next morning he came for us at our hotel and we went to see his friend, who showed us many coats until he showed me one I liked. It was of muskrat fur, trimmed with a big collar of wolf fur. Instead of buttoning down the front, it was designed with a flare from the right side trimmed with a wide band of wolf fur. It had been shown at a fashion show and was rather theatrical and I loved it, but the price was too high for us.

We left the store without the coat. That night our new friend came back stage with the coat. The furrier had agreed to meet our price. I loved my coat, and wore it for a long time.

The new women's hats, called a "cloche," looked somewhat like a helmet. Mother decided I needed one, so with my new fur coat and hat, I felt quite fashionable. We also went shopping for gifts for Alton and Daddy. At home Alton was working at a drug store. He sold cigarettes, cigars and pipes, and was becoming knowledgeable about tobacco. Since he had started to smoke a pipe, we bought tobacco and a handsome pipe for him. For Daddy, we purchased a big tin of Scotch toffee, and it looked so good we bought one for ourselves.

We went to a quaint tea shop for oatmeal cookies, scones, and a cup of tea. We talked of Grandmother and how she would have liked to be sitting with us. We were going to miss the English tea shops, but it was a good thing it was time to move on. Our trunk was running out of space.

The train arrived in Boise, Idaho, too late for a matinee, so we only did two night shows. It had started to snow after the last show. Mother and I went to the sidetracked coach and saw there was a snowball fight going on. We managed to get inside without being hit and watched the fun from the vestibule. When the gang came inside, they had kept snowballs, and there was laughter and screaming as they pelted each other. Mother and I managed to get to safety in my upper berth, and one of the girls handed Mother some snow. When my former adagio partner, Ed, went by, she dropped the snow down the back of his neck. He was certainly surprised when he saw who had done it. She had a look of satisfaction on her face.

Next morning, we were in Salt Lake City, Utah, the last theater of the tour. The marquee of the Capital Theater displayed, "The Lone Wolf's Daughter" with Bert Lytell and his co-star Gertrude Olmstead. It was an old theater and I noticed the larger-than-usual crystal chandelier suspended from the ceiling. It also had boxes on the sides like the one Abraham Lincoln was sitting in when he was assassinated.

On the day we closed, Mary and I had been at the theater in the morning packing whatever we could. Then we left for the hotel to join Mother, who was getting ready to check out. The sidewalks were crowded with Christmas shoppers. Mary squeezed my arm, and gave an elaborate wink as we neared a corner. She stopped, shook my shoulder, and pointed up into the sky. I looked and didn't see anything in the blue sky except for some white clouds, but I still looked to where she pointed. When I caught on to what she was doing I nodded my head. The people behind us looked up to where Mary was pointing. Soon we had a crowd around us. We left, trying not to laugh, and glancing back we could see the people still looking and even heard a couple saying they could see it!

There were more tricks that night at the theater. England Ong had been teasing the stage hands all week, so they figured out a way to get even with her during the last show. On the way to the wings for her entrance, it was easy for one of them to sweep her off her feet. He deposited her on top of one of the drinking fountains and turned on the water for a couple of seconds. Her satin pajamas were soaked at the seat. It was fortunate England just sang and didn't have to dance. She sidled onto the stage, sang her song, and sidled off again. We were all watching and laughing and, when she came off the stage, she laughed, too. Probably, the others in the show had the same thoughts I had. This would be the last performance and we would not be working with England again. I knew I would miss her.

The closing night was sad, but exciting, too. I had packed all I could into the trunk, and it had been taken out of the room before the evening shows. The next time I would see it would be at home.

When the last production number was over, the big curtain closed and the audience filled the aisles as they left. A few stayed to see the feature picture if they had not seen it. The main curtain parted and the picture began on the screen. Behind it, the scrims were lowering, and the stage hands were warning us, "Heads up." We tip-toed from the stage in a hurry.

In my dressing room, I took my costume off and covered it on its hanger. After

I dressed, I rushed the costumes and shoes to the wardrobe lady. I thought sadly, "This is the last time I'll be doing this." Our worn but still beautiful costumes would be packed in crates, loaded on trucks and taken to the station. In Los Angeles, they would go to the Fanchon & Marco warehouse. I quickly removed my makeup, and packed the kimono I had bought in San Francisco's Chinatown. I checked the room to be sure it was empty.

Mother was at the stage door holding a cab for us. We shared the cab and sped away. Getting on our sidetracked coach, we found the dressing room empty and undressed quickly. The others were at the station restaurant having coffee and a snack. We didn't drink coffee; instead, Mother always bought treats for us to eat in her lower birth.

That night I lay in my berth listening to the clickety clack the wheels made as they rolled along. I wondered if this would be the last time for me to enjoy this. Not only was this the closing night in Salt Lake City, but we were going home. It had been an exciting three months.

Daddy and Alton met us at the station in Los Angeles, and we all talked at the same time. Daddy said I was to call our friend Mr. Fountain the next day. He had some plans for me. I called him, and he told me he wanted me to dance at the West Coast Theater on New Year's Eve. I told him I thought that would be fun.

We did four shows that day and the people watching the last show were exuberant. After the stage show, cartoons and comedies were shown. At midnight, the screen announced the New Year. The screen went up to show the stage and an over-sized snowman. I was inside, and when an usher came and lifted the head off, I was able to throw cotton snowballs to the audience. After I was helped out of the snow-man, I threw snowballs from the stage. Soon the air was full of snowballs the ushers had distributed, and screams joined the clamor of the noise makers they had been given. Finally the organist played Auld Lang Sang and everyone sang the old nostalgic song. The last movie went on and Alton took me home.

My family's guests were leaving, and Daddy said I could have a small glass of an after dinner drink that Alton had made with his new cocktail shaker. I sipped it slowly so I could savor each sweet drop until I went to bed. Sleep wouldn't come. It seemed longer than a year since the last New Year. How could so much have happened to me in one year? I wondered what the next New Year would bring. Would I be in another show? Would I still be dancing with Mary? Perhaps Mother would not like to leave Daddy again? Would he change his mind about my missing my last years of high school? I sure didn't want to go back there. Traveling with a big show was so much more exciting.

Chapter 3

Mary had told us the Fanchon & Marco office would call, if I was wanted for another show. I hoped to have time to rest, and it was nice to be home for awhile with Daddy and Alton.

Mother and I were enjoying the luxury of home. When we were traveling on the train, we had talked about Minneapolis. Now I wanted to know more. One day I asked her, "How did you and Daddy meet?" She told me, she and her friends would dance at one another's homes, They had met on one of those nights. He played the harmonica for some of the dances and singing. When they played the record player, he asked her to dance. They found they both loved dancing. He asked to take her home and they started to date. They went together for awhile and one night he asked her to marry him, but there was a problem. She was taking care of her younger sisters while the rest of the family worked. She could not leave them. Daddy was a carpenter and the problem was solved when he enlarged the upper part of her mother's home. After they were married, they lived there. She was able to take care of her sisters besides doing the cooking and the housework.

Her sister Mildred loved dancing as much as Mother did, and she took dance lessons when she was old enough she became a professional dancer. By that time, Beatrice was in her teens and Mother and Daddy were able to move into their own home.

Daddy had told me about his family once when I was with him in the garage. They had immigrated to America from Oslo, Norway, where he had worked at the shipyards with his father. Their mother had been ill, even before they had left Norway, and passed away soon after they arrived in Minneapolis. Their father had not lived long after he lost his wife, and the boys were left on their own. The boys sold papers until they worked as apprentices doing carpenter work.

One day, Mother asked me if I remembered Mr. Lankis, I did. John Lankis had come from Greece and he and father had become friends when they were young. Mr. Lankis had started from a push cart selling vegetables and, after working hard and investing his money, he eventually had a large store. It had rows of attractive vegetables and fruit, and even had a glassed-in room with a large ice box to keep beautiful flowers on display for sale.

Daddy would meet us at the store after Mother and I had been shopping in town, and take us home. If we had to wait, I'd ask Mother to take me to the basement so I could watch the ice cream being made, or better still, see the girls making candy, because they would give us some.

While Mr. Lankis and Daddy would talk business, Mother and I waited in front of the white marble soda fountain, sitting at delicate tables on chairs of white wrought iron. Mother always had the new drink, Coca Cola, and I would have a dish of ice cream with different flavored toppings. Mr. Lankis always gave us a box of candy when we left. I wanted to talk more, but Mother would get tired of talking about old times, so I would try to remember the stories I had heard. I knew Alton was three years old when mother lost a baby girl. Her life was taken to save Mother's. If Mother could have had a Caesarean operation, my brother would have had a red-headed sister, and I probably would not have been born! She was happy a few years later when she again became pregnant, though she had been advised against having another child. The doctor became concerned when her baby was slow in arriving.

Before dawn on March 22, 1912, I arrived, in a hurry, because I was late! Not having a telephone, Daddy went to get the doctor. I couldn't wait for them, so Mother had to manage my birth alone. After they arrived, and Mother had been cared for, Daddy went upstairs to Alton's bedroom. He told him he had a birthday present, a baby sister. It was Alton's seventh birthday, and they hadn't planned for me to come that day, I was to have arrived earlier. That day was the first time of many, when I did not do what Mother expected me to do.

Alton never got in trouble like I did. All we had in common was our green eyes. Mother often had heard what an excellent mother she was because Alton was always quiet, kept very clean, and never wandered. He never would have embarrassed Mother as I did one night when I had just learned to walk.

Friends were at our home playing cards and before the guests arrived I had been put in my bed upstairs. Later I awoke because I was too warm, so I got out of bed and took off my nightgown. I heard the laughter and talking, so instead of going back into bed, I went down the stairs for the first time, holding onto the banister. When I walked into the dining room where they were playing cards, everyone laughed and made a fuss over me. Mother took her nude baby girl back to bed. She was not amused.

My uncle Willie had a lodge at Lake Minnetonka. Father had helped him build the vacation home between the lake and the forest at one of the lakes Minnesota is famous for. On the first floor there was a large kitchen, dining room and a comfortable room with a huge fireplace. A porch ran along two sides with plenty of space for dancing. The bedrooms were upstairs. We could hear the animals at night, especially the eerie sounds of the loons. Instead of a bathroom, there was an outhouse at the edge of the forest. The women and children would not go out there alone at night.

Our family would join other families at the lodge on weekends and during the evening, Daddy would play the harmonica while they danced, and I would cuddle next to him, listen to the music and watch the dancing.

Singing was popular during World War I, and everyone knew the current songs. I joined in when they sang, "There's A Long, Long Trail A-Winding." Then everyone would get livened up with "In the Good Old summer Time" and "The Bowery." My favorite was "Beautiful Katie" because the lyrics stuttered and I thought that was a fun thing to do. When they sang "Over There, Over There," I did not know where "Over There" was, except there was a war, and Mother's only brother, Uncle Clancy, was in it.

Daddy also played a Jew's harp, a funny little instrument he would hold at the side of his mouth and pluck with his finger. It didn't make a smooth sound like the mouth organ, but twanged. I had my mother's love for dancing and the men would dance with me even though I was a small five-year-old. I learned all the current ballroom dances, even the new Fox Trot.

Too soon, Mother would take me upstairs to my bed. One night I fell out of the bed and rolled under it to the wall to be warm. When Mother and Daddy came to their bedroom and saw my bed was empty, they searched through the entire house. Some of the men went to see if I had gone to the outhouse. With the aid of a kerosene lamp, they found me under the bed, curled up into a tight ball in the corner.

Daddy was my champion and would take me fishing in a row boat on the Lake. He taught me how to put a worm on the hook so it wouldn't come off when the fish nibbled it. I was told to be still, because Daddy said if the boat moved, the fish would not bite. I behaved for him, because he always explained why he told me to do something.

He had purchased several lots, built a home for us on one, and on the other lots he built homes to sell. I was not afraid of heights and I loved to be with Daddy. One day when he was up on the roof putting shingles on a two-story house, I called to him, "Daddy, I've got a splinter. Would you take it out?" He took me down the ladder and took out the splinter. After a spanking, Mother gave me orders not to climb up to the roof again.

I called him another time and he found me half way down the cellar, holding on to the rungs of a ladder for dear life. My feet were dangling in the air between the rungs. They had slipped from the next rung before I could get my footing. He rescued me, but not from another spanking. Even Alton, trying to save me from my frequent spankings would say, "Don't spank my birthday present." I still got my spanking, which was the way children were disciplined in those days.

Daddy would keep scraps of two by fours six inches high for me, and I made dolls from them. With pieces of material Mother gave me I would make dresses. I would draw faces and color their hair with crayons. On their flat bottom surfaces they stood up better than my real dolls. I could group them together and have whole families of different sizes. My real pretty dolls were always "sick in bed," which puzzled Mother because they always had lovely clothing she had made.

One day Mother asked our neighbor to keep an eye on me while she went into town. She saw I was busy with my wooden family and left. I went into the house to see Mother, but I could not find her. Panic-stricken, I looked for her, since she had never left me alone before. When I ran outside, the neighbor told me I was to ask her if I needed anything. My Mother had just left.

Running to the front of the house, I saw Mother going to the street car line that ended a block away from our home. There was just one track, so to change the direction the motorman had to take the trolley, the line the electricity follows to the wires over-head, to the back of the streetcar. The motorman had finished and was waiting for Mother to get on board before he started into town.

I ran as fast as I could, calling, "Mommy, Mommy." The conductor heard me and said, "Your little girl wants you." She turned just as I clutched her and held on to her. I wailed, "Mommy you didn't Tiss me goodbye." She never left the house without kissing me goodbye again.

The motorman knew me and had nicknamed me "Smiley." The street cars had seats that ran the length of the car with the aisle in between. I thought smiles made people happy, so when passengers would sit down opposite me, I would smile at them until they had to smile back at me. Mother didn't seem to mind unless they gave me a small coin, then she was embarrassed. I always smiled at people until I was older and realized it was not the proper thing to do.

My only playmates were older than me and were almost finishing kindergarten. When their teacher suggested they might bring friends to a party, they asked Mother if I could go. She told them, "Yes." When the students had finished their entertainment, the teacher asked, "Would any of our guests like to do something?"

One of my friends said, "Lucile can dance."

They had been watching me when I made up dances for my own entertainment as well as theirs. The teacher asked me, "What kind of music would you like?"

I told her I didn't need music, I just made my own. Then going to the center of the floor I hummed, while doing my dance.

The teacher asked Mother if I could finish the semester with the class. This suited me because of the activity it provided. I don't think Mother minded, because taking care of me was like holding onto quicksilver. The next semester I started in my own class of kindergarten and I enjoyed being with children my own age.

When all the houses Daddy had built on our block had been sold, including our home, we moved into Grandmother's upstairs rooms. Then Daddy bought a large garage where people would bring their cars to be repaired. He liked tinkering with machines, and now it was automobiles. When he bought our car, we were the envy of the neighborhood. It was a Liberty Sport Model and, compared to other cars, it was really sporty.

Living in Grandmother's house, the upstairs rooms were crowded with only one bedroom, so Alton and I shared a couch that made into a bed in the tiny living room. He didn't like the idea very much, but I did. He would always be my hero. Alton worried that the fellows would find out and tease him. It was bad enough that I trailed him all the time.

All of his friends, except Lila and her sister Bertha, became tired of my being around. Without any children my own age, he was expected to keep me out of trouble. When I learned how to read, I could sit still for hours, but before then I was always active. After Mother dressed me to go downtown with her, she would put me in a chair and tell me to sit still until she was ready. I would try to stay quiet, but then I would start wondering what Grandmother's chickens were doing. When Mother had finished dressing, she would find me playing with the baby chicks and have to change me to a cleaner dress. After I had my spanking.

Her fingers were skinny, and the spanking hurt. I decided if I didn't cry there would be no reason to spank me. It worked. Mother stopped the spanking when I just lay over her knees, not making a sound. Then she made her decision. If I misbehaved Mother called me "Naughty Lizzie," and said she did not love me. My middle name was Elizabeth after my Grandmother, but I hated the name Lizzie and, of course, wanted Mother's love. It worked for her. She controlled me by not showing her love for me. Many times later, I wished I had just taken my spankings, and cried until she felt I had been punished. It hurt, but keeping her love from me hurt me more. When I was older, I realized she gave me her love in her own way. She gave up many things so I could have my lessons and made my dresses and costumes for years.

When I was in first grade, my brother's girl friends, Lila and Bertha, would take me to their folk dance classes. Their dance instructor would let me dance with them because I did not need special attention. Learning the dances was easy for me, and I was always happy when I was dancing.

One day the girls and I were watching the rehearsal of a play, "Snow White and the Seven Dwarfs." The girl who was to do a solo as the Queen of the Fairies couldn't learn the dance. We had been watching for several days, and Lila went to the teacher and

56

said, "Lucile can do the dance."

The teacher asked where I was and told Lila to bring me to her. She asked where I was and told Lila to bring me to her. Then she asked me if I could do the dance. I showed her I could, then she said I was to be the Queen of the Fairies. The girl was demoted to being a fairy. She did not seem to mind. Mother was delighted when she heard the news and asked what kind of a costume I would need. It was the first of years of sewing costumes for me.

Mother asked Daddy if I could have dance lessons, but he said it could wait until I was older. He could not afford it, and he thought I was too young. If I took lessons, I would be expected to practice instead of play.

Father and I were alike in many ways. He didn't mind my hugs, and liked my companionship when he was making things out of wood in the garage. I loved to watch him when he was making furniture or toys. Then he shared his love of wood with me, showing me how the grain in the wood sometimes looked like scenery.

When he would go to the car, I was right there eager to help start it. A crank was in the front of the radiator and I would sit in the driver's seat while he turned the crank to fire the ignition. On this model, there was a lever on the steering wheel for feeding the car gas. When the sound told me the ignition had caught, I would carefully push the lever higher. He would stop cranking and hurry to get into the car, then warm up the motor until the car was ready to drive. Cranking a car was dangerous. Sometimes an arm was broken if the crank reversed fast. Alton wanted to crank the car but Daddy didn't let him. When Alton was old enough, Daddy taught him how to drive. He also told me all the things I should know about driving, but never let me drive when I was old enough.

When people started to buy more cars, accidents started to happen. A horse pulling a buggy would sometimes rear up and run away when it was startled by the backfire from a car. The people in the buggy would be terrified and the papers would tell of someone being killed in the overturned carriage. Automobiles were to change many things, and they were not accepted quickly.

I loved Grandmother's horse, Molly. Sometimes we would go for a ride with Grandmother in her carriage. The sound of Molly's hooves going clip, clop, clip, clop when she was pulling the buggy was more pleasing to me than the noise of the combustion of the new cars.

In the daytime Molly would be tied in the empty lot next to Grandmother's home and Mother would let me play near her. When I was a baby I had crawled around, even under her. She would be careful not to step on me when she moved.

When we went for a Sunday drive, Daddy would set me on his lap and let me help steer. He didn't think women should drive-it was not ladylike-so Mother never drove. I loved being near my father and driving was a real treat for me.

I would try to remember everything he told me, he instructed me to watch where we were, to remember where we turned, what was on the corners, and which way we went. Going home, I had to tell him how to get there. He taught me how to tell east from west by the shadows cast by the buildings and the trees. Then I could tell where north and south were. If I remembered all he told me, and I was careful, I would never get lost when I went any place.

He did teach me something that would help me the rest of my life. He told me to watch where we were driving, to remember where we turned, what was on the corners, which way we went. Going home, I had to tell him how to get there. He taught me how to tell east from west from the shadows cast by the buildings and the trees. Then I could tell where north and south were.

Ironically, the first time I became lost was years later in Minneapolis, when I was dancing at the Minnesota Theater. I had left Mother at the hotel and had gone to the rehearsal. Because I left from the front of the theater instead of the alley door, I couldn't remember which way the hotel was. I was not worried because I knew the name of the hotel and could ask where it was. The rehearsal had gone quickly, and Mother would not be expecting me, so I was looking into the shop windows. Then I heard a hostile voice, "Why are you following me?"

A disreputable old woman had stepped in front of me and would not let me pass. Her voice was venomous. I stopped. "I'm clean," she said. "The police better stop following me." She shook her skinny, crooked finger in my face.

"I don't know what you are talking about," I said.

"Yes you do, and stop following me."

She was shaking with anger and began swearing at me. People were looking at us and I was embarrassed and frightened, but I managed to move around her and hurried away.

The hotel was in the next block and Mother listened to my story. She could not understand the incident either. We thought it odd that we would be in Minneapolis and have this happen. From then on, I remembered Daddy's instructions and seldom got lost again.

In 1918, when I was beginning to understand events outside of my own small world, there was a terrible epidemic of the Spanish influenza, which killed thousands of people. Grandmother was seldom home because she was helping at the hospital. She wasn't a registered nurse, but when the country went to war, she had begun to help in any way she could.

On November 11, 1918, I was looking out of the window trying to find out what all the excitement was about. There was lots of noise with horns honking, church bells ringing, and I even heard guns being fired into the air. Some people were banging pots with big spoons to make more noise. I couldn't understand what it was all about.

"What's happening?" I asked Mother.

"The war is over," she said. "We have won the war, and an armistice is being signed. Times will be better. Uncle Clancy can come home with his Polish bride. Grandmother will be able to be at home more and we will start getting ready for our move to California."

I had not paid much attention to Daddy's talk of driving to California. Mother had not been too enthused, now I decided they were serious. When Daddy had time between fixing other people's cars, he began to prepare our car for the trip. No more Sunday drives. Mother and Alton were busy pumping gasoline at the curbside pump at the garage while Daddy was working inside. The doll I had brought with me did not keep me from being bored, and besides, I wanted to help, so I began to call out "Iverson's Garage" at the top of my lungs. Mother decided I should spend Sundays with Grandmother, who didn't mind my trailing after her and always found time for me to sit on her lap.

She had nicknamed me "Slakey." It was a Scottish name for someone who was affectionate, and I certainly deserved the name.

When I was about three years old, Mother dressed me in a pretty white dress with my new black patent leather shoes. My hair was washed and curled, and we went to visit Grandmother. I had just received a banana from her when someone came to the door. A man said he was taking pictures of children for a contest. Mother wasn't interested but Grandmother overcame Mother's objections and told the man to take my picture. Mother tried to take my banana from me, but I would not give it up. She gave in when she decided this was not the time or place for me to have a spanking, and let the man take pictures of me. The resulting picture showed a child, with a determined expression, and tiny fingers that were digging into a banana. It won first place in the contest!

Grandmother was given a large framed photo which went into her parlor. From then on, in her opinion, I could do no wrong. She had given me a small stein of my own that originally held German mustard but didn't hold much beer. When she took care of me, we would sit in the living room in front of the pot-bellied stove, sipping our beer. Then I would hear stories about Mother's childhood and about Scotland where they used to live.

One day I asked why I did not have a Grandpa. Other kids had one, why didn't I? She told me Grandfather and she had decided their children would have better schooling and opportunities in America than they would have in Dundee. I wanted to know where Dundee was. "It is where the Marmalade you like comes from."

I wanted to know where the children were. She laughed and said, "They are all grown up. Your Uncle Clancy is the oldest and he joined the Army. Your Aunt Nora was next. She comes here sometimes with her children, who are all older than you. Next was your mother, and then your Aunt Mildred. You have fun with her. Your Aunt Beatrice was born here, and your mother took care of her while the rest of us worked."

"Where is Grandfather and what did he do?"

"While we were in Scotland, he worked at a nursery where they grew flowers. He thought he could make more money in Minneapolis, but instead he could not find a good nursery job and had to take a job working with horses in a stable. He had a head injury one day, during an accident, and never fully recovered. He was taken to a state hospital and has never left it."

She had forgotten me and was sort of talking almost to herself. I slipped off her lap and went to the kitchen to see if there would be one of her wonderful scones so I could put some of that marmalade on it.

She came into the kitchen and said, "I had better start to cook our dinner." Watching her cook in the big kitchen was fun, and sometimes she even let me help. She

60

would bring in a big shovel full of coal and start the fire roaring again from the embers that still remained in the big iron stove. It was always warm from cooking breakfast or maybe just from making the tea that she and Mother liked.

The great big black stove fascinated me because she did so many things with it besides cooking. On wash days, she had a big oval container she would boil the clothes in. I wanted to help her stir the clothes with the long broom handle like she did, but she said I was too small. The kitchen would be hot and steamy and smelled of the soap.

The stove held the irons she used for ironing clothes. The iron itself had a top and two bottoms. Using the top part with a hot bottom until it cooled, she would take it to the stove and do something to the top making the first part fall off, and she would pick up the other hot one.

It seemed she was always baking something good to eat, like scones or oatmeal cookies. For Christmas, she would make Scotch short bread that melted in your mouth, serving it with apricot brandy. Daddy always gave me a bite of his shortbread and a tiny sip of his sweet brandy.

One day when I was underfoot in the kitchen as usual, she needed something from the store. It was easy for children to get groceries when there was a charge account and a list, which sometimes included a penny candy reward. She asked me to go to the store a block away. I loved to run fast, and I was back quickly and sat down.

She saw me and asked, "When are you going to the store?"

I pointed to the sack on the table.

She asked me, "How did you get it so fast?"

I said, "I put pep on my feet."

I was teased about "pep on my feet" for a long time.

I asked her if she would be going to California with us. She said "No. Leaving Scotland was enough change."

I didn't mind making a change at all. It sounded like a big adventure when Daddy talked about it. Mother said she did not understand why they had to leave all their friends. He said one reason he and his family had left Norway was because of the weather, and winters in Minnesota were not much better. He told her about the wonderful sunshine in California with no snow to shovel. Look how much money they would save not having to buy coal every winter. I asked him if I could take my sled, and he said I would not need it, that instead I would have a great big ocean where I could swim all year long.

I knew the time for our leaving was getting closer when Mother and I visited some of her relatives on their farm. I had never been on their farm for more than a day, and I loved the week we spent there. I would get up early, so I could watch the hired hand milk the cows. Not everyone had the new machinery that later would make milking by hand obsolete.

He would go into the barn and lead one of the cows out and tie her to the fence that went around the pig sty. He then sat on a little stool by the cow and placed a bucket beneath her udder. Reaching under her, he would start squeezing and pulling. The sound of the milk as it went into the bucket always brought the cats, who were mousers for the barn. It was fun to watch him squirt milk into the cat's mouths. They were expert in catching it too.

One morning he squirted milk into my hair. I squealed like the baby pigs and mother came running out to see what was happening. She was provoked when she had to wash my hair again after washing it the day before.

She was strict with me but could be fun, too. One day she played a trick on our host, who was in the habit of having a nip of whiskey on the sly before dinner. He had a hiding place in the pantry and Mother found it. One evening before dinner, she took the whiskey out and substituted cold tea in the bottle.

We all waited for the explosion. It came! Sputters from the kitchen were followed by some words I had never heard before. We tried to hold straight faces when he came into the dining room, but when we all started to laugh it didn't make him any happier. Besides the family, the men who came to help with the harvest sat at the table as well.

I had heard about another trick that Mother and Dad had participated in. Two of their friends, Mr. and Mrs. Torgenson had just been married. She was full of fun and liked to trick or tease her friends.

At the reception in their new home, the new bedroom set was much admired. Instead of the usual double bed, they had bought the latest fashion, twin beds. They had been asked what they were going to use the other bed for. They insisted they were going to use both beds. Then she explained how much healthier it was to sleep apart.

Her parents had given them a complete silver service for a wedding present. While they were on their honeymoon, their friends went to their home. They short-sheeted one of the twin beds by folding the top sheet half way down. They took all the forks, knives and spoons from the silver chest, and carefully put them between the folded sheets, then they smoothed the top of the bed.

The next card game was at their new home.

"How do you like twin beds?" they were asked.

She replied, "They're wonderful."

While serving refreshments after the card game was over she complained, "It's funny. We can't find our silver set."

She was mystified when everyone started to laugh. Then they showed the couple where their gift had been hidden in one of the beds. They heard about that for a long time.

Meanwhile, the time for our trip to California grew closer. Mr. Lankis insisted we stay at his orchard for a week. We stayed in a large and comfortable army officer's tent left over from the war. We spent a week there while Mother practiced cooking on the Coleman stove. We bought food from the neighboring farmers. Mr. Lankis liked Mother's cooking and she cooked everything she thought he would like when he visited. He would bring some of his wonderful ice cream and told us, "You can't be too full. It will go down through the cracks."

Daddy said we had to go home because the car was almost ready. Mother said I would have to make my own decisions on which toys I would like to have in California. My little iron stove, which looked so much like Grandmothers, had been given away, along with the doll crib Daddy had made. I decided upon Reggie, my teddy bear sleeping partner, and Freckles, who was dressed in overalls and wore a big grin on his face. I had much prettier dolls than Freckles but his smile made me feel good.

Aunt Beatrice was called Bea now that she was a young lady, and she was coming because she didn't want to be away from my mother. It was obvious they were sisters, with their brown hair and blue eyes, but their dispositions were entirely different.

Although there was several years difference in their ages, Bea accepted Alton at fourteen more than Alton accepted me at seven. She included him in some of her social activities, and I always felt left out. To make me feel better, Mother let me wear my fairy costume and go out to trick or treat, when my aunts, Mildred and Bea, had taken Alton with them on the previous Halloween.

Halloween had a real meaning then. Mother was not happy at all about hearing of an outhouse being pushed over by them and some of their friends. Anyone who still had an outhouse had to stand guard if they wanted their outside bathroom to be intact the next day. No one seemed to get awfully angry. Perhaps they had pushed over a few in their youth.

Daddy had done a lot of work on the car so that five of us could ride, eat and sleep in what was a forerunner of modern RVs. The back of the front seat had been made to fall flush with the back seat. Daddy's friends made fun about my folks "having their seats cut down." Daddy and Mother did not mind. They would have a comfortable bed. Daddy used his carpentry skills and made sleeping quarters for Bea, my brother and me. A long narrow box on the running board on the driver's side held the rolled up springs that we pulled out to make a bed. At night, a tent fastened to the side of the car, which was large enough to cover the bed Bea and I slept in and the cot placed alongside for Alton. We let Alton undress under the shelter of the tent first while we were still warmly dressed. He had to wait outside in his pajamas while we changed.

On the passenger's side of the car Daddy made a cupboard that fit the contour of the car's fender and the running board. With Mother's directions, he made shelves with spaces for containers for the food and utensils we would need for the journey. Everything had to be secure. The door of the cupboard hinged at the bottom and fastened at the top. A leg was attached to the front of the door and, when released, it came down and held the door which then became our table. Mother cooked there with the Coleman stove, then it was cleared for us to eat upon.

The folding chairs, linens, blankets and clothing were in a big box, fastened to the back of the car. Everything we were going to have in California for awhile was in that box. There were more boxes left in Minneapolis, which we would send for once we were settled.

Daddy visited Mr. Torgenson for the last time, taking "Torg," his water spaniel hunting dog, to his new home. Torg had short, tightly curled reddish brown fur and his brown eyes were soft and loving. I grieved over leaving him as much as I did for the toys I had to leave behind. Torg was a good dog and knew how to play hide and seek with Alton and me. He would "stay" while we hid. Alton would call, he would find us, and almost knock us over with his exuberance. He was our playmate until the hunting guns were brought out. Then he didn't even know us, but didn't let Daddy out of his sight, until they left to go hunting. Mr. Torgenson had given the dog to Daddy, who had named him Torg.

The Minnesota lakes were famous for duck hunting and fishing. Daddy was going to miss his companions who had gone fishing and duck hunting with him. His knowledge of carpentry had enabled him to make a special boat for hunting ducks. It was constructed in halves so the group could split and go in different directions.

Mother was worried about the condition of the roads we would be traveling on. Daddy reassured her they were being improved all the time. His sport was bicycle racing, and knew first hand when a different stretch of road had been improved. He talked to the different cyclists, whom he had competed against, about the road conditions where they had cycled.

Touring across the country was the least important reason for improved roads. Farmers needed better roads for their produce to be taken into town. Federal money was given to states and counties so there would be better roads for the new mail trucks to travel on. Daddy told Mother there was even a transcontinental road being built called the Lincoln Highway. It would go from coast to coast. Money from the government was available to the states, but there were not any universal rules about how the roads were to be built. Worse still, nobody could comprehend how much money was needed, and until the twenties, there did not seem to be much of a plan. Not too many people ventured to take the trip we were going on.

We traveled on old roads, some partly asphalt and macadam. Once in awhile, there were patches of concrete. Besides dirt, which became mud when it rained, there were rock and gravel surfaces. In towns, brick was a good surface but water and heavy traffic would wear it down, and then it needed frequent repairs. The larger cities started to have concrete roads connecting them. Steel reinforced concrete was enabling bridges to be constructed over rivers that had only known ferries, or were forded. A system of numbering U.S. routes was just beginning, which enabled maps to be comprehensible. Daddy had been collecting maps and marking them for our trip.

When we got into the car, Daddy gave me the box of maps and the job of navigator. I realized he had been training me for this for a long time.

Our Car Fording a River

Daddy Working Under Our Car

Hamlin Kiddie Revue, I am in Front, 2nd from the Left

Hamlin Kiddie Revue, I was a Newsboy

In One of Mother's Most Imaginative Costumes

Sweet Sixteen and Ready to Go

My Daddy, John A. Iverson

My Mother, Margaret Iverson

Chapter 4

Mother sat in front with Daddy while Alton, Bea and I sat in the back seat. It was really quiet in the car, because we were all thinking about the changes we were making. Mother and Bea were leaving their mother. Daddy was leaving friends he had made since he came to America. Alton was going into a strange high school, and I thought of the dolls that I had given away because they could not come with me. Daddy broke the silence by starting to sing, "It's a Long, Long, Way to Tipperary," and soon we joined in. He always knew how to cheer us up and singing songs helped us cross the country. If spirits were low, one of us would start to sing and we would all join in. We always finished with the song that made us laugh, "Beautiful K-K-K-Katy." Then we would talk about the scenery and the mood changed.

Daddy had planned the trip well. He would ask me questions about where we were or how far to the next crossroads. I helped him as much as I could. I had to be alert and watch for landmarks and road signs, so I really saw more than anyone else did. Years later, I realized what a favor he had done for me because I remembered more about the trip than anyone else. Also, I have been blessed with a good memory, because I can see what I am thinking of in my mind.

We traveled south going through Iowa and saw cornfields that stretched as far as the eye could see. We found our biggest trouble would be mud in the wheels. They were made like wagon wheels, with large spokes. The mud would pack into the spokes and Alton and Daddy would have to dig the heavy mud out. It was called gumbo mud, and from then on Mother was teased for her gumbo soup. Her soup was always like stew and her stew like soup, but always good.

If we had a flat tire, Daddy would fix it. He knew how to fix the car when something would go wrong. If we had to wait while Daddy was working on the car, we would take walks along the road. We were going though a small town in Missouri and Daddy stopped the car so Mother could go into a grocery store. The rest of us were walking, stretching our legs, when we passed a group of school children. Bea asked one of the girls, "Did you learn anything new today?"

The girl answered, "That's what we go to school fer."

We bought our fresh food from the farmers when we could, and it was lucky we all liked chicken. We had all the vegetables we needed and milk never tasted as good again. When we found the place to camp overnight, mother would give each of us something to do to help with the dinner. We never worried about having an appetite.

Almost every night mother would say, "Adolph, when are we going to stop to camp?

He would say, "Pretty soon. We still have lots of sun."

After awhile she would ask again or the rest of us would point to the places we thought would be good to camp in. When the sun had gone down and we finally stopped, we would make camp with a flashlight and Coleman lamp. Then it wasn't only the air that was chilly. Nerves can get on edge when five people, tired and hungry, are confined to a car for days.

After we had gone to bed one night, I was sound asleep until Bea woke me up and asked me, "Are you awake?"

I was awake and frightened, too, when I realized why she was scared. We heard something sniffing around our tent.

She said, "Is it a wild animal? Wolves? Or maybe coyotes?"

We had heard the wolves howling and the coyotes yipping while we were eating our dinner. We finally went back to sleep and the next morning we saw our wild animals. We were next to a cow pasture and they were curious about us. Alton laughed at us, but we insisted there were wild animals out there. Daddy proved it because the next day he stopped the car and shot a red fox. He skinned it skillfully and, after we arrived in Long Beach, he had it made into a stole for mother. She wore it for years.

One night, we camped in a narrow canyon, and when the car's lights were turned off, we could see the sky, full of stars that looked as though they were resting on the tall cliffs. It was quiet and peaceful while we had our dinner and went to bed. About one in the morning the wind awakened us, a wind that wanted to tear our tent apart. We knew the clouds hanging over the cliffs were full of rain. We had been warned of flash floods, and did not want to be caught in one of them. It did not take us long to break camp and pack the car. Traveling through heavy rain, thunder and lightning, we reached the last town we had passed before. We found a hotel that had a small light in the lobby. The sleepy clerk took us to two rooms, without any heat, but we were glad to be indoors.

Mother left Bea and me, and went to see if Daddy and Alton needed anything. When she came back, I was busy opening the dresser drawers to see if anything had been left in them. She got there just in time to snatch the "balloon" I had just found. She said, "Nasty," and took it down the hall to the bathroom to get rid of it. Bea was as curious as I was. I heard them whispering before I went to sleep. From then on mother made dresser drawers a "no, no" for me.

We didn't stay at a hotel often, but one Friday night Daddy decided that we needed a rest from traveling. He explained that the car needed a rest, too, and he intended to take it to a garage and work on it.

Saturday morning, when we were dressing to go to breakfast, someone looking out the window noticed that there were people going into the church across the street, dressed in their Sunday best. We soon found that it was not Saturday but Sunday! Daddy said we were losing a day's travel, but we had two nights in a hotel and an opportunity to look around the town. It was Tuesday before we were on the road again.

Daddy would ask what we could expect ahead of us when we stopped at the service stations. Information about the rivers we were to cross was most important. A river without a bridge meant we must ford it, and farmers would use their team of horses to pull our car across. We learned to look for the sign by a road leading to a farmhouse that said they would ford a car over the river. Once in awhile we would be offered a rest overnight in their home. Then we made the trip across the river in the morning before the farmer's chores.

One time was special. After a good dinner, the wife and my mother had talked for a long time and became friends. Evidently, Mother had asked her to take a picture of us fording the river and send it to us later. We had a hearty breakfast the next morning. Then, shivering from the cold, we climbed into the farmer's wagon. The team of horses towed the car with Daddy at the wheel. The picture shows the rest of us, bundled up in the wagon on a cloudy morning.

I was the only one who liked the ride across the river. Mother would tell me to stay in my seat, but I would go to the side to look down into the water. I did not think it was dangerous to cross a river until I was an adult and would see a movie with wagons overturning while fording a river, and the people drowning.

We were enjoying the warmer weather when we reached New Mexico and saw the railroad station in Albuquerque. We reminded Daddy that he had promised us we could eat at the Harvey House, next to the station. Fred Harvey had built many of these restaurants along the Santa Fe Railroad. They were famous, not only for their food but also for the attractive Harvey Girls, who had been hired for their character and appearance.

The dining room was filled with tables covered with snow-white linen and we had more knives and forks and spoons at our places than we had ever seen before. Our appetites overcame the formality and we enjoyed the delicious food. Suddenly, the room filled when passengers streamed in from a train that had stopped. We were curious and the pretty waitress told us the company also had chefs cooking for the dining cars on some trains. From then on we would look for the dining cars on the trains. While we were eating, Daddy told us that we could camp overnight on the outskirts of Albuquerque. Before we camped we went to see the missions and historical buildings and looked at the wonderful Indian and Mexican crafts on display. When we made our camp, we had our first experience with sand. The next day on our way to Gallup we saw lots of it. It was also hot! We were told we should be comfortable in the dry heat, but we were still hot.

The brilliant reds and golds of the plains fascinated us beside the intense blue skies and white clouds. The trees were starting to wear their autumn apparel, adding their hues of green with still more red and gold.

We saw many Indians with their tepees and adobe homes. We would point out these different dwellings to the others. Even the smoke from their fires smelled different, and I still like the fragrance of New Mexico wood burning. The desert land was not like the green Minnesota we were accustomed to, and the roads were endless. We traveled for a long time on what had been an Army road, part of which would become the famous Route 66. Now it was Highway 40 and it was endless. I think the scenery today is more or less the same, but there are more motels than there were in 1919.

In Minneapolis, we had gone to ceremonies at the Indian reservation outside the city. One time when, as usual, I was dancing by myself to the music, a handsome Indian man came to me and showed me how to do one of their steps. I didn't forget it and used it in a routine years later.

Before we reached Gallup, Daddy pointed to a sign and said to Alton, "There is a Harvey House in Gallup, and we won't be seeing any more of them. Do you want to eat there?"

We knew Daddy was teasing Alton because in Albuquerque he had made an impression on the waitress. When the winsome young lady had brought finger bowls at the end of our meal, he had carefully dipped his fingers in the bowl, then dried his fingers on his napkin. We followed his example, but we noticed she brought him extra mints.

Later, in the car, Mother said, "Alton, you had never seen a finger bowl before. How did you know what to do?"

"I was watching other people when they received theirs, but I wouldn't have done it if I had known that girl was going to make me feel so funny."

"She was complimenting you on your good manners. I was proud of you."

He changed the subject. "Look, a train is coming," and we turned to watch it.

The railroad tracks often ran parallel to the road, and one of our ways to while away the monotonous hours was to count the cars and read the box car signs to see where they were from. We saw the dining cars as they passed and I resolved that someday I would be traveling in a dining car like those people. Some years later, when I traveled with shows, I always enjoyed the diner, and when I'd see cars traveling along the road, I would recall our trip.

We were told there was an Indian reservation nearby, and we agreed we had never seen so many Indians. In town, we wished we could buy some of the wares spread out upon their woven blankets. Daddy was quick to explain there was not room for any pottery, jewelry or baskets, even if we were able to afford them. Each of us had a preference, but we could not persuade Daddy to buy anything. I did manage to acquire a tiny baby papoose that I had to promise to keep with me. I kept it for years.

At a garage, Daddy found the Arizona 1918 AAA tour book, and we learned more about the road conditions ahead. It helped, because it told us what we should expect. It said the road from Gallup to Holbrook was "sandy, rough, no bridges, steep grades, many arroyos washes." We agreed it was not an easy road to drive on, but we did manage it without difficulty. Seeing the west this way was something we could not have imagined. The altogether different sights fascinated us.

Bea found out the hard way that you don't touch the odd looking cactus when she touched one and a needle stuck into her finger. When she tried to bite it out, it got into her tongue. Daddy had a hard time, but finally got it out with a pair of pliers while we stood and watched.

From Holbrook to Springerville our tour book said, "Fair roads, easy grades, bad in wet weather." It didn't rain, so we made the 95 miles without mishap. Going to Cooley's Ranch, we saw spectacular scenery along the way, and a 9400-foot high mountain amazed us after the flat country we knew. We not only saw rocks of many colors but also wished the road didn't have so many rocks on it.

Daddy told Mother often that the scenery we were driving through made up for the discomfort. It was beautiful in its own way, but we would have liked to have been more comfortable. The roads had so many curves; we three in the back seat were tossed towards each other. At first we laughed, but after awhile it was not so funny.

At last we saw the sign, "Globe, the Gateway of the Copper World." It was a large town with streets that wound through mountain canyons, mountains which showed scars, evidence of extensive mining. Daddy's book said there were good garages, so he decided we should stay at one of the many hotels.

After checking into one, he took the car to a garage, and the rest of us walked around the busy town. Soon Mother found the mercantile establishments and was surprised to see the abundance of sewing materials on display with all the accessories. A clerk assured her that in this small town, there were five churches, six schools and 10,000 people. Plenty of necessary domestic articles were brought to the town by train.

We enjoyed the cooler weather and the comfortable hotel, but Daddy woke us early. The car was ready and soon we were on the "Ocean to Ocean Highway" toward Phoenix, our next goal. We saw many mines in the mountains until we started to descend the steep grades. When we saw Castle Rock, we knew we were headed for easier driving.

The scenery changed and was more like Minnesota, with cattle and farmland. We saw some palm trees before we reached the town of Mesa. Further on, we had to ford the Salt River, and after some more desert scenery, we arrived in Phoenix. Everyone but Daddy thought it would be nice to take a day off. Instead, Daddy said, "We have a 208 mile drive to Yuma ahead of us, and we need to travel while we still have good weather."

After one night of sleep, we were up early again, and I began to watch for Dome because then we would be nearing Yuma.

When it came in sight, I said, "Dome is over there. Now we have twenty miles to go."

Reaching Yuma, we went to a hotel for a good night's rest, and the next day we explored the town because we were advised to wait for evening to cross the desert. Daddy talked with people about the new irrigation ditches that were bringing water in from the new Yuma siphon. The water was coming from the Laguna Dam in California and would make the area a wonderful agricultural district. We could see where cotton and orange trees had already been planted. The orange trees were added to the list we had made of all the different plants: cactus, saguaros, yuccas, and the wonderful date palm trees. During the day we ate delicious dates and oranges and had our dinner at a Chinese restaurant, something else we were not familiar with. Mother made us take a nap before we started our trip across the desert.

We were curious when we started out for the sand dunes, west of the Colorado River, and wanted to see the road made with wood planks tied together. It had been built to stop the sand from obliterating the roads when the winds blew. It was narrow and felt different because of the sand it was on. Daddy made certain not to leave the road because it would be hard to get back on again.

We also drove slowly because of the radiator. The radiators in those days had a nasty habit of heating and boiling over. If they got too hot, we would have to wait until it was cool enough for water to be poured in. We always carried extra water in a canvas bag that hung on the side of the car. Occasionally, the radiator started steaming, but we were lucky on the desert, and it remained cool.

The dunes were not very high but there was nothing to see anyway. We were on the only highway between Yuma, Arizona, and El Centro, California. It was paved in 1925, and now an interstate highway takes you quickly across this desert. I still look for the plank road whenever we cross that area. There is a small piece of the road fenced in, marked with a sign but, if you don't know where to look, it is hard to see. Places in the road were widened, so cars could pass each other. Headlights helped. When we saw their beam coming, we pulled off to the wider place until the car passed.

We were unusually quiet; the land was almost mystical with nothing but sand meeting the eye. It was hot in the car, especially since we had been advised to put up our curtains because of the sand. If we needed protection from the weather, we had curtains that were made of a heavy cloth with snaps that matched big snaps on the car. The only windows were rectangles of a product called Isinglass. Daddy had told us it was a transparent, almost pure gelatin prepared from the air bladder of certain fish. It would become discolored so it was hard to see through, not at all like the windows we have now that you can open easily. At last, we left the dunes with sighs of relief, and after a few uneventful miles, we came to the Laguna Mountains. The road was steep and narrow and made many tight turns. The three of us in the back seat were rolled side to side again, making any sleep for us impossible.

It was dawn when we drove into San Diego. Five weary people gratefully piled into beds at the Hotel Stanford, our home for the next two weeks. It was wonderful to feel the cool air coming from the ocean. The fog that we were going to know so well felt wonderful.

The first day we were in San Diego, Mother said, "I never want to be called Maggie again. From now on I am Margaret. It will be easy since we will be away from old friends."

Only Bea and Daddy really had a problem remembering. Beatrice had become Bea and Daddy had already changed to Adolph instead of John. He did keep his initials: J. A. Iverson. Alton answered to Al without any trouble but to us he was always Alton. Mother had named me after a book of poems and made certain I was to be called Lucile, and nothing else. This was just one of the changes we would be making in the future.

The Spanish, Indians, Mexicans and eastern folk looking for gold had built homes reflecting their past. Some were adobe style and others replicas of eastern homes. Daddy brought our attention to the new one story houses with porches in front. He had been told they were called California bungalows.

Tijuana, Mexico, was only a few miles away, and we drove across the border to see this foreign country. The casinos attracted Daddy because he had played poker with his friends, and he wanted to see the different gambling tables. It did not take long before he was convinced the games were not for him, so we moved on. We saw a saloon, whose sign said it was famous for its beautiful mahogany bar. Daddy and I went in to see the long bar, and he helped me get on a tall stool. We both ran our hands along the wood that was as smooth as satin. I loved having him to myself, and when he ordered a beer he asked for a small glass so I could have some.

Mother wanted to go to Long Beach to see where her cousin Annie Green lived before we decided where we would live. On our way, we drove along the coast and were awed by the Pacific Ocean. Looking towards it, all we could see was the sparkling blue water and the white caps on the waves.

In Long Beach, we stayed at a hotel on Ocean Avenue that had railroad tracks alongside the street right in front of the hotel. We were discussing what kind of dinner we would have when Alton, Bea and I heard a train. We ran to the big window of our room. When the train reached the front of the hotel, there was a loud whistle and heavy steam clouded our window. It startled us so much we screamed and backed up. We were still laughing when we went to eat.

We found a small apartment not far from the ocean where we stayed until we found our new home. Alton and I had to start school immediately, and he was able to go into high school, but they made me repeat my last grade. They enrolled me in the grade I had just finished in the spring. Mother fussed but they said there was too much difference in the school systems, so they won.

When we found the house we wanted, I had to go to a different school. I don't know Mother achieved it, but I was placed in the same grade I had started in Minneapolis in the fall. I was happy to be with others my own age again. I had a long way to walk each day, at least a mile, but there was a library along the way. I started to take out books often. Alton's high school was still in the same area so he didn't have to change. He had to ride a bus until he was given a bicycle.

We were experiencing many changes and could not foresee the future, but we were all glad to be in sunny California at last.

Chapter 5

Daddy was enchanted with the weather in California. When he heard of the heavy snowfall in the east, he reminded us that now he would not have to shovel coal down the chute into the cellar or clear the snow so we could get out of the house.

Thanksgiving Day we commented on the fact that it was warm and sunny. Daddy suggested we go swimming in the morning. We had been invited to my mother's cousin's home for dinner later in the day. When we went down to the beach, we found the water was cold and did not stay long to swim. Daddy took pictures of us, and we accused him of asking us to swim so that he could send pictures of us in the ocean in November to the folks in Minnesota.

Mother wisely preferred sitting upon a blanket on the sand. Alton quickly learned how to ride the waves and became an expert. Jumping in front of a wave that was about to break, he would get a ride into shallow water. I was not able to swim, but I learned later how to ride the waves. Water splashing into my face scared me. I found diving into the waves was more fun. Then my face would get wet all over.

We were happy to be warmer when we reached Mother's relatives. They had moved from Blythe, California, a very hot town in the desert, several years before and were now living in one of the California bungalows near the ocean. Isabel, the daughter, was three years older than I was, and her brother, Eddie, was my brother's age. Ed Green,

Annie's husband, sold Franklin and Chalmers automobiles, and was one of the leading automobile dealers in Long Beach.

He had prospered, and when he needed a larger building, he had it constructed with green tile facing. People told him they were glad his name wasn't pink.

Bea stayed with us until she decided she would like to live in Hollywood. When she found work there, she moved into an apartment, but for awhile she came to see us each weekend. Her visits became less frequent when she made new friends. She started to smoke cigarettes and drink the cocktails that were becoming so popular. With new fashionable short hair and clothing, she had become a typical flapper of the twenties.

Mother never did approve, but accepted the fact that her baby sister had grown up and would do what she wanted. Mother did not disapprove of drinking, she just didn't like the taste of liquor. She never believed ladies should smoke. We were surprised when Mother said her own long hair was giving her headaches so she had her hair cut. We all thought she looked years younger.

Our family became comfortably established. After several months, Daddy joined the local chapter of the Knights of Pythias Lodge. Mother joined the Thistle Club where she could be with people from Scotland. They soon began to have friends who liked card games and dancing. There were many friendly people in Long Beach, probably because so many were newcomers and were anxious to make new friends.

Long Beach had a nice beach in front of the tall bluffs that ran along the coast at that point. The Pike, a large amusement center, was in front of the bluffs, next to the ocean, with part of it on a pier over the ocean. There were mostly sideshows and places where you could buy popcorn, peanuts and hot dogs, and games where the fellows tried to win prizes for their girlfriends. I would beg to ride on the merry-go-round and tried to capture the brass ring so I could have a free ride. Alton and I wanted to ride the roller coaster but Mother said we could do that later.   When we were finally allowed to ride on it, I would scream with the other riders on the second dip. I was not the only one that screamed because wherever you were on the Pike, you could hear others doing the same.

Another attraction was the large Long Beach Plunge with an inside pool. There you could swim and use the diving board, as Alton did. Steps took you down to the tunnel that ended at the walk extending the length of the Pike. Crossing it, you reached the beach where you could sit on the sand or swim in the ocean. I soon learned I could find shells in the sand, and I would look for the tiny sand crabs that would quickly dig into the sand as the waves came in. They would tickle my hand when I would scoop them up. It was a pleasant spot, especially in the summer time.

The water was cooling and the air was warm. The men's swimming suit pant legs came down almost to their knees and their chests were covered. Women's suits were modest with long sleeves, high necklines, and always a skirt over their pants that looked like bloomers. Most wore stockings except for a few who dared to show bare legs.

The ladies usually lounged under rented umbrellas. Those who were brave would go into the ocean with the men, then jump the waves and scream. When you wanted to go back to the Plunge, you had to go through the tunnel, wading through water that smelled strongly of disinfectant. Swimmers were obliged to go under the cold showers and rinse the ocean water and sand from their suits and bodies. The showers were so cold the tunnel echoed with shrieks all the time.

Further on the Pike, there was the Hoyt Theater, much bigger than the neighborhood theater we had gone to in Minneapolis. We saw movies with Mary Pickford and Douglas Fairbanks and laughed at comedians Fatty Arbuckle, Charles Chaplin, and the Keystone Cops. Zazu Pitts, a comedienne, was a favorite of moviegoers for a long time. Marion Davies became famous, too, not only because of her acting talent but also because of her liaison with William Randolph Hearst.

Mabel Norman was a favorite, and Pearl White was rescued many times in the popular serials. We would see the heroine likely to be run over by the train, where she had been tied to the tracks, and the hero get there just in time to save her. Fortunately, he would also be there to rescue her when she lay in the path of the huge saw at the sawmill. The camera would go from the saw to the terrified young woman, who thought she was about to be sawed in half! It was thrilling, especially for the youngsters.

I thought Tom Mix was brave and wonderful. The Western movies reminded us of our trip through New Mexico and Arizona. Pictures were filmed there, and when they did not need the mountains, they were filmed in California. The sand dunes along the ocean depicted the west or Arabia. Now this area is known as Malibu, with the homes of movie stars so close that driving along the oceanfront you know the ocean is there, but you can only manage an occasional sight of it.

Before "talkies," music accompanied the action on the screen. The Hoyt Theater had a large organ and the organist provided mood music. Improvising happy rollicking tunes, melancholy melodies and the chase music was as exciting as the action on the screen. Even after the talkies came, the Hoyt Theater kept its organist, who played for the audience's enjoyment before the vaudeville performance. Other theaters did not use organ music anymore.

The silent screen printed what the actors were saying, so they didn't need to memorize a script. I could not read lips, but those who could, said some of the dialogue would never have passed censors. We heard that sometimes the screen sweethearts kissing actually hated each other! Before the movie started, the words of popular songs were flashed on the screen, and we would sing along with the organ. Sometimes a bouncing ball would follow the lyrics to give the singers the rhythm. Some people would harmonize, and the songs sounded even better.

"The Sidewalks of New York," "After the Ball Was Over," "The Band Played On" and "On A Bicycle Built For Two" were a few of our favorite songs. When I was eight, I knew more words of songs than I would ever learn again.

Past the theater was the Majestic Ballroom. Harry Myers, the owner, hired popular bands that were in a shell at the end of the vast ballroom floor. Thursday nights were "Loge Nights." A chain covered with velvet was hung from posts in front of each section. Couples would come week after week and claim the same space. Inside there were comfortable large chairs, and divans. Mother and Daddy's group of friends enjoyed the ballroom dancing there for years, and they would take me with them. It was like fairyland to me. A large mirrored, revolving ball was suspended in the middle of the ceiling, and it reflected the colored lights on the dancers and the dance floor. The men knew all the latest dances and sometimes asked me to dance with them. I had already learned the Waltz and the Fox Trot, and when the Charleston became popular, I helped them do it. I participated in the Charleston contests and won too often. Mother was told I was a professional and was not eligible, so I could not compete any more.

Thursday night was a big event for me. When I would get tired, I would curl up on one of the couches. Mother would put her coat over me, and I could watch the big mirrored ball turning. The beautiful music and the sound of the gliding feet soon lulled me to sleep, and at eleven o'clock they would lead a sleepy girl to the car.

Mother noticed the pictures of tiny girl ballet dancers in the lobby and read the placard that advertised "Dorothy Baas dance lessons." Mother talked to Mr. Myers, who praised Miss Baas highly, and reminded Daddy that he had promised I could have dance lessons when I was older. He didn't have a chance to refuse. He finally gave permission, one Thursday night, and on Friday mother bought ballet slippers for me. Saturday morning, Mother and I watched the beginner's dance class, talked to Miss Baas, and enrolled me in the class. Mother wasn't wasting any time. She was afraid Daddy would change his mind. I don't know which of us was the happiest.

I could not have started with a better teacher than Dorothy Baas. She had been a protege of the famous dancer Anna Pavlova, a graduate of the Imperial Ballet School of St. Petersburg. Pavlova had been the partner of Vaslav Nijinsky before she left Russia to tour the United States. She was one of the first to defect from Russia. I doubt if Dorothy Baas was from Russia, but I do know she was an excellent teacher, and I was fortunate to have been taught the style of ballet that would enable me to perform in any class that I went into in the future.

Miss Baas told Mother that the world-renowned dancer, Pavlova, was appearing in Los Angeles. Mother received permission for me to stay out of school so we could see her. She was among the first to bring ballet to America. There were many girl students in the audience, and we gave rapt attention to her, especially when she danced her famous "Dance of the Dying Swan." In her snow white ballet costume with ostrich feathers covering the tutu and white feathers framing her delicate face, she appeared almost ethereal. Except for the music, the auditorium was quiet. Pavlova seemed to float above the stage floor as she did tiny traveling steps, called bourres, on her toes. She moved her arms with a soft, fluttering motion. It seemed we were watching a swan really dying and all too soon it was over. I knew I could never dance like her, but I resolved I would work and work until I could float above the stage on my toes, too. I left the pink cloud I was on and became an earth child who loved ice cream when Mother said, "Would you like some ice cream before we go home?"

Mr. Myers asked Miss Baas if she would present students at the Majestic Ballroom on the first of May. I was among those chosen for the maypole dance. She taught us to skip in a circle clockwise around a tall pole festooned with colorful ribbons. Each of us had one of the long ribbons that were coming from the top of the pole. Once around, then half of the girls turned and went counter clockwise. As each of our lines went forward in our own direction we wove in and out. We practiced until the ribbons were braided at the top of the pole and down to the middle. When we performed the dance, we were thrilled when the audience applauded loudly.

In the class, after the barre exercises, we did our center work, and I had not been there very long when Miss Baas placed me in front. Before long, she recommended I have private lessons. Daddy said he could not afford to pay for more lessons. Grandmother said she would pay for my private lessons if I would learn the Scottish dances. I was eight years old, in my first year of studying, when I entered a competition for the Highland Fling. Grandmother was pleased when I won second place after just a few months of lessons in Scottish dances.

When Miss. Baas said I was ready for toe slippers, I was very thrilled. With high arches and toes square across, I had an ideal foot. Toe slippers are made especially for dancing on pointe. Layers of glue and Hessian (hemp cloth) are shaped into a box form and are baked, for protection of the toes. Toe slippers, covered with pink satin, are the ultimate goal for ballet students. They are very fragile; the boxing at the toes breaks down and gets less protective. The toes must be protected from the inside of the box or a blister will form, break, and hurt. I found covering the toes with moleskin before I broke in new slippers helped. Lamb's wool was the first thing I was shown how to use. After I learned how to crochet, I made covers for my toes. When rubber forms for the toes were introduced, I did not care for them. They would not allow me to feel the floor.

Pink satin ribbons hold the shoes on, and they are sewn on in a special way. If the tension is not correct the ribbons will break. When I was in class, a broken ribbon wasn't so bad. On the stage, it was a different story. Usually, it was best in that case to bend down and remove the shoe entirely, finishing the dance with just one toe shoe. Not too easy to do gracefully! I don't know which is the most difficult, to break a ribbon or lose a shoe. I was lucky; I only lost a shoe once.

At last the big day arrived for me. Miss Baas tied the pretty ribbons around my ankles, and as we walked to the edge of the ballroom floor, she told me. "Walk across the ballroom floor on your toes. Remember to pull your muscles tight, and don't forget to smile."

She had been training me to tighten the muscles of my legs, calves, thighs, and buttocks to make them strong until I was ready for my toe shoes. With careful little steps, I crossed the wide floor, then turning around, I walked back, still on pointe.

I was happy, until one of the mothers said, "Lucile must have been walking on her toes before now. It's so easy for her." Mother told her that it was really my first time. I not only earned my toe slippers that day, but I felt for the first time, the icy looks of jealousy from some of my peers.

The next year Grandmother stopped paying for private lessons when I became more interested in ballet. Miss Baas wanted me to continue with the lessons. She suggested since I had started to dance in front of my advanced class, I could demonstrate in front of her other classes, and she would continue the private lessons in return. This benefited me, too, because trying to be perfect improved my own dancing. It was lucky that Mother could sew beautifully. Mothers of other students would pay her to make their daughter's costumes. That money paid for my material.

In my first year of ballet, I made an appearance with two girls at the southern branch of the University of California, in Los Angeles. We did an interpretive dance to music one of the university students had composed. Mother bought net material of different pastel colors for the ruffled ballet skirt. I asked for "Whispering" for my first solo toe dance. The music had become one of my favorites when I went to my parent's loge dances. It was a simple routine, and the first time I did it was on that slippery floor at the Majestic Ballroom.

Following my win at the Scottish picnic, I was asked to dance my Highland Fling and Sword dances at the Thistle Club. Other clubs asked me to dance at their socials, too. Besides the Scottish dances and the toe dance, one of my favorites from the classes was the Sailor's Hornpipe. Mother made a small sailor's suit, complete with a white hat. I know the men in the audiences liked it better than ballet dances. It was fun doing a dance that required some acting. Raising my hand to my eyes, I would look out to sea, then hitch my trousers and pull the anchor in.

My brother, Alton, was working after school at a gas station, and he and Bea gave Mother money for various expenses. The cost of my dancing had become a problem for Mother and Daddy. To prevent Mother from taking house money for lessons, Daddy arranged charge accounts at the grocery store and one department store. He gave her an allowance for herself, and I received enough money for Sunday school. He hadn't prospered since leaving Minneapolis, and he said he needed all his money for his business. There might have been more money if Mother had listened to his idea of buying property to build homes. He had been looking at lots on Signal Hill, about two miles from the ocean. Years before, signals were sent to ships out at sea from the hill, hence the name. We went to look at the lots, and there were already some residents there. Ants were all over the place making hills for their homes. Mother said an emphatic "No," and when she said "No," she meant it. Daddy never did buy any property. Within months, oil was discovered on Signal Hill. The people who had bought property suddenly became very rich. The oil companies bought the property or the mineral rights from the property owners. Unfortunately, some of the owners didn't know what they were doing. A percentage of them sold outright and spent the money until it was gone. I heard some became accustomed to high living and went into debt. Then they were worse off than before.

One oil well caught fire, and it was many days before they were able to get it under control. It burned so brightly a newspaper could be read at night from a distance away. The roar it made could be heard for miles, too, and everyone was glad when the well was finally capped.

It seemed Mother was always sewing for me. She made me black bloomers to wear under my dresses, and when Alton complained, Mother said; "Lucile is always doing cartwheels. Her legs are up in the air all the time. I have to do something about it." I not only loved cartwheels and skating but also would do cartwheels on skates until one day she found me doing them down the front steps of the four-family flat where we lived for awhile. The stairs extended across most of the front of the building, and I was making use of them. That was stopped. I had to give up skating because my knees were skinned from falling, and Mother said, "Knees with scabs don't look good with pretty costumes."

Without skates, I didn't play with the girls and boys in the neighborhood anymore. After dinner, I would see and hear the children playing games under the corner street light and ask if I could go and play, too. Mother never said I could, so I would read after I finished my nightly chore of washing the dishes. Reading became one of my favorite pastimes, and I visited the library often.

Miss Baas told us about the Russian Cossack dance, and said she thought I could do it. The dance steps are known as "squat steps" because that is the position you are in most of the time. I learned one of the hardest dances I ever did. It was usually a dance for men. A show in Juneau, Alaska, had girl dancers who did the real Cossack Dance in a production at dockside. After my entrance step, I had a routine composed of movements that kept me going up and down. There was a step where I jumped up with both feet outstretched and, while I was in the air, I bent over to touch my toes with my fingers. My last step was called "Winding the Clock." I would squat down with my right foot extended forward with both hands on the floor on my right side. With my hands, I lifted myself into the air and hopped over my right foot as it circled under my body. I practiced until I could do it fast, making it very effective. Staying down in a squat position, I would do the duck step around the floor. All I can say about this step is that it did look like a waddling duck.

My first Russian costume, made of turquoise satin, was trimmed with white marabou. The headpiece with beads and pearls made me feel like a princess.

Pictures of me appeared often in local papers. They sometimes called me "Long Beach's Baby Pavlova." The dances brought appreciative applause, and Mother was afraid I would become conceited, so she told me I was not responsible for my talent. It had been a gift to me from God, and it was my duty to practice and become a better dancer.

After I had performed, she would scold me. According to her, I had forgotten a step or changed my routine. I did not smile enough, or my hands were wrong. Instead of feeling I had performed well, I would become dejected. Seldom did she say I had danced well. She had her reasons. She did not want me to become like some of the brassy kids we had encountered. She meant well, but made me painfully shy.

We had to find a new dance teacher when Miss Baas closed her studio to devote more time to her studio in Los Angeles. The years with her had given me a solid background. Madeline Getts and Caris Sharp had recently opened a studio, and we watched one of their classes. They were fine tap teachers, but their ballet was much easier than the work I was used to. The only ballet teachers Mother felt I was ready for were in Los Angeles, and we could not afford their prices or the cost of the transportation for two of us.

I was enrolled in the tap classes and enjoyed them. I was lucky. Before long I earned private lessons by demonstrating the steps we had learned. As usual, I knew the dances because I was the only one who practiced.

Mother had a telephone call from the producer of the shows at the Exposition to be held in the new Long Beach auditorium. A contest for a queen and her attendants had been held. The Court would reign every night on the stage. The producer asked me to be the soloist at the Queen's Court. My cousin, Isabel, and some of my former Baas classmates had joined the tap classes, and we all had learned the Buck and Wing, the Irish Jig and the all time favorite, the Waltz Clog. We were asked to do these dances at the Exposition, doing a different dance each night. I did a different solo dance too. Otherwise, we sat on the stage with the Queen's Court.

It was exciting because of the large crowds. Mother, Daddy and I would walk around to see the exhibits, and we would have a bag of Salt Water Taffy, a new confection beginning to be popular. They said it had been invented in Coney Island.

After the Exposition, I became busier than ever dancing once or twice a week. Mother's Thistle Club asked me to dance so often, the members became like aunts and uncles.

There were the Allied War Veterans, the D.A.R., the Elks, Masons, Knights of Pythias and others. The Community Service program was held every Monday night at the auditorium. I'd be on the program frequently. My scrapbook contains reviews of different programs with the city recreational department and schools. The Junior Chamber of Commerce sent a letter saying I had contributed to the success of the Industrial Fur and Rabbit Exposition! I think seeing my pictures and reviews of my dancing in the paper so often isolated me from the other kids in school. My daily hour and a half practice also kept me from after school activities. My dance career, both for me and mother, was becoming our whole life.

Mother had been talking about how much she missed home, her friends, and the change of seasons, and, naturally, she missed Grandmother and Aunt Mildred. In the summer of 1922, Daddy bought tickets for us to go to Minneapolis. I thought to myself, I wouldn't have to dance in public for awhile. Then I saw Mother packing my costumes, and I thought it would be performances as usual. Instead, I would only use my costumes one time at a veteran's hospital. I was asked to dance wherever we visited.

We took the train to Minneapolis when the school summer vacation started. I was happy to be with Grandmother again and was fascinated when I would sit with her while she was knitting. She had made hundreds of the hoods the soldiers had worn under their helmets. They went over the head and had openings for the eyes and mouth, then continued down to their shoulders. Shawls and mittens had been in demand, and she had made hundreds of them, too. She never seemed to be watching her hands to see what she was doing, but would talk and knit at the same time. She volunteered long hours at the Veteran's Hospital. The Mayor of Minneapolis had given her a medal because of all she had done during and after the war.

Soon after we arrived, Grandmother asked Mother if I could dance for the soldiers at the Veteran's Hospital, so one night I danced for them. The soldiers had been given long stemmed red roses, and, after the show, many gave their roses to Mother and me. They talked with me and told me about their kid sisters at home, while others visited with my mother. It was a bit of home for them, I guess. These veterans were younger than most of the people I had danced for and I was happy they had liked my performance. I had never danced for veterans before but did many times later.

I did not find much to amuse me. The neighborhood didn't have anyone my age, so there was no one to play with. We did go to one of the lakes for a swim one day. The water was warm, but there weren't any waves to jump over or under. I decided the ocean was more fun.

Aunt Mildred was dancing in the chorus of theatrical productions. She treated us to a performance of the "Mutt and Jeff" musical in the theater where she was currently dancing. Mutt and Jeff were popular comic strip characters in the newspapers and the musical was about them. One of the men was tall and the other was short and their costumes and makeup made them look like the comic strip characters. We saw the performance from the audience and again from backstage after I begged to see it from there. I was allowed to stand in the wings after I promised I would not get in the way.

In the second act, the tall one came to me and said, "In the next scene, I am going to shoot Mutt. It will be a blank cartridge; don't be frightened." He shot the gun and I didn't make a sound. When he came off the stage again he said, "You're a good trouper," and bent way down to give me a bear hug. Even though he looked weird with all the makeup he wore, along with a false nose, I liked him. Later he, too, wished me good luck as a dancer.

I thought the ladies of the chorus were beautiful in their elaborate costumes. I am afraid I stared at the heavy makeup they wore. I never wore that much.

Someone asked me, "Are you going to be a dancer like your Aunt Mildred?"

Mildred told her, I was already dancing, and then to prove it, I had to do some tap dancing and cartwheels. I liked the atmosphere backstage so much I resolved to practice harder than ever.

Uncle Joe, Mildred's husband, traveled around Minnesota in a different part of the theater business. He met with managers and booked motion pictures in their theaters.

He stayed home for a few days around the Fourth of July and one day drove us to Hastings to visit Grandfather at the state hospital. We had brought a picnic lunch with us and we sat on a blanket on the large lawn while we waited for the nurse to bring Grandfather. I did cartwheels until Mother finally said I should rest. I had worn my kilts so I could do the Highland Fling for Grandfather before our lunch. I could hardly wait to see the Grandfather I had only seen in photos. Grandfather had never recovered from the head injury he had sustained working at the stable years before. He was just fine physically, but he was vague when he tried to talk to us. His mind wandered. When I danced for him, his face lit up with pleasure. I loved him immediately, especially when I found that, like Grandmother, he liked my hugs. We were a sad group returning to Grandmother's house. Mother and I were afraid we had seen my Grandfather for the last time.

Uncle Joe bought fireworks for the Fourth of July. When that night came, we went out on the front lawn and he shot fireworks in the air. He gave me a big box of sparklers and, while the adults enjoyed the fireworks, I had fun on my own.

The longer we stayed in Minneapolis the more Mother appreciated and missed Long Beach. Hot, humid weather made her ill. Going home sounded good to me, because everywhere we visited, I was asked to dance. I liked my audience at a distance-in someone's living room I was almost in their laps. Once I did a cartwheel and hurt my foot on a piece of furniture. I was more embarrassed than hurt and I just wanted to be a guest. We said goodbye to everyone and took the train back home. Shortly after we arrived, the telephone started to ring again. "Would I like to dance for...?"

When I danced at a benefit there would be acts from theaters or a Hollywood celebrity. I learned everyone involved would get paid, except the entertainers. The unions for the musicians and the stagehands, if needed, demanded minimum wages. The rental companies that furnished extra furnishings were paid. The prizes that were given were well covered by the publicity the donors received. Usually, I would receive a bouquet of flowers.

Among my cherished doll collection, there is a little doll I received from the Thistle Club. One of the members had made kilts for her, which the doll still wears. She was never a doll to play with, so she is still in perfect condition.

I learned how to cope with all kinds of obstacles, like floors that were as slick as ice, and often dirty. There was the inconvenience of dressing in the ladies' rest rooms, and transportation at my own expense to out of the way places. For years I was at their beck and call, and all I have to show for it is a doll and scrap books full of newspaper clippings. My profit was the valuable experience I gained.

Mother and I were faithful attendants of the Long Beach State Theater. At one matinee, the audience began to clap their hands in unison and even started to stomp their feet. I asked Mother, "Why are they making so much noise?" She explained, "They don't like the act and this is how they tell them."

Before long, the two men left the stage and the next act entered. I felt sorry for the two men and hoped it would never happen to me. A few weeks later I danced for the amateur night at the same theater. I was doing my Russian dance, and when I did my more difficult steps the audience started to clap their hands. Were they applauding me like they did that act we had seen? I looked at my mother who was in the wings and she was smiling, so I stopped worrying. I finished my dance and ran off stage.

She said, "Go take a bow. They like you."

I went back and did a simple curtsy. When I came back to the wings, a man standing beside Mother picked me up and held me up high in the air. When he set me down, he put his arm around me and started to talk to Mother. I wondered who he was. He was Lester Fountain, the new manager of the theater and he was telling Mother I was exceptionally talented. Before he said goodbye he told us we were to ask for him when we came to the theater next time. We did, and he arranged for us to attend future performances without paying. He also talked to the other theater managers who had vaudeville, and we did not have to pay at their theaters either. We didn't miss many shows.

I was able to copy what I had seen and learned many new ideas for my own dances. It was the middle of April 1923. I remembered because we had celebrated Mother's birthday a few days before on the tenth. I thought regretfully, we wouldn't have any more birthdays until June when Daddy and Bea would have theirs. I loved birthdays. Alton and I had celebrated ours in March, and Mother had made two cakes: Angel food for Alton, and Devil's food for me. When you are 11 years old and your brother is 18 you take second choice, but I liked chocolate so much that first really didn't matter. Mother said it was more appropriate for me to have the Devil's food cake and Alton deserved the Angel food. Perhaps Mother was teasing me, but I took her seriously. I thought I would never come up to her standards. I was just thinking about asking her if we couldn't have another cake when she looked up from the paper she was reading and said, "The Mission Theater is going to have a Kiddie Revue this week. It is a group of children who perform during the summer months when school is out."

Mother and Daddy decided to take me to see "Twenty Minutes on the Bowery." At the theater, I waited anxiously for this show with children like myself.

Finally the stage was set to depict a street scene in the Bowery, a poorer section of New York. It was the background for twelve youngsters of various ages in shabby costumes. One was a newsboy making believe he was selling papers. Other kids were pitching pennies at a large cardboard box. They all acted their parts until it was time for them to sing, play an instrument, or do their specialty. I noticed the newsboy tearing a newspaper into strips to the fold. Then he did something with a rope. When the spotlight turned on him I could see the rope ran through the paper fold making a paper Hawaiian skirt. He tied the skirt around his waist, then took off his cap. Long black hair tumbled down to his shoulders. It was a little girl and she did a lovely Hula dance. We saw they were all girls, dressed like boys. They sang and danced until a winsome young lady with long brown hair, sang "If I Were a Millionaire." It was a song, telling what she would do if she had lots of money. The stage lights dimmed with just one spotlight shining on her and the kids sitting around her. When her song ended, the stage lit up again and one of the girls started a soft-shoe tap dance traveling in a circle. As she passed the others they joined her. When they finished dancing in a straight line they took their bows and the act was over. We all agreed the act was especially good.

The program we were given announced an audition on Monday morning. They were looking for new talent. When we got home I was sent to bed and Mother and Daddy talked about my trying out. In the morning Mother and Daddy had agreed I could do it if I wanted to. Mother called the theater to get information about the tryout and Monday morning we went to the theatre and joined a dozen other singers and dancers. I did my Russian dance and one other girl and I were accepted.

That night I heard my parents talking a long time in the bedroom. When Mother came to my room and found me still awake, she whispered, "You can be in the show. Go to sleep. I'll tell you tomorrow what your Daddy said." In the morning, after I told Mother I wanted to be in the show, she called the manager of the revue, Hugo Hamlin. He gave her the address for his studio and told her to bring me there. Daddy said he would help all he could. In daytime, we would have to use the big Red Cars for transportation to the theaters. He would come after the show to bring us home.

Mother and I went to Los Angeles and found the studio. After we were introduced to everyone, one of the girls, Trixie, showed me the dance steps. The routines were not difficult, and I learned the soft-shoe dance the first day.

While I rehearsed, Mother left to shop for my new wardrobe. She bought overalls for me and spent that evening making them look old. Now, the same types of jeans are very popular. Mr. Hamlin gave me a derby hat that came way down to my ears and my hair was tucked under it. He told me I was to be a boot black, a boy who earned money shining shoes. Daddy made a box for me and painted it black. In the show, I was to mime shining shoes until I either danced with the group or did my two solos, one a tap dance and the other my Russian dance.

Mr. Hamlin and Mother went to City Hall to get the permit for me to join the show. I aged fast that day! From eleven, I was suddenly twelve, the age I had to be to get a permit. I am a year older when I am in Los Angeles! Child labor laws were beginning to be enforced. Mother didn't tell me about that until much later.

We toured around the Los Angeles County area performing in the small town's theaters. My experience had given me confidence, but I had seldom done more than one show a night. It was customary for these theaters to have three or four shows a day.

Mother and I rode the fast big red streetcars to the towns. On opening day we would have to leave early in the morning for the orchestra rehearsal, but otherwise we left later for the matinee about three o'clock. The night shows were around seven and nine-thirty and after the last show, daddy drove us home with me asleep on the back seat.

For almost two years, Mother and I followed the same routine touring with the Kiddie Revue. We were the only family that traveled alone and traveled so far. The others lived in Los Angeles or vicinity, so they shared rides. They did better on the traveling expense because they each contributed to the drivers.

On our drive back to Long Beach, I would enjoy the smell of the sweet odor of the orange groves. Our car was open, without the new glass windows that you could wind up or down, so the night air came in. The towns were far apart, and between them grew miles and miles of orange trees. Japanese farms occupied many acres of land between the small towns. Sometimes it was foggy. My parents would talk about what they had done that day, and I slept.

I never knew what the financial arrangements were with Mr. Hamlin. Under Mother's expert management, there was money left over after expenses to pay for more lessons. We did not perform as often or go as far away as he had said we would, but we didn't mind. It wasn't easy getting around to all the towns.

There were times when part of the show would perform at fraternal clubs, the Elks or Shriners in Los Angeles. Daddy or Alton would take us.

I was excited one night, when Bill Robinson, the wonderful tap dancer, was the star. He was famous then, but would become even more famous when he danced in Shirley Temple films. After watching my tap dance, he told Mother that I should just do tap dancing because I was a natural. We had different plans because ballet was my love. Mr. Robinson asked to see my tap shoes, and asked Mother, "Where did you get the split soles for her shoes?" She told him her husband had made them and she introduced him to Daddy. Split soles were made of a special wood that Daddy had carved to fit the shoe. He had copied my first pair. Bill Robinson said they were better than the commercial pairs he bought and asked if Daddy would make some for him. Daddy said yes, and made several pairs for Mr. Robinson. The wooden split soles disappeared when the metal taps started to be used. The metal taps were cheaper but I did not think they sounded as good.

Our revue was given a return engagement in Long Beach soon after my twelfth birthday. It was a lot easier to work in the same town where I lived. The hometown papers gave me a special write up and many of our friends came to see me dance.

Between the Hamlin Theater performances, I was still dancing at various clubs. At last I was paid small amounts of money which I gave to Daddy for gasoline. He was still building houses on the same scale he had used in Minneapolis to withstand more severe weather, and was losing money.

Before Christmas, Mr. Hamlin produced "Babes in Toyland." Across the stage, there were large boxes for dolls. The boxes had doors on them in front so we stepped through a curtain in back to wait for our turn. Mother had made a pink ballet costume for my toe dance. I would get into the box, and wait for my entrance, holding my hands stiffly in front of me like a doll. Santa's helper would open the door and make believe he was winding me up as the drummer made a winding sound on something they called a ratchet. On my toes, I would walk stiffly to the center of the stage. Then when my music, "The Doll Dance," started, I began my dance.

Mr. Hamlin had an idea for a special novelty number for the "Babes of Toyland" show using tiny tots. Some looked dubious when they found what they were to do. Mr. Hamlin had rented eight grotesque masked heads with different types of clown faces. They were not frightening, but I didn't think they were especially funny either. The huge heads rested on the children's shoulders and changed their height to somewhere around four and a half feet. They wore brown jump suits that fitted some of them quite snugly. It was hard for them to see anything because all they had to look through was the opening for the eyes and mouths of the heads. Their simple routine of marching in different directions was done to the "Funeral March of a Marionette." It was so unusual the audience was captivated by their performance. During one show one of our dwarfs did not turn when she should have and marched right off the stage into the orchestra pit, landing atop one of the big drums. There was a crash! She was unhurt but frightened and embarrassed. The drum hadn't been damaged because she did not weigh very much. For a few minutes the audience was afraid she had been hurt and laughed in relief when she emerged unscathed.

We had a military finale and wore white satin military costumes and played snare drums while marching to the "Stars and Stripes Forever." I left the stage toward the end of the routine and quickly took off my drum. Then running to the center front of the group, I did a kick routine. After sixteen front kicks, I turned around to face back stage and started kicking backwards, touching my head, one foot after the other. Mr. Hamlin off stage counted my kicks. He started softly but by the time I reached thirty, he made it sound as though I were really doing something. Kicking my head was so easy for me I thought it was a big fuss over nothing, but the audience started to applaud after fifteen. We continued with this show into the summer. For several years each summer Los Angeles had a movie parade similar to the New Year's parades. Popular movie stars rode in cars or on floats. That year, we marched in the parade, dressed in our white satin military costumes and playing our drums.

Mr. Hamlin wanted us to look spic and span from our head to our toes. He had ordered some white shoes, and they were given to us at the studio just before the parade. We didn't have a chance to break them in. They were not made of leather, but of material that had been stiffened.

We were hurried to where the parade began. It was a hot summer day and we all perspired. My heels were slender and the shoes rubbed up and down. Blisters formed on my heels, broke and bled. I took the pain as long as I could then went to Mr. Hamlin who was walking alongside of us and told him about my heels. He told me to get back into the formation; the parade would be over soon. I might mention here that Mr. Hamlin enjoyed being in the spotlight with us every chance he could be. I think he did well financially, too. The temperature was over 100 degrees that day, and we were all getting sunburned. I could hardly walk, but there was nothing for me to do but continue. I could not leave the parade and go into the crowd of spectators, and Mr. Hamlin had disappeared. He reappeared when our part of the parade was over and took us to cars that were waiting to drive us to the studio where my mother was. When I saw her I started to cry and showed her my feet. The back part of the shoes was not white any more. Instead both the heels were soaked with blood. She was very angry but was silent. She wanted to get me home. I walked barefoot, tiptoe, so I could keep my heels clean. It would have been impossible to wear my own socks and shoes. We took a cab to the Red Car station and when we reached Long Beach, we drove home in another cab. I was glad to be home, until Mother told me to lie down on my stomach on the couch and gave me a soft pillow. I think it was to muffle my screams. Scream I did when she poured rubbing alcohol on my heels until she thought they were clean. The flesh had been worn away to the bone. My threshold of pain was elevated that day. There wasn't any public dancing for me until my heels healed. When I was able, I practiced in my bare feet.

For many years I had to be very careful of pressure on my heels. The skin was like tissue paper and would just slide off. That was the end of my performing in Hamlin's Kiddie Revues. Daddy drove Mother to see Mr. Hamlin. I don't know what was said and I never saw him again. I didn't care.

It had been a valuable experience. Dancing in theaters was so different from the Club dates. Mother and I were happy to be at home all the time but probably not as happy as Daddy was. I just practiced and wondered what was going to happen next, and hoped it was going to be better. It was.

Chapter 6

Alton and I began to know each other better when Mother and Daddy would go out for the evening and Alton would stay with me. We would play dominoes or checkers and he always won. When I became older, I would win too. Then games were more fun. I liked it when I would sit on the couch and he would lie down with his head on my lap and I would comb his hair. Alton's hair was auburn, red, brown and gold, all mixed up together, and had wide waves. I thought his hair was beautiful and wished that we could trade.

Every night my mother would put my blonde hair up in rags to give me my curly hair. We didn't have Bobbie pins in those days. Instead, old sheets or pillowcases were torn into rectangles, about 1¼ inches by 6 inches. My hair was rolled around these rags and the ends tied in a knot. I slept on them for years. It was no wonder I envied Alton's naturally wavy hair.

When he became bored with my playing with his hair, he'd say, "Would you like an ice cream cone?" I never failed to say yes.

He knew I saved any money I could, so he would ask, "Shall we flip a coin to see who will pay for them?" He tossed the coin and said, "Heads I win, tails you lose."

I lost again until one day I was playing with a coin, tossing it up and down and there the explanation was, right in front of my eyes. Next time he tried to play the trick on me, I said, "Oh, no you don't." At last, I had a fair chance of winning.

The tap dancing I was doing was not the same type we were seeing in the theaters. Perhaps Bill Robinson's suggestion that I should do more tap had something to do with it. Mother said I could start taking lessons with Jack Carney. We had appeared on some of the same shows, and we thought he was an excellent tap dancer. He taught in a recreation room in the apartment house where he lived. The hallways were dark and smelled of food cooking. Whenever I smell boiled cabbage, I remember going to that apartment house for my lessons. Mother would always go with me. It was strange because in Long Beach I could get around by myself on the bus. She told me she had smelled liquor on Mr. Carney's breath. She just wanted to be certain I was not exposed to something unpleasant.

He had a jolly sense of humor and was fun to work with. One step he gave me was called "Wings." It was difficult. A matter of doing taps while you are coming down from a hop or small jump. The tap had to be put in fast and I practiced a long time before I could do the step over and over. Another new step was "jumping over the foot." Holding one foot in front of the other, about ankle height, you jump over it. Then you jump back, which is harder. After I could do several of them, I had a high-light for my tap dance. Now I was doing the same steps the dancers were doing on the stage. The steps he had taught me were good and I was sorry when Mother said she could not afford more lessons.

One day a man on crutches rang our doorbell. He wanted to see me. Mother asked him to come in after a few minutes. He told me he had seen my tap dance several nights before. Later at home, or perhaps it was at a party, he decided to try jumping over his foot like I had done. He said it looked easy but when he tried it, he had fallen and broken his ankle. He wanted to see me, to tell me that more people should appreciate what I was doing! He was a surgeon and gave us his card. He told Mother if I ever needed a doctor he would like to work on my well-developed body. This was not unusual. More than one doctor told me it would be like working on a live chart. No fat just well defined muscles.

The dancers at the theaters were doing something new called acrobatics. I was fascinated. I could do cartwheels but they were doing other tricks that I wanted to do. Acrobatics became another way to use up time on my hour and a half of practice every day.

I tried to do what they were doing and found it was fun but I took many falls. A teacher was in Hollywood, but he was too far away, besides being expensive. First I tried front limbers. I'd go forward into a brief handstand, go over into a backbend and straighten to a standing position. That was easy. There were walkovers that looked easy too, but I could not do them. Each day when Mother was fixing dinner she would hear me fall. She would come into the dining room and see me on the floor again. I'd tell her I wasn't hurt and kept on trying.

For a walkover you start a handstand but you travel. One hand precedes the other, and the feet come down one at a time. I couldn't get it right until one night, as I slept, a strange thing happened. I dreamt I was trying to do the walkover. I did it! Not once, but several times and they were easy to do. The next afternoon down I went, then I remembered my dream. Still sitting on the floor I rested my arms and head on my knees. With my eyes closed I went through the motions in my imagination. I remembered! I visualized it over and over. When I stood up and tried the walkover, it was easy. I called Mother and said, "Watch me." She was amazed and happy, too, when I told her how I had solved it.

Having conquered a walkover I worked on doing them in one spot, which is done just the same, except, instead of walking forward with the second step, the foot is brought back. Doing them rapidly one after the other made a splendid finish for my new acrobatic routine. I had accomplished spotters.

When "Stardust" became popular, I set my dance to it and, in time, I became well known for my "Stardust dance."

I was getting stronger from my dancing and acrobatic work, and Alton and I would have a great time wrestling. One time when Daddy saw me hitting Alton with my fist during one of our play fights he corrected my hand position. "Don't put your thumb inside your fingers. Squeeze them tight and then curl your thumb on the outside." I tried it and it felt better.

One day, the newspaper had a picture of a beautiful girl, Aida Broadbent, who was starting a dance studio in Long Beach. She was a student of Ernest Belcher, the teacher I had always wanted to study with in Los Angeles. Mother enrolled me immediately, and again I could concentrate on ballet. The picture in the paper did not lie. She was lovely, and she was a wonderful teacher. Aida needed barres, and other work done in her studio. Daddy made a trade for lessons in return for his installing the barres and getting the floor in better condition.

I progressed rapidly in my ballet, and before long I began to earn my private lessons again by helping with her baby classes. Aida began to dance at the social clubs, and often we were on the same programs. George, her brother, was an accomplished pianist, and he accompanied us when we danced on a show or at the auditorium when we had our recitals.

Our families became friends, and Aida, who also had red hair like Alton, dated him for awhile. On Sundays they went to the beach with Aida's friends, the Prine sisters. Mother and Daddy watched them having their fun, but I just sat and ached because I was not old enough to join them. Mother was always worried that I'd be hurt so I kept silent.

The Broadbent's had formerly lived in Canada, and Aida's mother had a very pronounced English accent. She was visiting Mother for lunch and Mother served a delicious desert she had made from our own figs. When Mrs. Broadbent heard we had a fig tree in our back yard she asked to see it. She stood on the back porch in silence, looking up at the tall tree. Finally she said. "Aye, is that all the bigger the fig leaves are?"

She shook her head and went back inside. I was puzzled then, but when I was older and went to museums, I remembered what she had said. I knew why my Mother and Daddy had been amused by her remark about the fig leaf.

Aida was an excellent teacher and I missed her when she sold her studio to Mr. Belcher and danced for Fanchon and Marco. Mr. Belcher, too, wanted additional work done in the studio, and again Daddy earned class lessons for me with his carpentry work. The studio was in a club building and the large room was used for meetings at night. The mirror had to be portable, so Daddy designed a frame that rested on a long, strong base with small wheels, so it could be moved out of the way. Years later, I told a handyman how my daddy had done it, and I had a portable mirror for my own studio. Mother made drapes and, with office furniture, the Ernest Belcher Studio looked more professional.

Madame Heloise came from the studio in Los Angeles to teach. A strict disciplinarian, she rarely smiled and looked brittle enough to break if you were to touch her. Mr. Belcher visited the classes once a month. He spoke quietly when he insisted every step be done correctly. While demonstrating a step he impressed me when he would lift his trouser leg just a bit to reveal his slender foot and pointed toes, showing us a step. He was so neat.

For years, I had followed the same routine. Coming right home after school, I changed into my practice clothes. To make room in the dining room, I'd push the table into a corner and put the chairs into the living room. The built-in sideboard was my barre. Holding onto it I would start with plies and for 20 minutes I did barre work. It is dull and repetitious but very important. It is some time before the center floor work starts, and even then, there are floor exercises to be done precisely before dances can be learned and practiced.

Sometimes when Mother was out of the house I would read while I did extensions. It's surprising how long you can hold one leg straight out in front, in back, or to the side, when you are engrossed in your story. This resulted in high extensions.

Pirouettes are a full turn on the tip of the toes or on the ball of the foot. I decided I wanted to be able to do many pirouettes. They look easy, but are hard to do. I did them fifteen minutes every day, five minutes turning right, five minutes to the left, five minutes alternating right and left. Several months later I could do five turns on pointe, landing in a perfect 5th position. I never did five in class, but when I did my pirouettes during the combinations, it was easy for me to do three turns.

One month, on visitor's day, Mr. Belcher asked Mother to stay after class. He told her I was ready for more advanced work and asked if I could come to Los Angeles to his professional class. It met twice a week on Tuesday and Thursday at five in the afternoon. Mother said she would try to get me there.

I wanted desperately to be in that class, but I didn't see how it could be managed. To my joy, my family helped. Alton and Bea said they would give us more money to help with the expenses. After working in the Kiddie Revue, I was considered a professional, and sometimes I did receive a five dollar bill from a club. Mother took me to the large studio in Los Angeles, but not for two lessons a week. Instead, if we were careful with our money, I had two lessons a month.

At first, Mother and I worried, thinking I would fall behind the class because the work was more difficult. Few of the others practiced like I did so I would know the new work better than they. Mr. Belcher would motion for me to go into the front line with others who knew the work, and we had the opportunity to see ourselves in the mirror.

My new project was to do thirty-two fouette turns on pointe. This turn must be reserved for the ballerinas because they always do it in their Pas de Deux solos. I could already do continuous releves in an arabesque,00 and all I had to do were releves while turning and making ronde jambes with the free foot.

Releve's are done by raising up to the ball of the foot or the pointe. Ronde-jambe is a circular movement of the working leg. Put them together while turning and you have Fouettes. Yes, hard to do! I did my 32 fouettes and pirouettes and never showed anyone. I was afraid I would be accused of showing off!

Mr. Belcher said I was talented, my feet were excellent, but I needed more work on my hand and arm movements. I would hear him call out, "Lucile, your arms, your arms!" He wanted me to work on being more graceful with my hands and arms. I tried every way I could think of to make my elbows round and my fingers long and soft.
We did manage for me to have one private lesson that cost us $15. (That would be about $100 now). The studio pianist played, and I went through the barre and floor work, and, too soon, the 1/2 lesson was over. Mother and Mr. Belcher had talked throughout it! Mother told me he had said I needed to perfect my arms, but I knew that. She seemed more confident about my future and sometimes let me stay for the night class so I would have three hours of class.

When I took the two classes, I had already walked at least two miles between walking to school, the Red Car, and then to the studio. I would barely have time to change into my practice clothes before I had to hurry into the classroom and find a place at the already occupied barre. After the 1☐ hour class Mother would bring me a chocolate milk shake, then I would go into the empty classroom and practice.

The seven-thirty class was much easier than the professional class, but it seemed I was corrected twice as much and told, "Drop your shoulders, don't point to the ceiling." It was funny, but I never felt embarrassed or picked on. Evidently my mind was too busy trying to do what I was being told to do. Going home was when I felt discouraged.

The next day, I spent more time in front of the mirror in the bedroom. I practiced dropping my shoulders, and rounding my arms until they ached. How could I do all these things at once?

One afternoon, after the professional class, I was sitting at my mother's feet in the dressing room, removing my toe slippers and trying to keep from crying. One of the mothers asked, "What is the matter, blisters on her toes?"

"No, we were just wondering if we should give up. Mr. Belcher keeps after her about her arms."

Her reply gave us hope. "Lucile is one of the best in the class. My daughter has been taking lessons here for years, and he doesn't even know her name."

Mother and I decided I had better keep working on my hands and arms. I was ecstatic the first time I was complimented on them. While I danced, I would mentally check the different parts of my body. What do I do with my head? Are my toes pointed, the knees straight and turned out, and don't forget your hands and arms. Each measure of the music I was to do different things. Every muscle was to do what I wanted it to do. Oh yes! Don't forget to smile! I decided my body was like a violin, and I had to make it perfect before I could make it perform beautifully.

The last 15 minutes of the night class we did Spanish dances with castanets, and I met with still another problem. After hours of practicing, "roll, roll, both, both." At night I went to sleep saying those words over and over. I had enough ability to use them in a Spanish Waltz that I added to my repertoire. Mother made a ruffled Spanish costume of white taffeta trimmed with red sequins. I was such a ham that whatever costume I wore would transform me into the proper character for the dance. I was so lucky to have so many theatrical attributes given me. I knew I was also lucky to have a mother who had patience and could make beautiful costumes.

Mr. Belcher would come in from his sitting room after he had his tea and watch me practicing my acrobatic work. He had told Mother that ballet dancers could not do acrobatic work because the muscle control was different. Yet he saw me doing it! Several months later, a new teacher, Sam Mintz, was added to the staff to teach tumbling and acrobatics!

Between classes I practiced my backbend, without hands. When my head was touching the floor, I slid out until I was in a prone position on my back. Still, not using my hands coming back up was harder. One night after the seven-thirty class, I sat down on the floor in front of mother while she tried to find out what I was complaining about.

She picked at a spot on my scalp and I said, "Ouch, that hurt."

"It looks like a speck of dirt," Mother said.

"It doesn't feel like a speck of dirt."

She picked at the spot again. "Does that hurt?"

"Yes," I said, emphatically.

By this time we had several interested bystanders. She was offered a pair of tweezers, and Mother pulled out a long, thick splinter from my head. From then on, I was more particular about floors that might have splinters.

The backbend without hands was in my Oriental dance to "Persian Market." The costume had a sequined and beaded bra, and a full, long chiffon skirt. Mother had made two skirts. One was red for floors that were not too clean and a white one with gold sequins that was my favorite. The arm movements were supposedly Oriental, but mostly it was ballet with the backbend and some crawling splits. Different types of turns also made this dance asked for often and it became a favorite along with the Russian and acrobatic dances.

I doubt whether I would have made it as a professional dancer if I hadn't added the acrobatic tricks to my ballet dances to make them unusual. Other acrobatic dancers did different tricks to a pretty waltz. Credit also should go to Mr. Belcher's training in doing multiple turns that made my routines very showy. I'd receive applause when I did them. My teachers had done a lot for me, especially Miss Baas, Aida and Mr. Belcher.

Ernest Belcher had come from England to Hollywood to teach dancing and was one of the first to become a choreographer for the movies. Others were Albertina Rasch, Maurice Kusell, Theodore Kosloff and Rita Hayworth's father, Eduardo Cansino.

Mr. Belcher's beautiful stepdaughter, Lena Basquette, was a famous movie star. She had started as a child ballerina in the 1915 San Francisco World's Fair and then became a child actress in films. She left films for Broadway as the Prima Ballerina of the "Ziegfield Follies." Giving up dancing, she again acted in films. Rod La Rocque, her current flame, was a handsome actor, and they sometimes watched me practice between the classes.

Margie Belcher, Mr. Belcher's youngest daughter, also became a professional dancer. When she was tiny, she would watch the classes before she started her training. Later, she was in two Disney Studios productions, a model for the heroine in Snow White and The Seven Dwarfs, and for the Blue Fairy in Pinocchio. In 1945 she met Gower Champion and they became a ballroom dance team and were married in 1947. Using the names Marjorie Bell and Gower Champion, they traveled from coast to coast dancing in major hotel ballrooms. When they danced in the 1951 film, "Show Boat," they were outstanding. During his career on Broadway, Gower became a choreographer for New York productions. He died when he was still a young man. Marjorie opened a successful dance studio in Hollywood.

Mr. Belcher was the dance director for First National Studio's "Twinkle Toes," starring Colleen Moore. The professional class performed the ballet in the movie. The star was portrayed day dreaming while drinking tea. She was the ballerina in a ballet she saw inside the teacup. The finished scene didn't look like the set we had been on, that hot summer day in Hollywood.

Mother, Daddy and I had driven from Long Beach early to the site. Instead of being filmed in a studio, we were outside, on a large stage. Reflectors were focused so the sun lit up the set. It was already a hot day and the reflectors made it hotter. Our ballet costumes had shoulder straps, so our arms and shoulders became sunburned. Our new toe slippers caused blisters that peeled off and many of us had bloody toes. We earned $15 for that long day, if I remember correctly. It seemed little money for so many hours rehearsing before the cameras rolled. When Mother and I saw the picture, it was not possible to find me in that little teacup. I decided I liked it better when I danced in front of a live audience.

The only time I was to see myself on the movie screen was when I was in the parade with the Hamlin Company. We were seeing a newsreel of the parade in the Loews State Theater, and suddenly, I appeared marching in my white military costume playing my snare drum and wearing a big smile on my face.

While in Franklin Junior High School, I enjoyed my classes, even General Science. In that class we had a demonstration about smoking and what smoke could do to the lungs. I benefited from that class.

After one semester, Mother managed for me to not have any sports. I had enjoyed playing baseball but had to stop. Instead, I was in a tumbling class. Miss. Mattern, who taught the class, was a cute brunette whom I admired. Leaving me to teach the class, she would go out on the field to coach baseball and basketball teams. I did almost more teaching in that class than she did. She did teach us pyramids, which must have helped the future cheerleaders.

I didn't do well in the typing class, because after school, I would always go straight home instead of going to her room to practice typing. At the semester's end, the teacher gave a party for other teachers, and she asked me to dance. I was surprised when

I received a B plus because I felt I did not deserve it. The class was good for me because I remembered the instructions and later I was able to type.

When I was 14, I was in a film in Long Beach. The name of the scenario was "My Sweetheart of the Screen." A home movie camera, quite a novelty then, was used to film a rose garden scene. Wearing a ballet costume, I was shown wandering through the garden, smelling the flowers and trying to look enraptured. When I saw my lover standing by the garden, with my arms outstretched I walked toward him right out of the picture. The night of the performance arrived. The curtains opened to show the screen. A pianist softly accompanied the tenor singing the verse while the film showed me in the rose garden. The verse ended, the curtain closed on the screen and I walked toward him from the opposite wing. Attired in the same ballet costume, I listened to his love song while in his arms, then danced for him and the audience. That was it. I still have a copy of the film. We certainly had not set the world afire, and we were not called to Hollywood.

On another occasion I overheard Mother talking on the telephone. I was full of curiosity until she told me, "The Elks are going to do a musical comedy for charity and they want you to be in it. If you are interested, there is a part for you doing a song and dance." The show was "The Girl from Honolulu," a three-act musical comedy and it was agreed I should do it. I took the role of "Patsy," and was supposed to be a flirt.

I did not know the dance director, Miss Ellis, and I wondered if she would give me a routine. She came to me during the first rehearsal and asked if I would mind setting my own dance? Mind! I was relieved. I had been making up my dances since I started to dance before kindergarten. It was years later, before I found I was unique in having this ability. There were two exceptions, I never altered Scottish or Hawaiian dances. They were traditional dances.

The script in this production had me cast as a glamorous showgirl without many lines to memorize but with an important song and dance. The costume was made of a shiny white satin with a short circular skirt banded at the bottom with a wide trim of white fur. The long chiffon sleeves were also trimmed with white fur. I had to have special engineering for the upper part. This glamour girl was supposed to have everything. My only makeup instructions were to be sure and have curly hair that would show around the white fur trimmed hat. I sang, "I'll be your Eskimo baby, if you come to Iceland with me."

I was told, "Be seductive, and flirt with the leading man and the audience." I was pretty young to be seductive, but I remembered the actresses in the movies I had seen, and I did my best to flirt and never was corrected, so I must have filled the bill. I loved the acting so much; it was a wonder I didn't want to change my career ambitions. But leave my ballet, never. I had one major worry. Would my voice be strong enough? The weakest of voices are heard now with the aid of microphones. But back then I was concerned.

The night before the real opening, we had a dress rehearsal. In the audience there were local dignitaries and the theatrical reporters from the newspapers. The director, voice coach, and Hazel Lindoft, the author, went to the balcony to hear how well our voices carried. The show was well received and we were jubilant. Then we saw the director and authors come backstage. Immediately they were surrounded by the cast, wanting to know how well they had been heard. Everyone but the leading lady had to wait his or her turn. We were surprised when we heard she was the only one who had to return the next morning. She had to rehearse until they could hear her better.

I asked, "Could you hear me?" They said, "You are just fine, Lucile. We heard you perfectly." Mother and I were relieved.

The performances of the "Girl from Honolulu" were on November 17 and 18, 1926, and I had enjoyed my part in the successful musical comedy.

I thought that if junior high school had given me so much, high school would give me more, but I was to be disappointed. The first day I entered Long Beach Polytechnic High School, I met with my counselor, who recognized me from my pictures and the reviews in the papers.

She said, "We will have to give you classes to further your dance career." After several minutes of going through numerous papers, she gave me my program. "This is what I have for you. For your English course we will give you oral expression. It has a little drama in the course. You would probably get more benefit from bookkeeping than higher math. Chorus will be good; I understand you sing. I am sure you will try out for the Glee Club. We have a good one here. We have a dance class you can attend instead of gym. You say you would like an art class. I can understand where some knowledge of art would help. Here is your schedule. Come to me if you have any difficulties."

What she had assigned for me had so few credits, I could see I would have to stay in high school for a long time.

I was late getting to my art class and found that the teacher had left a student in charge. She told me to sketch the rose that was on display. I had never tried to draw anything before. Going down the aisle, I looked at the other student's drawings, and I felt I was in the wrong class. If the teacher had been in the room instead of a student, it might have been different. Instead, I enrolled into a music appreciation class. It proved to be a lucky change.

I tried out for Glee Club, and that teacher recognized me, too. Many times when I had danced for luncheons, the Poly High School Glee Club had been on the program. They performed often, because they were above average. When I made the Glee Club, I was pleased. Now, I would be having voice training. During the class, I did receive vocal exercises, but every time they performed, I danced. Mother and I could not understand why it was so easy to be excused from my classes. Even on test days, all I had to say was, "I'm performing with the Glee Club," and I was excused from eleven o'clock on.

Oral expression was interesting, but I had trouble finding the time to memorize the assignments. The day came when we were told to memorize a fairy tale, and I just hoped she would not call on me, but she did. Fortunately, I had made up a story instead of memorizing one. I had outlined it in my mind while walking to school that morning. When I had finished telling my story, I returned to my seat and hoped I wouldn't be accused of lying.

The teacher asked me to stay after class and asked? "Lucile, who wrote your story?"

"It was anonymous." This was true. I was certainly anonymous.

She said, "I would like a copy of it, please."

The next day, I gave her a copy. When I handed it to her she said, "I liked your story; it was new and different."

She gave me an "A." I felt guilty, but I was too embarrassed to say anything. I had learned a lesson. Don't avoid telling the truth. I had worried all night, wishing I had told her the story was original. I had found that a lie can lead to more lies, and the truth was much easier to live with. I had never lied before, and it was a good lesson I never forgot. There were times when I would get in trouble telling the truth, but I wouldn't lie.

My favorite class was music appreciation. I was listening to music I loved and getting credit for it. For years I had been listening to classical music, choosing what I wanted to use for my dances. In this class I learned about the composers' lives and about different instruments.

A male classmate asked me for a date. He was older, and I knew he was a member of the same fraternity that my brother belonged to. I could hardly wait to tell Alton that one of his friends had asked me to go out with him. I did not expect the reaction I received. Alton said flatly that I was not to go out with him, and he gave me a long lecture, some of which I did not understand. He told me, "I do not want any fellow to talk about you, like I hear them talk about the girls they go out with. Besides, this fellow is already going steady with someone, and he probably wants to go out with you for just one thing." I wasn't too sure about what the "one thing" was, but I knew my brother meant what he said.

I gave my classmate a note to tell him I could not go out with him and got into trouble when the teacher saw me passing it. My first and only note to a boy in school, and I got caught! Lack of experience, I guess.

The interpretive ballet was more like modern dance. Sometimes the teacher gave us some work, and left me in charge of the class. I learned more about teaching than modern dance.

The class that took most of my study time was the bookkeeping class. We had to keep business books. I understood it, but it was hard keeping my books up to date. I worked on the books every evening but was always behind. I did learn methods I would use to my advantage when I had my dance studios years later.

My bookkeeping teacher was a favorite with the girls. He was an elderly, handsome man and looked like he played golf every day. His wavy, snow-white hair looked marvelous with his tan. Girls flocked around him and he loved it, but they were the type of girls I avoided. In those days they were called "fast." When the end of the semester was near, he told me to stay after class.

After everyone had left, he said, "You are way behind on your book work." I knew that, but I did not expect what he said next.

"I would like to help you. Why don't you let me know when your parents are not going to be at home. Then I will come to your house and help you. You will receive a higher grade." I walked out of the room stunned. I never took his offer. I was innocent but not completely naïve, and I didn't think his idea was good.

Mother let me stay up late at night when I told her I might fail the class if I didn't bring my work up to date. Probably, I should have told her about the teacher's offer, but I didn't. I did receive a C in the class. I studied hard in the study hall period instead of socializing with the other students. During the lunch period I would either brown-bag it or go to the cafeteria and buy a milk shake. Between the buildings, there was some grass where I would sit, eat my lunch and study. In this way, I could complete most of my homework, which gave me more time to practice. My grades were good. I have wondered, could I have been an A-1 student if I had not been studying so hard to be an A-1 dancer? I also had private lessons from a voice teacher. She had a small music conservatory, and I taught tap, ballet, and ballroom for her. The cost of my singing lessons was taken from my small salary. She developed my speaking voice, too. Two days a week after school, I went to her studio, taught dancing, and had my lesson.

I made one friend while I was in high school, Marjorie Hoyt, daughter of the owner of the Hoyt Theater. She invited me to go to the Virginia Country Club to play tennis. I didn't know how, so she taught me. After playing, we would go to the clubhouse and have a "Black Cow," a root beer, with ice cream. It was great having a friend I could talk with about something besides dancing. One day I twisted my ankle while playing and Mother decided no more tennis. I didn't see Marjorie anymore.

A boy from the R.O.T.C. asked me to go to a Sunday matinee with him. It was my only date in high school. I don't think I was much fun, and when he didn't ask to see me again, I wasn't surprised. I went through all my school years without making a lasting friendship. I didn't realize my loss until years later when I would come home and had no one to see.

In the summer I danced in parks for entertainment shows that were held there. A favorite of mine was a dance with a beautiful young lady. I played an artist with palette and paintbrush. She posed as the subject of a portrait, and I mimed painting the portrait while dancing.

One evening Mother looked up from the paper she was reading. "There is more news in the paper about the Exposition. Besides the water show they are going to have a Hollywood producer stage an extravaganza. Local dancers may audition for the show. It sounds good. Are you interested?" I was definitely interested.

The Exposition was going to be on the edge of town. A local bus took us to the site and signs directed us to the stage located at the end of a swimming pool. We climbed temporary stairs and saw a piano and some chairs besides the carpenters and electricians. The girls were wearing shorts and blouses, different practice clothes than I wore. Everyone seemed to know every one else. After I changed into my practice costume mother said, "We will have to do some shopping." I was glad she had noticed my little ballet outfit did not fit in with this group at all.

Two men climbed the stairs and the older one went to a chair and the younger man said in a loud voice, "Girls, form a straight line according to your height."

He looked like the dance instructors I had seen in the motion picture musicals. The girls were all older and I envied their casual manner. Going to the end of the line he began asking questions and writing on a pad on a clipboard. He barely talked to some because he obviously knew them. When he reached me, I gave my name, address, phone number and experience. He gave me a second look when I told him my dance experience, but he went on writing. I was beginning to lose confidence. He had looked at me the same way my brother looked at me, his kid sister. When he was done, the audition started. I went into the back line, where there was more space. Besides I didn't know how difficult the steps were going to be. I felt better when I found they were the type of tap I knew.

He gave a command. "Come up here in the front line." I realized he was gesturing to me. I went to the front line and the girls I had been following moved over so I had some room. Soon, the steps became so easy I tried to put some expression in them. "Blondie, you aren't doing a solo. You are doing just fine, but tone it down a little." He watched us dance for awhile then talked to the man making notes. We were told to "take five." Some dashed off to the rest room. I was thirsty and some of us found some water. At the fountain I found out the older man was the choreographer.

Returning to my mother, I asked, "Am I doing all right?"

"You are doing fine but you might be too young," Mother said.

Then the dance instructor said, "Take your places for the ballet work." I relaxed, because it was simple ballet. The combinations were easy. Then it was time for another break. When we were told to take our lines again, they had decided whom they wanted to keep for the show. Our dance director went down the line and some were told to step over to the side. I was still in the line. When he had finished choosing, he told the girls who were on the side, "Thank you. If we need some replacements in the future you may be called." He turned to the rest of us and said, "Girls, we will start the ballet routine first."

When the rehearsal was over, future rehearsal hours were given, and we all changed to go home.

The next day, when I came to rehearse, we were told to take our make up cases to the dressing rooms. Sixty of us would share three long narrow rooms. The makeup table was a long, waist high shelf with mirrors and bright lights above them. I went to the back of one of the rooms and hung my street clothes on the hooks on the wall, feeling like I was in a movie scene.

"I guess the girls who wanted to be closest to the door don't know the old superstition." It was the girl next to me talking to Mother and me. "They will cut down the number of dancers they need when the show gets closer to the end of the engagement. Those nearest the door are cut first."

It did happen that way! When the attendance started to drop off, they let some of the dancers go. The girls closest to the door! My neighbor and I were still there closing night. Show business superstitions are scary sometimes.

During a later rehearsal, I had made friends with the Arabian tumblers in the show. Mother had asked one of them to look at my original acrobatic work. These tumblers, who were not really Arabians, were the best I had seen. Doing some fast flips backwards they finished with layouts, soaring through the air with their bodies opened out, as though they were lying in the air. My new friend, Eddie, helped me when I tried to do a back flip. I knew how, but had never felt confident doing them.

Most of the time we rehearsed hard, especially the ballet. The dancers were Hollywood girls who had worked in movies before, and the ballet they had done previously hadn't been too advanced.

Opening night was a new experience for me. Huge searchlights scanned the skies and famous people attended the performance. The newspapers had given the Exposition, pages of publicity. They said, "The Exposition will put Long Beach on the map!"

That night a handsome young man came backstage to talk to the Arabian Tumblers. Archibald Leach had worked with some of them before his acting career had started. Eddie introduced him to us. He was polite and I did like his smile because it was special. When he became famous as Cary Grant, I remembered how pleasant he had been to my mother and me.

The show started with our tap dance. Between the acts on the stage, there were exhibitions by famous divers and swimmers in the pool. After their swimming and diving, they swam towards the stage and dived under the mirrors slanted in front of the stage reflecting the water. The finale of the show was spectacular. The stage set looked like an ice cave decorated with fringes of silvery cellophane, a new product. The one-piece leotard costumes were decorated with silver sequins and more cellophane fringe. The symphonic sized orchestra played the "Dance of the Hours." It must have been beautiful. The audience applauded enthusiastically.

When the music started, the stage lights came on and revealed us in small groups under what must have looked like large chandeliers dripping with icicles. When they were lifted, we did our ballet dance. We finished the dance by forming two straight lines across the front of the stage in front of the pool. The water in the pool below us was still rippling from the swimmers. Each line walked forward and disappeared! Actually, we descended narrow steep steps that were behind the slanted mirrors. Our arms were extended over our heads and we were not to look down. The combination of the mirrors and the water gave the illusion that we entered the water. It was fun because we could hear the audience murmuring in surprise. I wished then, and I still wish, I could have seen it.

Mother was with me each night, and while I had my nose in a book backstage, she became friendly with the dancers. Later she told me they had said I should audition for Fanchon & Marco. I knew Daddy had always wanted me to finish school, but maybe she had managed to change his mind. She asked me if I would like to audition for Fanchon & Marco. If I were accepted, I would not go back to school. I had to do some serious thinking about that. I didn't think I would do any better in school than I had in my sophomore year. My dancing came first.

I asked, "Mother what do we have to do to find out about auditioning?" When she told me, I was surprised how much advice the girls had been giving her. She made the telephone call, and on the following Monday, we were on the Red Car bound for the audition that would change my life.

113

Chapter 7

The Monday after New Year's Day I was told to report to the rehearsal for the "Waltz Idea." It was 1929, and I was looking forward to my seventeenth birthday in March. Daddy realized he had lost his girls to show business. It was obvious Mother loved the new life because it was all she talked about. When I would start to tell my version of something she was talking about, she would say, "Lucile's on her soap box again." The familiar popular political saying would silence me. At first my feelings were hurt, then after awhile, it didn't matter. I let her talk.

I expected to see strange faces when I opened the door to the rehearsal room. Instead, all the chorus girls from the "Orientale Idea" were in the room. Mary came to me and said, "We are to be partners again, and the Tom-Tom number is going to be in the new show."

When I returned to the room after changing, Alice told us we were to learn the opening dance, too. She told everyone we were to do a Tiller dance. Some of us didn't know what a Tiller dance was, and she explained it was a precision line number, popular in England. Alice introduced a pretty young girl with long legs, and a lissome body to go with them. We found she was like a drill sergeant, with a delightful English accent. She was determined we were to learn in one week a routine the Tiller girls had probably been dancing for months. Fortunately, the girls had been in several shows together, were better than most, and were willing to learn. I had more trouble than the others did because it was new to me. With our arms around the next girl's waist, we were taught to do high kicks forward. Then we were given different directions for the kicks while hopping on one foot. The entrance step was difficult, and when we were told we were to travel onto the stage doing that step, we groaned. That was when our drill instructor smiled for the first time.

Part of the dance was sitting on the floor; we held our upper body weight by leaning on our elbows in back of us while our legs were making patterns up in the air. The costumes were high-waisted royal blue velvet trunks attached to gold satin blouses with full sleeves. By the end of the week we knew we had achieved our goal when Miss Fanchon gave us a rare compliment after she had seen our dance.

Our dance was a novelty for a short time. Then it seemed to be everywhere. Universal and other film studios began producing musicals, with Busby Berkely staging some big ones using similar dances. When Gene Kelly entered the scene, he produced wonderful stage dance productions. Even casinos now have large shows using chorus lines. The Rockettes are famous for their line dancing in Macy's Christmas Parade in New York and can be seen on television. Now, high school cheerleaders do fabulous routines. Times have changed.

The "Waltz Idea" opened at the Loew's State Theater in Los Angeles. The much talked about Greta Garbo was on the screen with John Gilbert in, "A Woman of Affairs." The critics said the sex scenes were the best part of the picture. The Tiller routine to "I Can't Give You Anything But Love," a popular song, opened the "Idea." Quoting the review, "The 16 line girls peddled some nifty steps and kicks down front in unison...Sam and Sam, did a Buck tap dance, which demanded an encore. For this they offered a Military tap without music. It was all good and well sold by the two boys."

Gene Morgan, a popular Master of Ceremonies, was billed as the "Ceremony Jester." Our show gave him the opportunity to shine. We only had two acts with us at this time so Gene had time to put his talents to use. He had two spots in the show and the press and audience loved him. Jess Stafford and his Brunswick Band were on the stage and they offered a medley of "Sally" numbers, with Stafford featured with his trombone. Two band boys sang "Sally, Girl of My Dreams."

The Tiller routine and the Tom-Tom production numbers were prominent parts of the Idea. Neither of the dances was a waltz, which really didn't make much sense to us. We were happy when the Tom-Tom number was given better reviews than we had received the first time when it was in "Orientale Idea." The acts were changed often, sometimes after just one week with us.

Fritz and Jean Hubert, both dressed in men's tuxedos, did a drunken dance that always tickled the audience. They mixed eccentric steps with some falls and seemed not to have any bones in their bodies. They won many laughs from the audience when they fell into ridiculous positions.

For our finale, our singers, Helene Hughes and Roy Smoot, sang the theme song from "Lilac Time," a motion picture starring Janet Gaynor and Charles Farrel. "Jeannie, I Dream of Lilac Time," was a waltz, and was one of the first songs from the sound tracks with the new talkies. While the duo sang, I did a ballet dance, a welcome change from everything else I had been doing.

The orchestra men occupied an area in the back of the stage that had a roof, which provided a second, and smaller stage. A silvery scrim was lowered down to it. When raised, it showed stairs and pillars that were covered in gleaming white oilcloth. When one chorus of the song had been sung, the stage lights dimmed and light was focused on the upper area. The scrim lifted to show the chorines in a line at the bottom of the stairs facing the stairs. The girls wore silver bras and trunks with large heavy scarves of a metallic material woven like a fish net, draped across their backs. Mary and I also wore silver, but our costumes were a different style. We all wore white wigs, which I felt made me look like I was doing an imitation of George Washington. Mary joined me on the stage and we held a pose when the girls slowly went up the stairs while the song continued. The set had subdued lighting, with pastel colored spotlights shining on the girls, resulting in iridescent shades. One critic likened the finale to a motion picture set, with maidens in a Grecian Temple.

Sometimes, in the larger theaters, there were windows across the back of the last row of seats. Closed drapes were on the lobby side of the theater, so it created a mirror effect and reflected the action on the stage. We could see what the audience was enjoying so much.

On closing night, Mary asked Mother, "Can Lucile stay over night with me? We will see you in Glendale tomorrow." This was news to me, and Mother surprised me by saying, "Yes." She was pleased because, if Daddy would be bringing her to the theater later, it would be easier for her to bring our clothing for the week. We had decided we could afford a hotel instead of going home each night.

When Mary was certain they had left, she said, "We have dates after the show." I was not too pleased, and when Mary told me it is all arranged and there will be another couple, I asked, "Who?"

Mary and one of the chorus girls had become acquainted with two of the ushers from the front of the house. They had arranged for me to have a blind date with another usher. I knew Mother would have never allowed all this, but now I did not have any choice.

After thinking it over, I thought it would be fun to go someplace and have something to eat. Perhaps it would be a place with an orchestra and we could dance. The boys were waiting for us when we finished packing and were ready to leave. We got into their car and we were on our way. To my surprise, the car went into a residential district and stopped in the driveway of a house. I reluctantly went into the house, the home of one of the young men. His mother was a nurse and would be gone all night on duty. He mixed drinks for everyone and then the other two couples vanished. My date and I had been left at the open door of a bedroom in the rear of the house. I put my untasted drink on the sink. There was a small broken down uncomfortable chair, a dresser and a bed in the room. We had decided to sit on the bed. I just sat on the edge. Here I was with a man I had just met, alone and wondering what was going to happen? Nothing happened. My date realized the situation from the start, and because he had a younger sister my age, he tried to put me at ease. He had not expected his blind date would be so young. We could not find a subject to talk about. He probably could talk about sports, but sports were foreign to me. Dancing was all I knew. I doubt if he had ever before experienced such a dull companion and finally he said, "I'll be back in a minute," and left.

I heard him arguing, and when he came back he smiled and told me, "We are leaving." We not only left, but we were taken to Mary's home. I went to bed without talking about the evening. I thought, perhaps she was thinking it was Mother who was keeping me from men, and I would be different on my own. Well, she was wrong. I had my own ideas about what I wanted to do.

When I was with Mother the next day in Glendale, I did not know how to tell her about the night, so I didn't say anything. If she were to confront Mary, I was certain there would be tension between us and that would not be good for the partnership. Mary was relieved, I know.

The opening day at the Glendale Theater was without incident. Then after the last show Mother and I went for a walk. Before long we heard the sirens of fire engines and saw them stop at the rear of the theater. We found out a fire had started downstairs in the chorus girl's dressing room. The fire was extinguished quickly and we were allowed to see how Mary and my dressing room had fared. It was smoky but otherwise everything was all right. The chorus girl's room was a mess from the sprinklers. One of them had hung her metallic scarf over one of the light fixtures above the make up table. It had caused a short and the fire. Dumb!

Early the next morning Mary and I had to go to the Fanchon & Marco business office to pick up our contracts. While we were travelling on the Red Car to Los Angeles, Mary tried to explain the previous night. I told her it had been my first date, and if that was a date, it would be a long time before I dated again.

After we had signed our contracts, we were about to start on our trip to the Glendale Theater when we heard someone say, "Lucile and Mary are here. They can take the costumes to Glendale." They showed us boxes almost as big as we were. We looked at each other, how would we manage them?

The optimistic seamstress put two large boxes in each of our arms saying, "You acrobats are strong, you can manage. Here is the money for the cab fares you will need. We have one waiting for you at the curb downstairs to take you to the Sixth Street station. Take another cab from the Red Car to the theater."

The boxes were not heavy and contained replacements for the costumes damaged from the sprinklers during the fire. The costumers had worked all night. Laughing, we struggled on our way to the curb where the taxi was waiting. It helped remove the tension between us. Arriving at the station, our struggles with the awkward boxes attracted two young men, and they offered to help us. We bought our tickets and the fellows persuaded the man at the gate they were needed to help us onto the coach. Our unknown benefactors left after they deposited us in our seats with the boxes surrounding us. We collapsed in laughter to the amusement of fellow passengers. Our plight had interested them, and we had all the help we needed to the taxi for the trip to the theater.

119

We managed to get the boxes into the dressing room without casualty. The wardrobe lady had performed wonders to the rest of the costumes, and before long, the smoke odor was almost gone. Mary and I were spared the "advice" given to the girls.

We were booked for split weeks in two more theaters in the vicinity of Los Angeles, so Mother and I were back home in Long Beach and riding Red Cars with Alton coming after us. He did not mind at all, probably because he had begun to talk with one of the girls in the chorus. The girls had become friendlier when they found I had a good-looking brother. Mary had flirted outrageously, but she was my age and lost out to an older girl. Alton and Daddy saw us off at the train bound for Fresno before a romance had a chance to bloom. .

While we were there, we were told Al Jolson, the famous Jazz Singer, would be performing with us at the Warfield Theater in San Francisco. The Tiller dance would open the show and we would do the Tom-Tom production number, which was considered strong enough to close the show. After Mr. Jolson sang, we would do the finale. Every one was impressed by the thought of seeing Al Jolson, but I was hoping to see Ruby Keeler, the tap dancer. She had been starring in a New York show, not too common for a dancer. She and Mr. Jolson were reported to be engaged to be married.

San Francisco was to be a hard week. Large crowds wanted to see the great Jolson in person. We did six performances every day, each for a full house. The line outside the box office stretched for most of the block. The production numbers, with the singers, Mary and I, and the chorus girls, were all that was left of our show. We never did see the other acts again. We rehearsed and went downstairs to the dressing rooms to unpack and get ready for the first show. One of the girls from the line came into our dressing room to talk a few minutes. She started to whistle and we hustled her out. It was considered bad luck to whistle in the dressing room and bad luck was on its way!

Mary hurried into her costume, and went into the hallway where I heard her talking to one of the musicians. I knew she was asking him to help her get limber in order to do better splits. Mary would stand with her back against the wall and have the fellow take one of her legs and push it up until she was doing a standing split. It was the same stretch that the young instructor had used when he pulled the muscle in my leg. I thought it funny that Mary would have to have someone do this for her when splits were so easy for her. This time, she was backed up against the wall next to our dressing room door. I had finished my makeup and was ready to change into my costume. I said to her, "I'm going to shut the door so I can get ready."

The heavy fireproof door slammed shut, I heard Mary scream. I quickly opened the door but the damage had been done. Her thumb had been in the hinged side of the door and was smashed. She had to have a doctor, so Mother and Mary went to a hospital in a taxi.

I stood in the hallway shocked, but the minutes were ticking off. The manager of our show came to me and said. "Stay out of the opening number. You will have to change your acrobatic dance to a solo."

The 15 minute signal had already been given; the five minute signal would be buzzing soon. I did a lot of mental choreography before the Tom-Tom number went on. Instead of Mary's special tricks, I had to insert difficult tricks of my own. I ended up with a very energetic dance.

Mary was pale when she returned to the theater after what seemed to me forever. Her broken and bruised thumb was in a splint and she was not to dance for a few days and no acrobatic work for weeks. Mother and Mary reassured me it was not my fault, and Mary and I vowed we would never let anyone whistle in our dressing room again.

Doing six shows a day was not easy. I lived on the milk shakes Mother brought to me. I didn't have time to eat a real meal. After the last show, the only places we could find open were Delis and Chinese restaurants, which suited me just fine.

Al Jolson was in top form, and a wonderful performer. He "wowed" them that week and was on stage for a long time. Each audience wanted more encores. I would watch him from the wings, enjoying his terrific delivery, and was careful to stay out of his way. It was plain the rest of the cast did not exist for him. I heard Ruby Keeler had come to see Mr. Jolson, but to my disappointment, I didn't see her.

It was a tired group of girls that opened in the new Fox Theater in Oakland the next week, and we were glad it was not the old T & D Theater. Everything was up to date in stage equipment and the dressing rooms even smelled good. On the corner, next to the theater entrance, there was an ice cream parlor whose hot fudge sundaes were famous. Every night, between the third and fourth shows, the three of us had a treat. Mother even gave up her Coca-Cola for the sundaes. Mary had been doing the Tiller routine and the finale with a small bandage on her poor thumb. She didn't have any trouble with the hot fudge sundaes!

The show was completely different. Chirot and Mercado were the new singers. Conlin and Glass were advertised as Vaudeville's "Funniest Comedy Team." The picture starred Reginald Denny and was supposed to be very funny.

In every city where we were playing Mother would watch the paper for events we could attend. In Sacramento she suggested we should go to the State Fair Grounds. Mary went with us, and we saw the trainers exercising horses at the racetrack. The horses were pulling sulkies, tiny carriages with large wheels, and we stopped to admire them. A trainer approached us. He asked Mary and me if we would like to ride around the track. Of course we did. He explained we each would be alone as they carried only one person, and we would not be going fast because we would go opposite the usual race track direction. He reassured mother it would be quite safe. It was a slow ride but still thrilling, sitting behind a horse going clip clop, clip clop, around a big track.

In Oregon we played Medford and Salem, and finally we were in Portland, and there was Ronnie. He seemed different. He asked Mary to go out with him and barely talked to me. The young man I thought I had fallen in love with was gone. This man wanted a girl for a different kind of relationship.

Mother was sympathetic and she tried to turn my mind to other things. One day we were taking a walk before the first show and stopped to look into the window of a toy shop. It was opposite the park where Ronnie and I had walked. I think Mother wanted to distract me so she drew my attention to the baby doll in the window. When we went inside, the sales lady let me hold him. His head wobbled so I quickly held it like I would have held a real baby's head. He was soft to hold and seemed to cuddle. Mother was pleased to see I had remembered her instructions on how to hold a baby. She surprised me when she said I could have him, and I walked out of the store holding him. I named him Tommy. When I came back to my dressing room after the first show, Tommy was wrapped in a pretty baby blanket. Mother said she had found it. I'm sure she did, in a store. We took Tommy traveling with us. I still have him, and for years he sat under the Christmas tree. Now he resides in a small cradle in my studio room. Somewhere along the way, he lost part of a toenail but otherwise, he is still intact and does not show his age of seventy years a bit.

In Seattle, the chorus girls had become friendly with some young men from the university. One night, Mary asked if I would like to join her in a double date. I hesitated and was about to refuse, but Mother urged me, "Go and have some fun. The boys seem to be nice."

When I said I would join Mary, I hoped we might really go dancing some- where. I was introduced to Shorty, who was not only short, but plump. Mary's date drove a new sports car, and although it was a cold night, the top was down. Shorty and I were in the back seat where we had a good view of Seattle and the sparkling lights on this crisp, clear night. I thought it was going to be all right. We were out to take a ride and see the city. But I was wrong. Instead, as I was enjoying the trip through a lovely section with large homes and landscaped lawns, we drove into a driveway, and my heart sank. We entered the house and went into a library room with leather furniture and more books than I had ever seen in a private home. I refused the drink I was offered and asked for some water. These were prohibition days, and Daddy had told me to avoid anything that might be "bathtub gin."

Before long, Mary and her date disappeared and I was alone with Shorty. When he asked if we were going upstairs, I said, "No." He sat down on the couch, patted the place alongside him, and said, "Why don't you come over here on the couch beside me?" I told him, "No, I am quite comfortable here in this chair."

He came over to me and tried to kiss me. I avoided his lips. I had not had many kisses, and I did not want one from him. I protested, "I don't kiss boys I don't know." He said, "Let's start to get to know each other." Again I said, "No. Please let me alone."

Shorty said, "Well, guess this isn't going to be my night," and he stretched out on the couch. In a few minutes he was fast asleep and started to snore. I tiptoed to the book- cases, and, recognizing titles of books, I opened them. Apparently they had not been opened often. I thought how much I would love to read them all. Settling down in my leather chair, I started to read one. It was quiet, except for Shorty snoring, until I heard a door open in the back of the house and heard the voices of young boys in the kitchen. I thought they might give me a drink of water. I was still thirsty. Entering the kitchen I saw several boys near my age opening bottles of beer that smelled just like my father's homebrew.

"How about a beer?" they asked me and I said I would like to have a small glass. I thanked them for the beer and went back to my chair.

I could hear them laughing and talking as they approached the library. Seeing Shorty asleep on the couch, one said, in a manner I did not like, "Guess Shorty got tired out."

Then they surrounded me, sitting on the arms of the chair, at my feet and one stood in back of the chair. It was as if it were planned. They attacked different parts of my body, or tried to. I had to fight all of them at the same time. I kicked at the fellows at my feet as their hands started reaching under my skirt. I flailed out at the two who were trying to reach down the front of my dress. I was glad I was strong as I battled the five of them saying, "Stop, stop it."

The commotion awakened Shorty, but instead of coming to my rescue, he laughed, and I was afraid he would join them. The boys left. The futile assault was over quickly. Instead of the frail girl they expected, they were picking on a girl almost as strong as any one of them. Their fun game had not turned out as expected, so they left making unflattering remarks. At that time, I didn't realize how lucky I had been that they hadn't done more to me.

I did know I had enough. I went up the stairs to the next floor. I walked down the hallway until I heard Mary's voice. I shouted, "I want to leave NOW!"

I was ready to go to the hotel but the others decided they were hungry and started to drive to a Chinese restaurant. Shorty tucked me in under the blanket, and at first I thought he was trying to be considerate. He tried to kiss me; his hand went beneath the blanket and was going up my leg. I was completely fed up with all this hanky panky. I began to hit him, hard. My fists landed on his nose and eyes. When we reached the cafe his nose was bleeding. They decided they didn't need any Chinese food and took me to the hotel. I was glad I had roughhoused with my brother when we were growing up. Daddy's showing me how to make a fist had come in handy. I was also glad that Shorty hadn't decided to hit me. He had been too surprised. Mother was half-asleep and only awakened enough to say good night before going back to sleep. When I thought what could have happened, I had to overcome the desire to cry. When I said my prayers, I thanked Him for protecting me. That was the last time for me to double date for many years.

When our week was over in the Seattle theater, we kept the hotel room an extra night because we were playing in Bremerton again. Mother decided to stay in Seattle.

Our trip on the ferry was more enjoyable than the one on the fishing boat had been. The manager was, as usual, making the last show late. Mary and I read the ferryboat schedule and decided to try to make the last one.

We asked Beth, one of the girls, if she would put our shoe bags and costumes in the crates. She said she would. We arranged our street clothing for a fast getaway. As soon as we finished the show, we dressed, and ran out of the theater and down the street. We could see the ferrymen preparing to leave the pier. The ropes that held the boat to the pier were being tossed aboard. Perched, almost tip toe at the edge of the pier, we watched the swirling water from the propellers widen. The wharf men had run toward us because they thought we were going to jump across, but we knew better. They shook their heads as they walked into the ferry building. Defeated, we went to the hotel, and went up the stairs to the lobby. The entire cast was milling around the desk. Beth, our fellow conspirator, was peeking out of her room, down the hallway.

She whispered, "Come in with me and wait."

She barely opened the door and we slipped in. In her arms she held her small dog. She said, "I was afraid he would say I could not have my dog in the room. I don't know what I would have done if he had said I couldn't." The line registering for rooms was taking a long time. Beth said, "Why don't you stay with me?" We had one small dog, and three of us in one bed.

The clock's alarm was set. A ferry would leave at 5:00 am. No one was at the desk, and we were as quiet as mice leaving the hotel. We enjoyed the early morning ferry ride. Mother was surprised to see us so early.

Later, Mother and I were standing on the station platform waiting for our train. The girls were laughing and talking with the university fellows and Mary's friend came up to us. "Mrs. Iverson," he said, "Shorty sends his regrets. He couldn't come to the station to say goodbye to Lucile. He is nursing a black eye and a swollen nose. You never need worry about Lucile's taking care of herself."

He turned and left. Mother asked, "What did he mean?"

I told her, "He got fresh."

After asking if I were all right, she said we would talk about it later. I never told her about the incident with the boys or what Shorty had attempted with me. I didn't tell her about the first time in Los Angeles either because she was shocked enough as it was.

I agreed we would keep our distance from Mary in the future, and we would not be partners in any more shows.

After a split week, we went back to the Strand Theater in Vancouver. Jackie Souder was still there, and we were happy to see him again.

On the 22nd day of March, Mother had a surprise for me. While I was reading between the two night shows, she left the dressing room. One of the girls came to my door and said, "Lucile, come out here for a minute." She led me to the Green Room and, as we entered, most of the cast was singing "Happy Birthday." I was certainly surprised. We had cake and ice cream and I had presents to open. It was a great seventeenth birthday. The friend who had arranged for my fur coat was there, too.

Later that week, Mary and I and the chorus were told we were going to dance at the Vancouver Hotel. A big ball was going to be given for important dignitaries from London. We were to dance the Tiller routine and our Tom-Tom number.

That evening, after the last show at the theater, we went to the hotel and were shown to a large room where we were to change into our costumes. After our arrival, two cartons of champagne were delivered to us with trays of finger sandwiches and pastries. We performed and started on our goodies. It was my first taste of champagne, and I loved it. I was thirsty, so I had more than one glass. I looked around for Mother who was to meet me. Instead, someone called me to the door. Our friend was in the hallway. He told me that Mother had said he could take me back to the hotel. When the girls were all decent, he came into the dressing room and had some champagne and goodies, too. Of course I had more wine with him. It was not too far to the hotel so we decided to walk, instead of taking a cab. I felt I needed the air.

"Would you like to see my store? It is close by." His arm had gone around my waist and he was guiding me down the street.

"Yes," I said, thinking, "Why not?"

I had never had such rubbery legs, and I giggled all the way to the haberdashery store his father had given him. I could see he had really attractive clothing displayed.

"It isn't too late. Would you like to go inside?" I said, "Yes."

I wanted to see if there was anything for my Daddy and brother when Mother and I went shopping. It was warmer inside than it had been out in the cold March wind. He helped me out of my coat and took me to a corner where he helped me onto a high stool. I snuggled against him when he put his arms around me. He turned my face to his and kissed me, several times.

"Gee," I thought, "Kissing can be nice."

He had turned my body so I was facing him. Then his hand was on my leg going up my skirt. I started to struggle and push him away from me. I was woozy from the champagne but was beginning to feel alarmed. He knew what he was doing, I didn't. It was like the fellow I knew had turned into a stranger. Suddenly I felt a stab of pain. I pushed him away so hard that he almost fell into the showcases.

"What's wrong with you?" he said in an angry voice.

Surely I had made it clear enough. I had no interest in yielding to him. I said, "You know what is wrong. Take me to the hotel."

My head was clearing from the effects of the champagne, and I felt confused and angry. I just wanted to get to my room and Mother. The hotel was near and before he left me in the lobby he said, "I'm sorry. I didn't know you were a virgin."

I went into the elevator. Mother let me in the door of our room and I said, "Go back to bed. I am sorry I woke you up." She asked me how the dances had gone over. "Just fine. I'm tired, I'm going to take my bath and get some sleep."

She got back into bed. I ran water into the tub and quickly got undressed. I felt so dirty, I scrubbed over and over. I found my undies were soiled so I put them into the tub and washed them. As I lay next to my mother in bed, waiting for sleep. I vowed it would be a long time before I would let a man get close to me again.

The next morning, Mother said, "Why did you wash your undies last night? I planned to wash some of our things today."

"Oh, they fell in the tub when I undressed so I washed them."

I did not want to tell her what had happened. She might have blamed me for going into the store. I had realized my mistake already. It was obvious the stool he had helped me onto was just high enough for his sexual exploits and had probably been used many times before. He had been so considerate; I had been taken in. I thought, "The first time Mother had allowed anyone to be my escort and I got into trouble."

Years later I was to hear about date rape, and I understood how it could happen. If only I could have spoken more openly with my mother about this subject! Perhaps she could have warned me about the effects of drinking, and that most men were different from my brother. The events of the past few weeks influenced my feelings about men.

Next day, Mother said I could have my haircut, now that I was seventeen. It had been curled every night for longer than I could remember. She asked me if I had changed my mind when I did not seem to care. I should have paid more attention when the beauty operator started to cut my hair. She almost scalped me! It wasn't her fault. It was the fashion to have short hair with little feather like tendrils coming toward the face. Mother took tucks in my silver headdress because during the matinee performance it had skidded around and almost blinded me. My hair grows fast, and before long I could curl the ends and fluff my hair. Mother was right; I did look better with curly hair.

We shopped and bought toffee for Daddy and another pipe and tobacco for Alton. Then we had our afternoon tea and scones. Mother asked why I looked so gloomy. I could not tell her that I was unhappy about my two losses. My hair and the other thing I was trying not to think about.

When we left Vancouver, Mother said, "We will be home soon."

I was homesick and told Mother, "When we get home, maybe Alton and I can go to some dances."

Before the Exposition, Alton and I had sometimes driven to Balboa, a summer resort by the sea, where name orchestras played at the ballroom, and dancers would drive there from all over southern California. When we had been home a few days Alton consented to take me to the Balboa Ballroom. When we were driving down the coast it seemed a long time since we had gone dancing; I just wanted to be with my brother. I understood now what he had been hinting about, when he had said, "Some men want just one thing." I realized I was not being considered a teenager anymore. I decided growing up was not much fun.

In the "Orientale Idea" we had traveled through winter snow, now it was spring-time. Would the next show travel longer than the "Waltz Idea"? I didn't know I was to have new and different experiences before my next big show. We had not been home more than a week when something did occur.

We had finished breakfast one Sunday morning, and I was washing and drying the dishes. I could see a bus go by from the kitchen window but didn't expect to hear the sound of cars crashing a few moments later. I threw down the towel I had in my hand and ran out the front door. Looking to the left corner I saw two busses stopped and a small Ford car in the street between them.

I ran to the corner and saw children's bodies in different places in the intersection. It was such a horrible sight that I stopped in my tracks and then realized Mother had come to stand beside me. She said, "Go to the little girl in the grass by the sidewalk across the street."

I went to the small girl who looked about twelve years old. She was unconscious but there was not any sign of blood on her. Kneeling beside her I thought there was nothing I could do but watch over her until help came.

Two ambulances arrived and after one of the men talked to my mother, they put a small child into one of them. An elderly lady and my mother also got into the ambulance. One of the men came to where I was and called for help. Another man came and they carried the little girl to the second vehicle. I could see people still gathered around inert bodies. I went closer and someone told me what had happened.

The car had been full of children from a large family. The eldest son was home on leave from the Navy and was taking his sisters and brothers to the beach. The young man had tried to cross in front of the bus, which he hadn't seen until it was too late. That bus sent the car into a bus that was just pulling away from the other corner and that bus sent the car to the middle of the street.

This was long before seat belts, and the children just flew out of the car in all directions. When the last ambulance left, I went home and told Daddy what had happened. He had been working in the garage in back of our house and had not heard anything.

Mother called from the hospital and told me the little boy had died. The family was distraught and alone in Long Beach so she had offered to stay with them. I was to pack a suitcase and Mr. Urban, the father, would come by and pick it up. She stayed with them for several days. It seemed losing the baby boy and an older child was more than the family could handle. The little girl had been operated on for a broken pelvis. Others had been more fortunate. Mother took care of the family until they became more stable. She always knew what to do, and as always, she helped those who needed help. It was not the first time I had seen this side of her and I tried to follow her example whenever I could.

Chapter 8

I had just answered the telephone. I told Mother, "Mary just called from Los Angeles and said she will be here in two hours. She caught me by surprise. She wants to go to the beach. Perhaps she thinks we live close to the beach." We had thought we would never see Mary again. Mother looked as surprised as I felt and she told me, "We had told her to come to see us at one time, so be nice to her. I don't think it is wise to go to the beach on a week day; there may not be life guards around."

I had barely spoken to Mary after Seattle, staying out of our dressing room as much as I could. She had evidently forgotten all about my dislike for her kind of a date. My disappointment must have shown in my face. I had been bored without anything to do. Mother probably realized I needed a change because she said, "Why don't you go to the plunge? You can swim there, and also go down to the beach." When Mary arrived I told her we were taking the bus downtown to the plunge. After Mary had talked to Mother for a few minutes, we were on our way.

Mary had been doing club dates, too, since coming home from the "Waltz Idea," and agreed club dates were not much fun. I had started getting acquainted with the different theatrical agents in Los Angeles and Hollywood for the first time. Mary told me about a few more.

I did not mind the club dates when I did them in Long Beach because I felt comfortable with people I knew who were pleased to see me again. Away from Long Beach, I was just a dancer there for their entertainment. They were not rude, but they made me feel as if I were not a normal person. This feeling of being an outsider was something I was to feel often. Mary said she felt she was treated as though she was different, also. We were happier when we traveled with a show, and every one was different. Mary told me her brother was taking her to wherever she was working so she did not have a transportation problem.

Daddy's attitude had changed. He was proud of his dancing daughter. He didn't mind driving us wherever I had to go. When I danced in Los Angeles or in any of the surrounding towns, he would plan his work so he could take us there. It was a lot of trouble for ten or fifteen dollars, less ten percent for the agent. Of course living expenses were much less at that time.

I was dancing at the usual clubs. Sometimes the rooms would be so full of smoke, I could hardly wait until I could wash my hair and get rid of the smell. These were social nights when the wives were present. The agents were careful not to book me for a "stag night" because of my age. When I got older, I still would not do stag nights. They were for the strippers, now called exotic dancers. The material the comedians used on these occasions was pretty racy and has not improved. Speakeasies also hired dancers but the theatrical agencies used only older girls for them. The agencies did not even consider me. Mary and I agreed it would be fun to put all these worries aside and be carefree kids for a day. Arriving at the plunge, we quickly changed and went for a swim. Unlike Mary, I still did not know how to swim but I tried a few strokes. We alternated between the ocean and the plunge all day. I know Mary was disappointed, because there were not any men around. It was early June and they were probably getting ready for graduation or working. We were both tired when she caught the Red Car, and I took my bus home.

The telephone rang when the family was seated at the dinner table. It was a call for me from an agent at the West Coast Theatrical Agency. He asked me if I was working. When I said, "No," he explained, "The O'Neil sisters, who produce the stage shows at the Golden Gate Theater in San Francisco need a toe dancer for the show opening tomorrow. When I suggested you, they told me to call you." After a quick consultation with Mother, I told him I would like to go, and Mother and I did some fast packing. Daddy drove us to the station in Los Angeles, arriving just in time to make the eight o'clock train. The agent at the station window gave me our tickets for the trip, a lower berth for Mother and the upper berth for me.

He said, "You will have to hurry, Miss."

A depot porter had put our bags on a cart and we had to run to keep up with him. Quick hugs were exchanged with Daddy, then we boarded the train. The coach porter put our bags in the vestibule and the train moved. They had been holding the train for us! We were ready to retire when the porter asked if we wanted our berth made up?

Mother said, "Yes. And please let us know when it is six-thirty."

When I had to climb to the upper berth my legs felt funny, sort of rubbery. Finally, the familiar clickity, click, of the wheels over the tracks lulled me to sleep. After arriving in San Francisco, we took a taxi to the theater and I went backstage. Mother stayed with the cab and went on to the Governor Hotel to check in.

The O'Neil sisters knew me, or at least they knew my work from the "Ideas." When I had danced at the Warfield, I couldn't see their shows, but I had heard about them. They asked if I would need any help setting my dance.

"All I need is to hear my music and know how long the dance should be."

I found my assigned dressing room and quickly changed into practice clothes and toe shoes, but when I tried to stand on my toes I found I could not do it. My muscles did not respond. The swimming the day before had relaxed them. Fortunately, after I explained my problem, I was allowed to do my dance on demipointe in ballet slippers. Between shows I did barre work and happily, the next day I could do my dance on pointe. The third day, I fulfilled their expectations and all was well.

We were staying at the Governor Hotel again because it was convenient to the theaters. They catered to theatrical people so it was almost like a club. Every one had late working hours, so the management was more lenient about noise after eleven.

The next week, the production went to the El Capitan Theater, a theater further from the downtown area. Some shows were transferred there after the week at the Golden Gate. It was an easy ride on a streetcar, so we stayed on at the Governor hotel.

A young comedian, Morey Amsterdam, was staying there too. Sometimes, when I was having my breakfast in the Hotel coffee shop, Morey and I would share a table. His work was just starting to be recognized. Through the years I have followed his career, and was happy for him when he had such a long run with the Dick Van Dyke and Mary Tyler Moore show.

I had to cope with the stage at the El Capitan. In back of the apron, the floor was covered with a taut, heavy canvas, and I have a scar on my chin from that canvas. My acrobatic dance contained a chest roll. Starting with two quick turns to the right, I did a front walkover, and a very fast split, right foot in front. I brought my right foot back to my left foot and that put me on the floor on my stomach. Then I rolled forward, kicking my feet over my head onto the floor. I held my face to the side and used my hands to bring me into a back bend, then came up to an upright position. My face rubbed against the canvas and I scraped my chin the first show. Each show I tried to protect my face, but it always touched. The second day, I had a slight scab, under my chin. It rubbed off and when I reached my dressing room it was bleeding. No matter how I tried to avoid it, I always rubbed that spot. It did not hurt; perhaps if it had I would have taken the chest roll out of the dance. The scar that was left was under my chin so I never had to conceal it with make up.

I shared a dressing room with Benay Venuta, a singer who knew how to deliver a song. She was excited, and I did not blame her. The following week she was going to New York to rehearse in a musical.

I was asked to stay for a second week at the El Capitan and I was glad I had brought several different costumes. To my surprise I received a contract for the same week from the West Coast Agency in Los Angeles. I was to open at the Grand Lake Theater in Oakland. I telephoned the agent and explained my predicament. He sent a new contract for me to start in Oakland the following week, which I did.

We decided we would stay at the hotel because the streetcar would take us to the ferry building. We went to Oakland by taking the ferry across the bay. The Bay Bridge did not exist then and large ferryboats transported the passengers across the bay to a pier. While crossing the bay, we would go to the upper deck to see the many different sights. I enjoyed the cool ocean air and, after finding a place to sit, we watched the ships sailing to the docks where they would unload their cargoes from the far away foreign countries. The deep blue water was ruffled by the wind, making little waves that sparkled in the sunlight. Noisy sea gulls followed the ferry and swooped down to snatch the food thrown out by the galley workers. The deep whistle warned us to hurry to take our places in the lines disembarking. Large streetcars, similar to the Red Cars in southern California, were waiting at the end of a long pier to take us into Oakland. It was not long before we reached our stop in Oakland and we crossed the street to the Grand Lake Theater. It was a nice theater and a pleasant week.

Lake Merritt was across from the theater and between shows we walked down the pathways of the large park that surrounded the lake. When we crossed back to San Francisco at night, the lights of the city were beautiful. Twin Peaks lights looked like they were mingling with the stars.

The ferry building was at the foot of Market Street and streetcars originated there for districts all over San Francisco. Ours went up Market Street and our short trip went fast as we passed many different kinds of interesting shops. I would have liked to ride a cable car but it was too late.

When the week was over, Mother and I decided to travel home by bus. We could go directly to Long Beach and avoid having Daddy go to the railway station in Los Angeles. Besides, we would save money. We enjoyed the ride because it followed the coast, and was more scenic than the train ride. Open spaces enabled us to see the ocean and the beaches that were filled with people enjoying themselves.

A few weeks later, I received a call from the agency again. They were putting acts together that would be playing split weeks at theaters. Was I interested? I was not too fond of doing a three or four day engagement instead of a full week but there were few theaters that still had a full week's engagement. Our transportation would be in automobiles provided by acts on the show and we would travel as far north as the San Francisco Bay area. Mother and I were glad to know it was taken for granted she would accompany me. Our show would be starting the next week and it meant several weeks of steady work. It was late June, and we had fair weather as we played the towns around southern California. The Long Beach papers said, "Local Gal makes good."

We had telephone calls from reporters, and they not only printed the information we gave them but added some improvising of their own. They knew the schools I had attended and where I had danced and taught. One reporter said that I was considering becoming a comic dancer. News to me, but many times I have wished I had tried it.

The publicity and my picture in the paper did bring friends to the theater, and a few came backstage. The Glee Club teacher from high school came to congratulate me on my performance. I was surprised and happy to see her.

"Two Weeks Off," staring Dorothy Mackail and Jack Mulhall in their first talking picture, was the movie at the West Coast Theater in Long Beach. They were a popular comedy team. Slim Martin, a Long Beach favorite, was the orchestra leader and M. C.

Cliff Clark, an excellent comedian was the manager for our group. We were to go to him with any problems we might have. His wife, Mary Sweeney, recently from the Hippodrome Theater in New York, was known as "The Queen of the Air." I recall two parts of her act. Cliff held a rope that was suspended from the loft higher up. She climbed the rope, inserted one hand in a loop and turned over and over. The stage was blacked out except for the spotlight on her. The drummer played a drum roll with a cymbal crash each time she threw her body over her own arm. She did this thirty times before Cliff lowered her to the stage for her well-deserved applause. She went up the rope again, and an object was lowered beside her. It was a mouthpiece that she inserted into her mouth while she was high above the stage. Below, Cliff made the rope revolve and soon she was spinning at a rapid speed, hanging just by her teeth. The audience loved it because it really was sensational.

Mother and I traveled with Mary and Cliff in their car, and it wasn't long before we became good friends. Other acts were tap dancers, Wallen and Barnes, who, in show biz parlance, "wowed them," and Mabel Hollis, who sang popular songs, making a hit with the audience.

The tour lasted several pleasant weeks, a different experience from the hustle and bustle of the big cities. Too soon our miniature revue closed at the Grandlake Theater in Oakland. Their new orchestra, Horace Heidt with his Band of Renown, performed solos and they became famous for their novelty numbers.

Mother and I enjoyed the walks in the Lake Merritt Park again. One day, we returned to the theater and went to my dressing room next to the orchestra room. There was some time before the show and mother started to read while I was busy with my embroidery work. We were quiet, and at first we did not pay any attention to the voices which carried through the ventilator that served both rooms. Hearing my name mentioned made us listen. One of the men had asked Al if he was making any progress with Lucile. "No, her mother is always with us."

We recognized the voice of the violinist who had taken us sightseeing in his car. We heard him say he was enjoying being with us. We continued our friendship, and he took us in his car to places we would not have seen otherwise. Mother and he did most of the talking. We stayed in touch, and the next time we came to San Francisco he took us around to see the sights. The relationship the fellow musician had alluded to never took place.

After that week, we returned home, and I again looked for work. When it was possible, I went to Belcher's studio. He told his secretary to call me when the studio learned about motion picture auditions. I would go to these auditions but usually the girls hired were the ones the dance director knew by name. I did not fit in with the Hollywood dancer image. I had not become a party girl, and this made a difference.

When I had a call to go to the First National Studio in August 1929, I expected the same treatment, but I was wrong. There were not many girls auditioning, and they were more my age. Each one was asked to show her acrobatic ability and four of us were chosen.

The dance director marked a small rectangle with chalk on the floor. We each had to take turns doing spotters without stepping outside the chalk lines. When he was satisfied, each girl was given her own rectangle and told what to do. One girl did slow spotters. Next to her, another girl did back spotters. She did not have to worry about the speed. They are hard enough to do without worrying about doing them fast. The third girl did faster front spotters. Then turning to me he said, "Okay, Lucile, see how fast you can go," and he gave me my space.

He had a stopwatch in his hand and he told us when to start and stop. I thought he was never going to say stop. We practiced staying inside our spaces over and over.

He was satisfied at last and told us to come back to the studio the next day. We were told to go to wardrobe to be measured for our costumes before we went to a certain sound stage. The three girls were in the Wardrobe dressing room when I arrived next morning. We were measured for costumes and then were told where the sound stage was.

The buildings reminded me of the airplane hangers I had seen. The immense buildings were numbered with huge letters, so finding the correct one was relatively easy. The door we were to enter was of normal size, but it seemed small compared to the building. A red light was flashing above it and a sign said not to open the door when the light flashed, so we waited because it was blinking. When it stopped we tiptoed inside to one of the sets that was flooded with lights. Fortunately, we found the dance director there. A sign read, "Lilies of the Field, Corrine Griffith." When she came onto the set, she was surrounded by so many people I hardly saw her. The set looked like a night club scene with a stage at one end. The black and silver stage set looked very modern. It had little depth but was tall. We were told to go to the four small platforms that were at different heights. The girl doing the slow spotters went lower left. The girl doing back spotters was higher on the right. On the left, still higher up, the medium speed girl took her place. My area was about twenty feet high on the right. The back of the set had two large wheels. Actually, they were huge, about ten feet across. When I had reached my position, a voice called out, "Let them turn boys." The wheels began to spin. I moved away from the wheel beside me, as far as I could which was not very far because there was a ten foot drop on the other side. At my back there was the twenty-foot drop. I wondered what I was in for. I was glad to obey the next command, "Come down, get warmed up and we will rehearse."

I carefully made my way down the narrow steps to the lower level. I looked up at the wheels. Each of the wheel spokes had gathered, lightweight cloth inside it, black and silver cloth alternating. I could see my main concern would be not to get any part of my body tangled in that wheel. I did not even want to think about what would happen if I did.

The chorus girls, chosen at a separate audition, were rehearsed for hours, which turned into days. There were times it seemed, when nothing happened for anyone. The four of us watched the rehearsal and talked quietly. Silence was one of the main rules on the set. The chorus girls would play cards and smoke. I tried to practice, but it was so hot in that building, I would get too limber, so I read the book I always had with me. When it was lunchtime, we followed the "old timers" to the place to eat.

Vainly, we looked for our favorite stars. Someone told us they usually had their food sent to their dressing rooms. I realized that some of the cottages I had seen were really dressing rooms and others were offices. The lot looked like a small village.

Busby Berkely, the popular dance director, was also rehearsing a musical in the area. A note was given to me the last day when we were filming. Mr. Berkely wanted to see me on his set. I could not leave, so I asked the bearer of the note if I could return the next day to see Mr. Berkeley. He said I should show the note to the gateman, and he would let me in. I knew I would need identification to show because only those with their names on a list at the gate were allowed to come on the lot. The security was very tight.

The Thursday that we filmed was one of the longest days of my life. We were given our costumes, which were silver to match the set! This time, unfortunately, I did not have anything with me to sew on the edges to protect my skin from the scratchy cloth. In the makeup room, not only did we get face makeup but also the makeup girl applied Wheatcroft, a body lotion, on our exposed flesh. When we occasionally had a moment to sit, we were so hot we left a pool of Wheatcroft, then a girl would dab more on us. I wished I had a natural suntan instead of having Wheatcroft put all over me.

We were told to climb to our own platforms. There was a call for "LIGHTS," and the set became brilliant. We were told to start doing our spotters, then, "CAMERA … ACTION." The curtains in front of the set were drawn to the sides. The chorus entered from the wings onto the set doing their dance steps. We kept on with our spotters. I thought my lungs would burst as I went over and over until finally the blessed words "CUT" came. The heat from the lights on the set made me more limber than usual. I was taking a smaller space for my spotters than ever before. Considering how much room I had been given, I was glad there was a little more space left around me. We would rest while different orders were being shouted at workers, then they would shoot the scene again and again. I believe we were paid fifty dollars a day. We earned it.

Every night when I got home I threw myself on my bed and cried I was so tired. I told Mother, if this was an example of working in motion pictures, they could have it. I remembered to tell her about my note from Busby Berkely. She said I should go and see him the next day. It might be a big break for me. I sighed and said, "All right."

Well, it was not to be.

The telephone rang at seven the next morning. It was Alice from Fanchon & Marco. She reminded me I had been asked to go into an "Idea" when I first started at First National. Mother had told Alice where I was working.

It seemed they had tried to use two girls in the part they had planned for me. At the Manchester showing the night before, the girls had not been satisfactory. Could I at least work the week at the Loews State? If I wanted to go back to the studio work they would try to find someone for the rest of the tour.

Mother said, "Why not go in the "Idea" for the week?"

Daddy had not left the house yet so I hurried and packed what I needed in my makeup case. He took me to the Red Car line, and I was on my way again.

When I arrived at the theater, I was introduced to Mayme, the wardrobe lady. She worked on the costumes until they would fit me. She told me the show was "Screenland Melodies Idea" and I was to portray "Ramona" and "Coquette." The first costume looked like a Spanish Shawl that had been attached to a leotard. One arm was bare and the other had the shawl draped over it. I thought to myself that I wouldn't have too much freedom with that arm. When she brought in the second costume I thought, "Oh no, not again!" It was composed of a silver leotard that was bad enough, but the rest of it seemed like a bad dream from a dancer's viewpoint. The half skirt on the left side went from the middle of my waist in front around to the middle of my back. It had row after row of pastel colored ruffles from top to bottom. On the right side, the arm from the shoulder to the wrist was covered with more of the same ruffling. It was attached to the front bodice and back of the leotard. The half skirt was full enough for me to have a band of elastic on my wrist with the skirt fastened to it. This outfit was for my toe dance to "Coquette."

The tenor and I rehearsed the Ramona spot together for a few minutes with the orchestra. It brought back memories of another tenor who had wooed me with a song, but this time I was not on the screen first.

The set was composed of different levels. A dance team would be on the first level and I saw him helping her become accustomed to coming down the narrow stairs. He was holding her hand. For Coquette, I was on the level above, and did not have a hand to hold onto when I tried the stairs. I would have liked to practice going up and down, but there was not enough time, so I just hoped I could do it gracefully and not fall. There were two finales where I was to dance. The end of the Spanish sequence came first.

I was told, "Lucile, you are center stage. What can you do there?"

I remembered I would have only one arm to use. I tried one handed walkovers and then a quick split. It worked. When something was needed after the walkovers I thought of my kicks to the side of my head. I tried them and hoped when I had the shawl on, they would work. In the dressing room I tried it successfully.

When I was asked, "Do you have some kind of turn you can do in one spot?" I remembered a turn I had learned during the men's time in one of Mr. Belcher's classes. It was when the men had their own more masculine turns but Mr. Belcher had never stopped me from joining them. This turn was done with one foot extended straight out in front while doing continuous hops on the other foot. It was fun because a lot of speed was generated and when it was finished you could do at least a triple pirouette to end it. The male dancers in ballets often feature that turn. It is a good finish for a solo. In this instance, I only had to make certain I left enough room for the soprano to cross from one side of the stage to the other, upstage from me. This staging was done in the space of two hours before the theater opened. Different than rehearsing for two weeks!

"Screenland Melodies Idea" had two excellent singers, Sherry Louise, a soprano, and Roberto Guzman, a tenor. The first number he sang was a lively Spanish song, "Cadiz," while the chorus girls did a dance full of turns and strutting steps to show off their elaborate costumes. After they left the stage, Roberto sang "Ramona." I came on for the chorus of the song, and danced. It was easy, nothing spectacular. Just some Spanish type steps I borrowed from the Spanish dances I had learned at Belcher's, besides doing some pantomime towards the singer.

The next act, Billy Randall, was a novelty dancer who played a violin while he tap-danced. While he played Russian music, he did the Russian squat steps, even working in taps. Variety said about him: "It was a sure fire applause getter, going over big."

The singers were on stage for the long finale, and sang songs from current motion pictures. When the first scrim was lifted, Everts and Lowry, a lovely dance team, were posed on that level. Miss Lowry wore an exquisite white organdy ruffled gown, and Jack Everts wore a military uniform. Her face was delicate and she wore her long blonde hair in a bun in the back. He had red hair slicked down with so much goop it looked dark. If he hadn't, it would have been messed up when he picked her up and turned around. They danced to a medley of war songs beginning with "Charmaine" and ending with "I'll Always Be in Love with You." She was lucky, I think she had two gowns of organdy and Jack ironed them, a lot of work because they had full skirts with ruffles. Whenever we passed their dressing room, it seemed Jack was forever ironing an organdy gown. Her gown was always immaculate. We seldom saw this pair other than at the theater or on the train. They had a cute Pekinese dog, and we would see one or the other of them exercising him. Someone had a terrible temper and sometimes after they had performed their waltz, they would argue so loudly we couldn't help hearing them.

My scrim was next. There were a few steps down to the team's level. I crossed it and then went down the longer flight of stairs. I walked down all the steps on my toes holding my ruffles carefully out of the way. Again quoting Variety, "Guzman then swung into 'Coquette' and Lucile Iverson offered a toe routine which was extremely effective. 'Pagan Love Song' was next, offered by Miss Louise, bringing on Franklyn and Warner for a South Sea Island acrobatic and adagio dance which was well conceived and was well executed."

There were two more levels above mine, on which the chorus girls were arranged. They all had different pastel leotards that were covered with rhinestones of the same color. Each girl held two gorgeous ostrich plume fans in the same color as her costume. Every show, when they appeared, there was a small flutter from the women in the audience. Once, when I tried out the fans, I was impressed because it was not easy to handle them. The girls with the fans danced to "Painted Doll." The critic should have said more about them because their number was lovely. The critic continued, "The audience really got their money's worth this week. Stepin Fetchit made a personal appearance." Stepin Fetchit was a popular black actor in motion pictures.

The "Meglin Kiddies," were also on the bill and they received a good revue, which they deserved. That week I learned Fanchon & Marco had sold their dance studio to the Meglin Studio, one of the leading dance studios in town.

The reviewer had seen the show early in the week. That was fortunate for me. I was not at my best later on. The weather had been exceedingly hot-nothing new for Los Angeles in the summertime. I had neglected to soak my feet in Alum water for a couple of weeks. Sitting with my feet in a basin of cold water, with a couple of tablespoon of Alum, helped toughen the skin on my toes. I did not have time to do this when I was at the motion picture studio. Blisters formed on my toes. When they broke, the skin slid off, and I really had sore toes. I wrapped them in moleskin and thought I would be all right. Then, for the first time, I had soft corns develop between my toes. When I tried to medicate them, they festered. I went to a podiatrist, and he did what he could before the first show each day. I could not even wear my toe slippers much less dance on pointe. My experience at the Golden Gate Theater in San Francisco had come back to haunt me.

Mr. Morgan, the Capezio shoe representative for Los Angeles and Hollywood, was sent for. He had been fitting me for all my dance shoes since I had started dancing and no one could dye shoes as well as his store personnel could to match a costume. He had my size for shoes on record at the store. Fortunately, the white shoes he brought went with the costume.

Now I had to come down the stairs with the new shoes. They were shoes normally used for tap or Spanish dances. The Cuban heels were about an inch and a half high. One matinee, my right heel caught on the edge of the step and was pulled off as I came down the stairs. I ignored it and went on with the routine. During the dance I would kick my left hand with my right foot coming over my head. When I saw a stream of blood running down my arm, I realized the nails left in the shoe when the heel was torn off had punctured my hand each time I kicked it. When the dance was over, I found the wardrobe lady, and she cleaned the costume while I took care of my hand. It was not a good week for me.

I decided to continue with "Screenland Melodies" and went in for my contract. Alice asked me if Mother would be traveling with me. She had a proposal. They would pay Mother's train fare if she would assist the wardrobe lady with the costumes on opening days. In the Spanish production number the costumes the chorus girls wore had many tiers of ruffles on their skirts and all had to be ironed. There was too much ironing for one person on opening day. I knew Mother would do it and told them she would. Alice seemed relieved. The motion picture studios were making many musicals, and using more experienced dancers. Fanchon & Marco were obliged to take younger girls for the "Ideas." Some of the chorus girls in our show were only sixteen and this was another reason Alice wanted Mother to be with the show. Mother became a surrogate mother for the young dancers and often I would leave the dressing room so she could have some privacy with the girls when they brought her their problems.

My contract read: "the entire run of "Idea" including all eastern bookings, opening at Loews State, August 8th, 1929. First 12 weeks to be prorated as follows: 6 @ $87.50, 6 @ 77.50 thereafter all dates at rate of $87.50 weekly. West Coast furnishes 2 tickets for Lucile and mother and furnishes reservation for Lucile, one berth. Her mother the lower and Lucile the upper." The usual five per percent would be taken out of each check. I was delighted because I had been given a raise. Maybe being hard to get paid off.

Opening day, I was enjoying the luxury of my own dressing room when my buzzer sounded. I went to the stage door and was told someone wanted to see me. The doorman pointed to a fellow who introduced himself and gave me a bouquet of flowers. I thanked him and he said he liked the show, and I was a wonderful dancer. He came to see me two more times that week, and after I introduced him to my mother, the three of us would talk. He never asked for a date but seemed to be satisfied just to talk to us for a few minutes. Wherever I was for the next few weeks he would appear: Glendale, Pasadena, and even San Diego on the weekend. About the third week of the tour, we played in the new Warner Brothers Theater in Hollywood. My mysterious friend appeared there one day and gave me an envelope. He explained it contained a pair of tickets for a theater in the vicinity. He thought my mother and father would like to see the play while they were waiting to take me home. He finally persuaded Mother to accept them. I had been enjoying the small gifts of candy and flowers he brought me. We did wonder a lot about him, but he never asked anything from me except a picture. Each day Mother and I wondered if he was going to ask for a date but he never did. We were always polite to him and gave him time to tell us about himself.

The O'Conner act was on the same bill, and the little boy who was running down the hallways with his buddies between shows was to become famous as a wonderful dancer and actor, Donald O'Conner.

In Fresno I found my troubles were not over. I had an accident during a matinee that would cause me trouble the rest of my life. Everything was going as usual. When we went into the Spanish finale, I went to center stage for my one handed walkover with the slide into the split. I started into the walkover as soon as I turned, but my right hand caught in a fold of the shawl over my shoulder. My body was already starting in the downward motion and I could not stop, so I landed on the top of my head. It did not knock me out. I was able to get up and run off stage. I put my hands to my neck, heels of my hands under my chin, and stretched my head up as hard as I could. Nothing happened, except some dizziness, so I ran back on to the stage to finish the finale.

Mother was reading in my dressing room, and when I told her what had happened she wanted to know if I hurt or felt dizzy. After I reassured her I was all right, she helped me change into the Coquette costume and I finished the show. I did have a headache for a few days. Now I had two injuries to my back, one from falling when I was doing adagio with Ed and now this one.

I was in my forties when my arthritis started. The pain was in my neck and shoulders. Finally, I went to a doctor. The X rays were completed and he called me to his office. Pointing to them, he said, "Arthritis has gone to the old injury where you broke your neck. It was a fracture." I thought back to my various injuries and remembered when I had landed on my head in Fresno. This accounted for the stiff necks that had bothered me for years. I told him about them, and he said, "It was a wonder, you only suffered from stiff necks." However I was able to continue in "Screenland Melodies" without any further complications.

Who should appear at the Oakland Theater but my mystery man! He brought me flowers and candy, and that was the last time I was to see him. He left a note for me with the doorman, wishing me good luck and thanking me for our visits.

The picture that week featured Will Rogers in "They Had to See Paris." We received a fair review but he was the big attraction. It was a "talkie" and I would sit in the wings to hear him. I still have the record Daddy bought. At that time, I shared my Daddy's admiration of Will Rogers. The record is still timely! What a tragedy when he was killed in a plane crash in Alaska!

The reporter who reviewed our show gave a different twist to his comments about me. "Lucille Iverson is a tall and attractive blonde who could, should she so desire, kick the lights out of anyone's chandelier." The theater advertisement said, "High Kick Record Holder to Fifth." (It was the Fifth Avenue Theater.)

One matinee, two weeks later, we were doing the finale of the show, and I was in the middle of my rapid turns in the center of the stage. Miss Louise was to cross from one side of the stage to the other behind me. We were in one of the larger theaters so there was plenty of room for her crossover. I was intent on my turns when she ran into my extended foot. She walked right into me! When turning, a dancer sees only the spot she is using for a reference point. The spotlight was all I could see. I had not known she was near and her bump sent me towards the footlights. Fortunately I regained my balance in time, or else I would have landed in the orchestra pit. Maybe I was getting too much publicity and she was jealous. This was not a lucky show, but this time I wasn't hurt. The episode had a funny result, though. The chorus girls were hardly civil to Miss Louise from then on. They told me she had deliberately run into me. She never apologized, and I never went near her. Mother said it was her problem, not mine, and to try and forget it. Louise had a beautiful voice but was a lonely person because of her odd personality.

In Bellingham, Washington, I had another "Stage door Johnny." An attractive young man asked the doorman if he could see me. We talked in the Green Room, the three of us (Mother was always there). He visited the next night and brought a box of candy, then he really surprised us. He explained he did not live in town but had to leave on the last train to his home. He wished he could be our escort, but would we please go to a restaurant after the last show where he had arranged a dinner for us. Mother and I were reluctant at first, but he insisted. He would love to accompany us but that was impossible, and he wanted do this for us. We had an excellent dinner that evening at one of the better restaurants in the town of Bellingham. Closing night he came back as usual between the first and second shows. After we had thanked him and talked for awhile, he left. We shook hands and I felt something in my palm. I was surprised to find a golden crucifix. Mother and I were equally bewildered because religion had not been in any of our talks. We could not figure what had attracted him to me in the first place. Perhaps he had intended asking me to go out with him, then decided I was too young. We thought he might be in his late twenties, and I was just seventeen. Maybe he had just liked to be with both of us.

While in Bellingham, Everts and Lowry, the ballroom team, and I were chosen to represent our show at a Gala program at the opening of the new Leopold Hotel. It was a beautiful hotel, and we were treated royally. They had danced in hotel ballrooms before, but it was a new experience for me. The polished dance floor made my toe and acrobatic dances most difficult and dangerous. I was relieved when it was over.

We thought Spokane, Washington, was beautiful. It had snowed and everything had a Christmas card look. We were at a restaurant having our Christmas Eve dinner when someone appeared at our table. It was Al, our violinist friend. We were certainly surprised to see him, especially when we learned he had made the trip from San Francisco just to be with us for Christmas. He made our Christmas away from home more festive. He was, as usual, pleasant and we enjoyed his company. I still have his Christmas gift, a Kodak camera that I have enjoyed for many years. It still opens well, and I recently experimented and had success with a roll of film. The lenses are good, and I had the aged bellows replaced with new ones. It started me on a hobby that has given me pleasure all my life, and it even resulted in a side occupation years later.

The city of Denver was celebrating the reopening of the Tabor Theater. Another dance team, Jack and Betty Weller joined us. They were a comedy team and added more variety to our show. Our "Idea" received more than the usual publicity along with the picture starring Colleen Moore and Frederick March. The picture was "Footlight and Fools," a theater story. The inside of the theater was renewed to look like it did in the old days. Lots of gingerbread, almost to the point of being garish. Money evidently was of no consequence out front, but they certainly economized on the dressing rooms for the performers. I hope they were improved later because, when we were there, it was the T & D all over again. Even the rats looked like cousins of the Oakland rats.

The next clipping I have is the ad for the Wisconsin Theater in Milwaukee. We had a new act, Lamberti. He played a xylophone, but that was frosting on the cake. His costume made him look like a high-class bum with a clown's makeup. The audiences loved his jokes. Sometimes they were off color but he managed not to offend. He gave a number on his xylophone that showed he was an accomplished musician.

Another fine act joined us. Karavieff, who took up where Billy Daniels had left off. He did not play the violin, but he made up for it with his tap dancing. He did Russian squat steps with additional taps. We also had another new tenor. They seemed to change often. I wonder why?

When we appeared at the Fox Theater in St Louis we enjoyed hearing the wonderful banjo music of Eddie Peabody whom we had enjoyed in Long Beach. It was Easter time, and a miniature recital from a local dance studio had been added. They were lucky students because obviously their teachers were of high caliber. We had dancers from a studio in Detroit the following week, and again I was impressed with the performance of the children. I enjoyed a new experience both weeks. The little girls evidently admired my dancing, and I signed autographs after every performance.

Niagara Falls enchanted Mother and me. The falls were in winter garb with a fairyland of shimmering icicles and glistening snow with the falls themselves making such a roar you had to shout to be heard. Mother and the lady manager of the hotel found much to talk about and Mother enjoyed herself during our brief stay.

Utica was the other half of the split week. After finishing there, we were off to the New England states. Now we could compare the Atlantic Ocean with the Pacific Ocean.

Chapter 9

Traveling toward the East Coast, we worked in theaters in Hartford and Waterbury, Connecticut. We went on to New Haven and the first night between the evening shows Mother and I took a walk. There was new snow on the ground, and we enjoyed the rare sight.

Mother and I were shivering when we returned to the theater, and I quickly changed to my first costume, went backstage and started my warm up routine. When I did a walkover, one foot gave way and I fell. I tried to get up and found I could not stand on my right foot. I asked a stagehand to get my mother, and when she arrived, she could tell from my face I was in trouble. I was trying not to cry but was in obvious pain. Our company manager came and when he found I could not support any weight on my foot, he called for the line captain and orchestra leader. They were told changes would have to be made in a hurry. The fifteen-minute notice had already been given. This time my misfortune was affecting the rest of the show. The tenor, David Reese, would be alone in the early Ramona episode, but that wasn't a problem. The chorus girls in the background of the Coquette dance would just dance without me. There would be empty spots where I had been in the two finales.

Mr. Perutz, the theater manager, came to my dressing room and said, "When you are ready, I will drive you to your hotel."

He was anxious that I should be taken care of and told us he wanted his doctor to look at my foot. He would call me in the morning to tell me when my appointment would be. Mother said that it would not be necessary, but he insisted and said the theater would take care of the bill. In the morning, after a restless night, my foot had become badly swollen and discolored. I couldn't wear a sock, much less a shoe, when I left for my appointment with the doctor. After examining my foot, the doctor told me I had sprained all the toes on my right foot except the big one. He bandaged my foot and told me, "Keep off your foot, keep it elevated, and come back in two days."

Mr. Perutz said he had talked with the doctor and said I was to follow his instructions. He assured me I was not to worry about the show. This was the first time for me to miss any performances. Before now, no matter what was wrong with me, I had been able to cope. The next day we went to the theater to see the "Idea." I did enjoy it, but it was really strange, being on the other side of the footlights. The chorus captain had added more steps to the Coquette routine and, while I was relieved the spot was covered, it was strange not being there.

When we returned to the hotel, we found a message from our friend, Oscar Taylor. He was the singer in the "Idea" ahead of us that was playing in Bridgeport, Connecticut, not far from New Haven. He was tall, handsome and always fun to be with, and we had enjoyed his company whenever our paths crossed. He was closer to Mother's age than mine. He called again and asked Mother how I was getting along with my injured foot and wanted to know if I could travel to Bridgeport? It would be a short trip by train. His show only had one matinee and he would like to take us to see a performance at another theater. Mother found he meant a Burlesque show, and she rather reluctantly said we could go. I had never seen anything like it. I think Mother and Oscar were more amused by my reaction than the show's entertainment. I was reminded of the night when I had heard stories in the crowded berth of the train that was going to Fresno. Oscar certainly had managed to take my mind away from my foot. For the first time, I saw the burlesque type of dancing. Oscar said they were doing "bumps" and "grinds." As bad as these movements were, they were mild compared to some of the dancing that would be popular some years later. Not only on the stage or T.V., but also by dancers of all ages. Even little tots wiggle and squirm like they are being tickled when they are showing off.

For the remainder of the week, I used the crutches the doctor had loaned me and, with Mother, visited the historic sights. There was much to see that I had read about, and I was thrilled to see places I had only visualized when I had read about them. To stand where our forefathers had stood was a wonderful experience. I would shut my eyes and imagine what it must have been like to have been there then. Even though Mother knew I read whenever I had a chance, she was surprised that I knew so much about the history of our country. I kept her busy with the crutches because I wanted a picture of everything and couldn't hold them and the camera and take pictures, too. We did laugh when we were juggling everything, and had a nice afternoon. Oscar wasn't the only one who knew how to take my mind from my disablement.

When our show moved on to Bridgeport, the manager told me Mr. Perutz had called him on the telephone. He had said, "Even if she insists differently, she is not to do the toe dance." I finally persuaded the manager I could do my Coquette dance in ballet slippers, beside my Ramona scene, but I still could not do the two finales. My foot was getting better fast. Mother had used some of her old fashioned remedies for it. I had to soak it in hot and cold water frequently, and she applied warm Arnica to the bandage. It did not smell nice but did wonders for my foot.

We went to the Fox Theater in Brooklyn after Bridgeport, and I was disappointed when we did not perform in New York. Mother and I stayed in a hotel near the theaters in New York. We were planning on seeing New York before we took the subway to Brooklyn. We saw a few stores, but not as many as we had wished. Going to Brooklyn on the subway took us longer than we had imagined because the directions confused us. We made the rehearsal on time and were warmly greeted by Rube Wolf who was the orchestra leader at the beautiful Fox Theater. Sunny had sent a message, promising we would see her the next night and have a night lunch together.

My foot was almost well, and I did all my dances. Going back to the hotel the first night, Mother and I took the subway and became completely lost. It was cold and windy down at the underground level. Papers were swirling around in the icy air, and the lights were not very bright. We wished it were not so late. We could hear the rumbling of the trains coming from the dark tunnels. After trying to understand the directions posted, we still boarded a train going in the wrong direction. A kind stranger, noticing our confusion, helped us and we left the car at the next stop, used the overpass to the other side, and arrived in the right place in New York.

The next night we had our night lunch with Rube and Sunny and met Bill, a musician who played the cello in the orchestra. Rube had invited him to join us. After we had eaten, Bill offered to take us home. Before saying goodnight, he offered to take us around New York, to see the sights. We thanked him, and for the rest of the week we had an escort to show us anything we wanted to see before the first show.

Getting to the hotel wasn't a problem anymore. There were no more night subways because Bill drove us to our hotel each night after taking us to different ethnic restaurants. One night we went to Dave's, a favorite restaurant for Broadway show people, where cheesecake originated. Bill ordered the delicacy, and we could see why it was famous.

"Lilies of the Field" was being shown in a theater on Broadway. Twice we hurried to see it, but were too late each time. We never saw it because it was shelved. I will never know if my spotters landed on the cutting room floor or if I was seen on the screen.

Two motion picture magazines had pictures that had been taken on the set. There I was, in a backbend as usual, without identification. The "Lilies of the Field" that was filmed later was a huge success. It was an entirely different version, only using the name.

A letter from the Capezio office was in my mail at the theater. The letter read: "Please call this number and make an appointment to meet with Mr. Capezio one morning this week!" If it had been an appointment with the President, I don't think I could have been more excited. Mother and I found the famous shoe company in a building in Manhattan and entered the salesroom where we saw all the familiar dance shoes. When Mr. Capezio came in, I was thrilled to meet this wonderful man who immediately put us at ease. He explained he wanted me to try out some new toe slippers that he had designed. He was trying to make the toes of the slippers more durable because the satin wore out too soon. The shoes he showed us had different kinds of material on the tips of the toes. After pulling up the seat salesmen used, he sat down, and measured my foot. Now I felt like a real star.

He looked at my foot and said, "I made slippers for Anna Pavlova for many years. You have the same type of foot; it is strong with a high arch." That made my spirits soar but they came down a bit when he said, "Your foot is larger."

He told us stories about Pavlova, and we told him we had seen her "Dance of the Dying Swan" when I was first taking lessons, and how it inspired me to be a good dancer.

He asked permission to send slippers for me to use for a certain number of performances and then to return them by mail. I confessed to him about my bad habit. It was difficult to "break in" toe slippers. I would get painful blisters. I wore my slippers until they were shabby and so soft at the toes that my toenails would crack from working on the hard floor. Packing lamb's wool under the nails helped some and I did that regularly, despite the fact that Mother complained about the wisps of lamb's wool I left around on the rug. Mr. Capezio scolded me and said I would permanently injure my toes. He asked if I had to pay for my toe slippers that I used in the show. I told him they were furnished. He said I would have plenty of shoes for the remainder of the tour, and I was to change my bad habit. I promised to try. After talking for awhile we left. My knees were shaky and I felt as though I was walking on air. I was glad Mother had done most of the talking to this famous man, and I could just look at him. The next day, on our way to the theater in Brooklyn, we made a quick visit to the office to leave our itinerary and also an old pair of my toe shoes so they could match the orchid color. Now, whenever I see toe slippers with the improved toes I think, "I had a part in that."

The week sped by and we left New York for Philadelphia. I am reminded of an amusing incident. On opening day, I was crossing in back of the back curtain, tiptoeing, because the feature picture was on. I was startled when a man confronted me and whispered, "Does your belly button show?"

I said, "No," indignantly, but he insisted we go into the light so he could see my Spanish costume that certainly covered me. Then he went on his way.

I asked our manager, "What is going on?"

He told me, "If you have a bare middle, you have to cover it up."

I saw the chorus girls had added an undershirt for the opening production number. The costume had a bra top and those big ruffled skirts. Personally, I thought the under-shirt under the bra was ridiculous. Nowadays, more than the belly button shows!

Two days later we had a day off because it was Sunday. The "Blue Law." was still in effect. Bill had asked us to catch a midnight train Saturday from Philadelphia to New York. He met us at the station and drove us to our lodging for the night. It was a darling apartment in a lovely, old restored home. We regretfully said goodbye to the comfortable apartment the next morning. Our stay was so brief there was hardly a sign that we had been there.

Bill had taken the day off from the theater, and we had a full day of sightseeing. When we drove around the theatrical district, we saw the theaters I had read about in Variety. I thought the theaters were small, even the Palace, because I had become accustomed to the new Fox theaters in San Francisco, Hollywood, Portland, Seattle, St. Louis and Detroit. They did not have the charm of the New York theaters, but they were certainly more modern. The Bowery we saw that day reminded me of the show I had been in, "Twenty Minutes on the Bowery." The setting had been fairly accurate.

We had gone to the Chinatowns of San Francisco, Boston, Seattle, and Vancouver and were pleased when we had our dinner in the New York Chinatown. This time I could have a scrumptious dinner, all I could eat! Bill had found we liked Chinese food. We had an exciting drive to Philadelphia because of a ground fog. Mother moved to the front passenger's seat, and I looked out the back window to help Bill. When a large truck passed us, Bill followed it and we traveled faster. When we reached Philadelphia, Bill said he was looking for an automat. Bright lights led us to the location of a large one. Considering the time of night, there were many people in the big room. This was quite different from any cafeteria I had ever been in. Instead of having a long line to stand in we went to glass boxes along the wall. They were stacked one on top of the other like the boxes in a post office. Every kind of food you could think of was on display behind the windows. Bill put change in a slot, the window opened, and he reached in for the apple pie I had asked for. He took us to a table and went for my glass of milk, my mother's hot tea and his own food. While we were eating the food Bill told us of his plans for the future and hoped we would approve of them. He said he would like to spend his vacation with us and would join us in Washington, D.C. and travel to Atlanta, too. I glanced at Mother. She didn't look as happy as I was. He was getting serious, and she worried I might be also.

The following week, Mother and I tried to see all the historical sights of Philadelphia. We thought nothing could top our stay there, but then we went to Washington, D.C. The weekdays had only one matinee, giving us time to explore. One morning we arose early and rode a bus to Mount Vernon. It was interesting to see how the meals were cooked in a separate cottage. We decided we were much better off in Mother's kitchen rather than having to cook over an open fire in a large fireplace. The compound was composed of many small cottages, all connected by passageways. The main house, with its small, gracious rooms reminded me of a large dollhouse. I wondered how the ladies had been able to come down the narrow stairways with their hoop skirts.

We were to live in a bit of history ourselves. The man that I had heard of often as I grew up had passed away. William Howard Taft was President when I was born. He did not disappear from sight when Woodrow Wilson became President, but continued an illustrious career. He was a professor of law from 1913 to 1921. At the same time, he was called upon to do many duties for our country. He favored the League of Nations that was for years the subject of political arguments. Warren Harding appointed William Howard Taft Chief Justice of the Supreme Court in 1921. He retired in early 1930 because of ill health and passed away in February. We were among the throngs of persons who witnessed the funeral of this great man. It was a gray, cold, rainy day. Black umbrellas held by most onlookers added to the somber scene. The procession of grim military men, mounted upon their handsome horses, moved slowly and majestically down the avenue towards the Capitol. A deep hush came upon the observers when the flag covered casket came into view. In later years, I have seen on the movie news, and then on television, this ceremony repeated for later dignitaries of our nation, and each time I relive that occasion when I stood there in the rain watching Taft's funeral. I'll always remember the slow cadence of the drums.

In March of that year, I would be eighteen years old, and for many of those years, I had heard many political discussions in our living room. My family had given me a strong sense of a citizen's obligations. Women won the right to vote and as soon as I was old enough, I began to vote. I have rarely missed an election when I was eligible to vote. I get upset because of the low percentage of people voting. Why the people of our nation neglect this privilege is something I will never understand. We read the newspapers about people in other countries chancing the loss of their lives when trying to vote.

The funeral had made me depressed, but then I put my sadness behind me. Bill was at the theater on our closing night and had arranged for his trip with us. The next day he left his coach, and we enjoyed looking out at the passing landscape together.

Uncle Joe was now a movie distributor around the southern states. My Aunt Mildred had moved to Atlanta and had an apartment there. Mother and I stayed with her and Bill took a room in a hotel on Peachtree Street near the Fox Theater. He rented an automobile, and every morning we drove miles seeing the places of interest in the country.

Besides playing a cello in the orchestra, Bill was a customer's man in the Stock Market. At that time, I did not understand exactly what that meant. When we opened at the Fox Theater, we would take walks between shows. I soon realized I did not dare admire anything in a shop window. If I did, it became mine. Evidently he had more money besides his salary from the theater.

We celebrated my eighteenth birthday that week. On the big day, Bill and Mother arranged a party between the evening shows. The cast enjoyed the large beautiful cake and punch and they admired the Aquamarine ring Bill gave to me. When we were alone later, he said he would like to give me a diamond engagement ring with the same size stone. I told him it was too soon to talk about our becoming engaged.

It was a long time before I was to know anyone like Bill again. He understood I was not ready to trust a man but did want affection. Perhaps he knew I did not have the same feelings he did. I liked him. Who wouldn't when she was being treated like a princess, but my dancing came first and would for a few more years.

Mother and I didn't talk about the possibility of my returning to New York to work. I think she was waiting to see how much I cared for Bill. If I did go to New York, and Bill and I were to marry, she would essentially lose me. Even if I pursued my career, it would be unlikely she would be there to share it with me. She had been willing to sacrifice so much to further our mutual love of dancing, she might do anything to keep me with her.

We closed the show in New Orleans, a place I thought very romantic. I was looking forward to seeing Daddy and Alton. It seemed a long time since we had left. When we said goodbye, Bill and I had reassured each other we would be seeing each other soon. I wrote an answer to every letter he wrote and was puzzled when he began to scold me for not writing. By the time the tour was over and we were back home, his letters had become very chilly.

Mother told me she had sent a registered letter to his address in an effort to find out what was happening. Bill's mother had only heard about me from Bill, and probably I was not her choice for a wife for him. She probably wanted him to marry girls of their own faith. We could only surmise my letters to his home never reached him. His mother may have intercepted them. The last letters I had received were not so nice. Finally he stopped writing, and it saddened me that he had accused me of using him. If it had been a few decades later when long distance telephone calls were more common, this story might have had a different ending. Then I realized every letter I had written to Bill had been between shows, and Mother had mailed them. Or had she?

When I returned home, I realized the depression that I had been hearing about was going to affect me. I was still lucky in finding work, but it was hard work for not much money. The Depression of the thirties was to change lives forever. Young people cannot understand why their grandparents worry so much about saving money for the future. The future did not hold much hope for them. It took a lot of fortitude to live through those days and it was then people realized the value of money.

The Fanchon & Marco Agency called me one morning. Mother and I were to go to the Huntington Hotel in Pasadena that night. We were not to talk to anyone except for giving directions to the leader of the orchestra. Mother should act the part of my dresser. The agent told me the name I was to respond to. It was the name of a famous dance star in New York. They had scheduled this appearance for her but she could not make it, and I was to fill in for her.

He told me, "You can carry this off and have fun doing a little acting."

While it did seem like fun to impersonate a star, I was not sure I was not being involved in something that was not right. But surely Fanchon and Marco would not ask me to do something wrong. Mother and I decided that if he said this was all right to do, it must be all right. Looking back I am not so sure. Daddy drove us to the imposing Huntington Hotel and stayed out of sight. We were given a warm welcome and an elaborate suite of rooms for a dressing room. The orchestra leader came to the suite and I gave him my music and instructions.

The introduction I was given must have been excellent because of the audience reaction when I entered the room. The hotel ballroom was elegant but I was more concerned about the dance floor that I found to be as slippery as ice. I managed without mishap and my ego went up a few notches with the attention and applause. Too bad

157

I had only earned part of it with my dancing. The rest of it was for another person who had a famous name.

When I received the $13.50 check in the mail I wondered how much the agency had made from my deception. They could have skipped the 10% commission at least. There was to be a day when I was told I was the most gullible person that he had ever known. Perhaps my head was in the clouds from reading so much, or I loved dancing so much I was just happy to dance.

Now that I was home, I was delighted to see Mr. Fountain again. He was the district manager for several theaters in the area, with his office in the Long Beach West Coast Theater, and he gave me permission to practice there. The stage was wonderful for my ballet and tap dancing with lots of space because the only object to avoid was the standard holding a large, strong light that was there from the time the theater closed until it reopened again the next day. It did shed light over the area but not enough to keep me from feeling spooked by the shadows it caused.

I always finished practicing with my acrobatic work using the mezzanine that had a nice thick carpet, soft enough to work on. Mr. Fountain's office was nearby, and he would tell me to come to his office when I had finished. He found time for me and we would sit and talk. His son had drowned a few years before, and would have been my age had he lived. I think he talked to me as he would have talked to his son.

The tragedy had made him philosophical, so I learned many things that were to affect my outlook on life. I was so lucky to have his friendship and his good advice while I was growing up. I wondered years later why I had never talked to him about the business aspect of my career. We never discussed what I was earning. I wish we had. Generally we went to the corner ice cream parlor to have a "cackleberry," a milk shake with an egg in it. Mine was always a chocolate shake. Only Mr. Fountain called them cackleberry shakes, I found out later when I ordered one. Sometimes I had to tell the Soda Jerk, how to make one. Soda Jerks disappeared when eating or drinking at a drug store became passe. Perched on the stools at the soda fountain we would watch with fascination when the fellow would jauntily prepare our sodas, sundaes or shakes. They kept the different spigots of flavors highly polished and proudly reigned over their domain. When you needed something more substantial there were sandwiches, salads, soup, pies and cakes. For some reason tuna sandwiches never again tasted so good, even the ones I make for myself.

Sometimes on Saturday Mother would join us around noon and have her usual Coca-Cola. Then we would return to the theater where we would enjoy the current show.

Some local theaters could not afford to have live entertainment. Mr. Fountain worried about attendance at the several theaters in his district. The West Coast Theater went to a split week policy with stage shows on Friday, Saturday and Sunday. Only feature pictures were shown the rest of the week. His largest theater in Santa Ana had the same policy. Mr. Fountain explained that if he could "make the nut," (cover the expenses) with the four days of pictures, and if he had a good show on the weekend, he could turn a profit. The smaller theaters showed feature pictures, short subjects, a cartoon and a newsreel.

Stage shows had become a luxury. The musicians union and the stage hand unions were strong. They would not work unless they had a set number of employees. The performers did not have any bargaining power and received what money was left over in the budget. The musician's rules did not bother me as much as seeing able-bodied men doing only a simple chore backstage. The electrician did his work. The fly men did theirs and there was not much cutting down of men backstage.

I began to hear more and more about the American Guild of Variety Artists, known better as AGVA. Performers were getting their own union and it was getting stronger, especially in the eastern states.

To bolster business, several theaters in town would resort to giveaways. "Tonight, Country Store," would be advertised and patrons would be given tickets when they entered the theater. A lucky number could mean receiving dishes, groceries, or pots and pans. The grand prize could be furniture, even refrigerators or stoves. Stores and manufacturers benefited from the exploitation.

Mr. Fountain tried a different approach I was to find out. One day, when I went up to the mezzanine to practice, I found some of the space was occupied. A large colorful tent had been erected. There was a light on the inside and a woman dressed as a Gypsy came to the opening. She asked if I was one of the current performers. I told her I was local and was allowed to practice my dancing in the theater before it opened for the day. She asked if I would like to have my palm read. I had recently had my palm read when I had been on the Pike, the amusement center. This would be free, so I said, "Yes." I thought I would be careful about giving the Gypsy any hints and see if she really could foretell the future. Since she saw I was practicing dance at the time, I was not surprised when she said I would be successful in my dance career. She told me it would be difficult. This I already knew. Then she told me the same thing the previous Gypsy had told me.

"You will have a wonderful life but it will not be easy. Your dancing will be your greatest pleasure. Your real happiness will come to you in your later years." I thanked her and went back to my practicing.

One day Mr. Fountain came by and asked me to come to his office before I went home. He said he was going to Los Angeles the next morning and if I wanted to make the rounds of the agents, he would pick me up at home and drive me to Los Angeles. Mother gave her permission when I called her, and we set the time he was to come for me. The next morning, we drove to the offices where he would be booking future pictures for his theaters. I boarded the streetcar going further in town, taking me to the theatrical agents. We did this whenever it was convenient, it saved me money, and better still, it was another opportunity for us to talk.

I was nervous going to the agent's offices. When they began to know me, it became easier, but it never became a casual thing for me. I used a trick I had invented to lift my spirits when I was about to enter the stage. I do not know why it worked, but it did. I would open my eyes wide and roll my eyes a couple of times when I was alone in the hall before entering the office. It helped, maybe because I would laugh at myself for being so silly. I'd open the office door and the secretary would greet me with, "Here is the girl with the Iverson smile."

Mother kept me on a practice schedule, took care of my physical needs, and budgeted the money that I gave to her when I was paid. She seldom allowed me to go to work by myself, so I was sheltered more than the average showgirl.

Talent is not enough; I found that an influential parent, either with money or contacts, made a big difference. Just having a lot of nerve and the ability to brag on yourself helped also. I had neither of these attributes. I also was not going to lower my morals to get a job.

There is another way, through an angel, a person who opens doors for you in return for other favors. While I never became a star, I never regretted my choice of doing it my way, even if it was not easy, and it wasn't.

Chapter 10

Rube Wolf appeared at the Loews State Theater in Los Angeles in the fall of 1930. Sometimes Mother would go to Los Angeles with me, and we would see the agents and have lunch together. In the afternoon we would visit Rube. We were disappointed we could not see Rube and Sunny together. One day he called her on the phone and then said we were to have lunch with her, and he was to set the date. We planned a day when I would be coming in town to see the agents and Mother could come with me again. It worked out as we had planned and we went to their Hollywood home, had lunch, and visited with Sunny and the baby, who was now a lively little boy.

Rube loved Mother's Angel Food cake, and we would take one to him backstage after we had seen the agents. We talked for awhile. Then he would take us to an entrance that led into the theater, and we would see the show. One day when he realized I was not working, he suggested I see a New York producer who was casting a new "Idea" for Fanchon & Marco. He evidently telephoned him, because the next day the office called, and I was told to go to where he was rehearsing.

When I arrived, I was told to wait until the lunch break, then the producer would talk to me. Everyone had left when he motioned for me to follow him to a door which said, "Exit." I thought we were going to another room. He opened the door, and motioned me inside to the stairway. He turned to shut the door behind us, and when he turned back to me, he suggested a sexual act. I pushed him away from the door so I could go back into the rehearsal room. If he hadn't been so surprised by my abrupt movement, he might have restrained me, but I managed to evade him and opened the heavy door and went back into the room. After picking up my rehearsal bag, I started to leave. He came into the room, and as though nothing had occurred, said, "You can start rehearsing here tomorrow at nine."

I was unable to say a word but I wanted to get away from him fast. I was trembling and didn't want to wait for the elevator but went down the stairs as fast as my shaky legs could take me. My only thought was to get out of the building and go home. When I arrived home, Mother asked, "How did your meeting go?"

I only told her I was to start rehearsing the next morning. If I had told Mother I wasn't going to go to the rehearsal, she would have asked why. She might even have blamed me for getting into the situation, or tell me not to go back, and I would never be able to work for Fanchon & Marco again.

I thought of going to Alice but realized it would be his word against mine, and he could say I was trying to make trouble. Then, there was the embarrassment. No, I could not do that. There was not much sleep for me that night while I was trying to decide what to do.

The depression was affecting everyone. Daddy was not doing well because people did not want new homes. My Mother was trying to find work but did not have enough background to find anything. Alton was helping Daddy with household expenses.

I needed to be in Los Angeles. Living in Long Beach, I was missing out on available work. I would be closer to the agents and to my casual club dates. I might even be able to work at a nightclub, and there were a few theaters having live entertainment. But I was running out of savings and didn't have enough money to keep me in an apartment. It did not seem I had much choice. If I went to the rehearsal, I knew I would be with the dance instructor more than the producer, and I really needed the work. I decided I would try it.

The next morning, I danced for the producer. Afterwards, I kept my distance. I wasn't happy when I was told I was to be in the chorus besides doing solos. When all the routines had been set, I was doing eight dances. I went to Alice and told her it was too much work. She made promises.

Nelcha, one of the chorus girls and I became friends. She was engaged and working to earn money for her upcoming marriage. I had noticed she did not mingle with the rest of the girls either. They were much more sophisticated than we were. We planned on becoming roommates when we started touring. She was sympathetic to my problem and a better companion than I was because I was tired all the time and very unhappy.

Neither of us smoked, drank or used bad language. The producer, who was also the choreographer, was always telling the other girls stories, and I guessed some knew him intimately. I noticed the dance instructor kept his distance and didn't participate during the break periods.

Each day I went to the office and complained again. I was told they were trying to find a suitable dancer. When the "Top of the World Idea" opened at the Loews State Theater, no one came to rehearse, and there was no one in San Diego. It never changed. We went to new theaters, and there would not be a new girl. My calls to the office brought more empty promises.

Mother knew I was overworked. I will never understand why she did not try to help me. She probably believed Alice was taking care of me. I had been trained to do my work without question, and I was so naïve, I never thought they were acting in their own interest. I thought they had trouble finding anyone to do the unusual routines.

If I had known about the professional union, I could have taken it my story, but at that time it was not too well established in the west, and I don't think very well publicized.

Our opening started with the other girls doing a kick routine, finishing in a formation resembling the shape of an airplane. Their heavy silver cloth costume resembled a flight uniform. Sequins covered my similar costume. I ran from the wings to the nose of the plane and stood with my arms held rigidly over my head in the place a propeller would be. Two young men entered, dressed in a similar costume, only they wore trousers. Some planes were started when the propeller was moved side to side as though to ignite the motor. The fellows moved my arms side to side until I turned and started to do spotters in place. When the girls moved as though the plane was turning towards the wings, I also traveled, keeping at the nose of the plane. They moved forward and I had to do my spotters traveling sideways. The spotlight flickered, giving the appearance of a plane in flight. It must have been realistic.

We were stowaways in the next dance. Wearing white satin blouses and blue velvet trunks and tap shoes, we also wore chains. They began on our ankles and we had to attach the short length to a string of chains on the floor. The end result was a long line connected to each other. Many hours had been spent rehearsing the tap dance to avoid hurting each other, either by colliding or letting the chains between us hang loose, bruising our feet.

Next we were imitating a Chinese dragon. We wore black satin pants and ducked under a dragon form made of a heavy embroidered material. The material also covered coils of heavy wire about nine inches in circumference, into which we put our arms. The end of this sleeve had ties that were attached to the girl's arms ahead of us. We didn't dance but shuffled across the stage, raising and lowering our bodies, while moving our arms up and down. Our arms showed bruises where the coils nipped us. My Russian Cossack dance represented that country. It was difficult and exhausting.

I know I did acrobatic work besides three other routines that I can't recall. There were eight costume changes in a forty five-minute show. I had my own portable dressing room because there was not enough time for me to go to a dressing room offstage. Sometimes when we were in opening in a new theater, the stagehands did not have time to make my portable dressing room for the first show. I usually could only turn my back to everyone.

When we started traveling, the girls went on dates and knew better than to ask Nelcha and me if we wanted to date, too. There were always those who were in show business, not for any love of dancing, but because it was a good way to have a good time. I guess because we were not having boy friends, Nelcha and I heard there was a rumor we were lesbians, and to dispel that idea, we had to be careful of our actions. We did not put our arms around each other's waist, like normal teen-age girls.

I envied the relationship between Nelcha and her Polish family. Her fiancée was also Polish and she would tell me about the fun they all had together. I was worried about my family. Although the letters from Mother did not have any complaints, I knew she was not happy.

When we were on the northern part of our tour, I began to have trouble with my stomach. Mother had always said I had a nervous stomach and had watched my diet closely. The problem worsened, but I did not feel like going to a strange doctor who would probably blame what I was eating. I knew I was working too hard but did not know what to do. I was not hearing from Los Angeles anymore, my letters were unanswered.

In St. Louis, on our previous trip, Mother and I had met Bob, a young man my own age, and I called him when we arrived. He had an older brother and sister who had cared for him after their parents had been killed in a car accident several years before. Bob and I had lunch together one day. He was as enthused about swimming as I was about dancing. His picture had been in the paper recently when he had won a competition, and he proudly showed me the picture of him and a beautiful cup.

Ice hockey games were being held in St. Louis, and he asked me if I had ever seen it played. I told him I hadn't, so one night after my last show, we rushed to see what was left of a game. I found it exciting and wonderful to relax for a few hours away from the show. When the week was over, I was sorry to say goodbye to Bob and his small family, who had given me a glimpse of a loving family life.

Sophie Tucker, "The last of the Red Hot Mamas," was with our show in Toronto, Canada. Sophie Tucker was a favorite in Toronto, and there was never any doubt about her being a star. Normally, Ted Shapiro was her only accompanist, but for this engagement, she had two pianists. Ted noticed me in the wings when they were playing a duet together. We talked, and I told him how much I loved hearing the piano played.

Nelcha and I were asked to go sightseeing with Ted and the other pianist. The young man hadn't been there before either and enjoyed it as much as we did, even though we had to brave the snow. We only went out with them before the first show. Nelcha and I were glad they didn't ask for a date after the show. As we continued on the tour, my physical condition worsened. Even walking was painful. I noticed more pain after I did the spotters, moving sideways which was not natural. When I told the manager that I was not feeling well, he told me I would be better in a few days, and I noticed he was avoiding me.

We opened at the Fox Theater in Detroit, and our manager called the house physician because I was so weak. The doctor came to the dressing room Nelcha and I shared. I told him of my pain and that every step I took hurt. The doctor went to the manager and asked him what I did in the show. Later I found out that he had been lied to. He had been told I was doing very little, mostly posing! He left, after giving the manager a prescription. I was unable to have it filled because it was too late after the last show.

After a sleepless night, I told Nelcha I was going to see the doctor at his office. This time he examined me and told me he was sending me to the Grace Hospital because I was suffering from gastritis and my internal organs were being pushed out of place. He apologized and said that the manager had not told him how sick I was. He instructed his driver to take me directly to the hospital; someone could bring my belongings to me from the hotel. For ten days I had complete bed rest. They gave me chicken soup and vegetables mashed like baby food. Each day Doctor Feldman came to see me and said, "Well, I see you haven't jumped out of the window yet." He knew I was deeply depressed. I felt lost and neglected. They were trying to restore my body and also let me have complete bed rest. I needed the rest, but I also needed word from my Mother.

I looked in vain for a word from her. I had written a letter to her as soon as I entered the hospital. I wrote her about what I was there for and that I was receiving good care. The son of the woman in the next bed was visiting her. I asked him to mail my letter and gave him money for a special delivery stamp. Mother never received the letter. Why? Who knows? I wrote to her again, but I don't think I put a heading on the letters or a return address on the envelopes. I had told her not to worry. She didn't call the Fanchon & Marco office to find my whereabouts. Not hearing from her didn't help my condition. Nelcha brought my luggage but only stayed a few minutes because the visiting hours and the show schedule conflicted.

I was in a ward of eight beds. When visiting hours came, I took the sleeping pills I had hidden the night before and slept. It was too painful to be so alone when everyone else had visitors. The night nurse, Dorothy, became my friend. When I began recovering my strength, she brought a wheel chair to take me to her office so we could sit and talk.

On the tenth night, a telegram came to me from the district manager. He told me to leave the hospital the next day, and go to the railroad station. My ticket would be there, and I was to join the show at Niagara Falls. Dorothy called Dr. Feldman, and he arranged for my release the next morning. I was in such a daze that I did not think about the hospital bill. I imagined the theater was billed. Perhaps, I was having what they then called a nervous breakdown. Now, they call it stress.

I had not been on my feet for ten days and had trouble managing my luggage and purse. The taxis, getting to the train, all passed like a dream. I was grateful to the people who noticed I was not well and helped me.

In Niagara Falls, I went to the hotel where Mother and I had stayed previously, and they remembered me and allowed me to stay in the room with the personal luggage that would be picked up after the show. After a brief rest, I went to the theater to report to our manager. All he had to say was, "Come back in time to go with us to the train." Before returning to the hotel I went to see Niagara Falls. Looking at the water rushing over the edge, I thought how easy it would be to go over the falls. I left before I had any more foolish thoughts. I remembered a restaurant Mother and I had gone to and went there for a bowl of soup before I returned to the hotel to rest until the last show.

I returned to the theater to wait. That wasn't a good idea. There had been a horse act the previous week, and, as usual, the "perfume" was still in the air. It nauseated me, and I barely made it to the train. No one ever wanted to follow a horse act.

Nelcha had a letter for me from Mother. She said, "I hope you are well again. Sorry, I didn't know where to write you besides the theater." With Nelcha's help, I got to the train and into a bunk with a sigh of relief. I was glad to have her help because no one would talk to me. It seems they thought I hadn't really been sick, probably because Nelcha was the only one who did know what I had been going through. The manager knew, but he didn't care except for the trouble I was causing by my absence. I don't know how they had managed when I first left, but later I heard that it took three girls to take my place in the show.

We arrived in Utica, New York, and while the rest of the cast went to the theater to rehearse, Nelcha took me to a hotel near the theater. When I heard a knock on the door, I said, "Who is it?" A man's voice said, "I am the theater's house doctor and I came to see if there is anything I can do for you?"

Opening the door a crack I peeked out. A tall good-looking man stood there. I was going to shut the door but he gave me a card. It did say "Doctor," so I let him in. He not only was a doctor, but for me he was an angel.

For the next three days he took care of me, arranging for medicine, the right food, and he took time to talk to me. The manager did come in to see me everyday, but he just shook his head and left. No one else came, and I would have been entirely left alone except for Nelcha, my roommate. Never again would I know people who were so unfeeling. My doctor benefactor was in the room when the district manager phoned me from New York and told me if I did not get back into the show they would leave me in Utica without pay. The doctor knew I was disturbed and asked what I had been told. He phoned the district manager and told him I was unable to work and would not be for some time. He threatened trouble if I were not given my fare home. My ticket for traveling was arranged for by my doctor. No money was given me except for several dollars the cast had donated, Nelcha's doing, I'm sure. My new friend, the doctor, said I was not strong enough to make the journey all at once. I told him my Aunt Mildred and Uncle Joe were now living in Chicago. He phoned them and arranged for me to stop over a week with them. He asked me if I knew anyone else between Chicago and Los Angeles. I told him about Bob and his sister and brother in St Louis. He phoned them, and they assured him I was welcome to stay overnight with them.

I never completely recovered physically from my stomach problem. For a very long time I was on a diet of bland foods, no raw fruit or vegetables, and I still don't eat spicy dishes. Practically my only visits to doctors over the years are for the same problem. The episode did not help with my trust of people either.

When the doctor shook hands with me when saying goodbye, I felt something in my hand. After he left the room I found a folded twenty dollar bill. I don't know what happened to the card he had given to me, and I never heard his name, so I could not write to him later except through the theater, and I never knew if the letter reached him. He remained nameless but never forgotten. He had done so much for me. I was sure my guardian angel had sent this kind and generous doctor to care for me.

Aunt Mildred and Uncle Joe met me at the station and informed me we were going to the racetrack in Aurora. He was a gambler and frequented the races whenever he could. I had never seen a horse race before. Just before the finish in an early race, two horses collided, causing other horses to fall. Jockeys and horses were strewn all over the track in front of the grandstand. I was appalled. I heard a gunshot and I was devastated when Uncle Joe told me they probably had to shoot one of the horses. They took me home, finally realizing that I should not have gone there in the first place. After a week of sleeping on their couch, I was ready to leave. I had not realized my aunt had a drinking problem or my uncle was unable to think of anything but gambling. I was not having the rest I needed. They put me on the train (happily, I think) and I was on my way to St. Louis. After my friends took me to their home, they immediately started to spoil me. The next morning, they didn't want me to leave, and I should have followed their advice. I just wanted to go home.

The train ride to Los Angeles was a nightmare. I don't know how I would have survived if the other passengers hadn't come to my aid. In Tucson, Arizona, the train was held while a doctor came on board and examined me. After telling the matron what to do for me, he left, reassuring the conductor that I didn't have appendicitis. A porter was waiting for me with a wheelchair when the train arrived in Los Angeles. I'll never forget my Mother's shocked expression when she saw me being wheeled toward her. She said she hadn't known I was so sick. I told her I hadn't wanted to worry her and maybe should have told her more about my condition. I was surprised when she said had she known, she would have come to me and taken care of me.

Under her care, I recovered. I rested and she fed me the type of food I needed, and my strength came back. She wanted to know why I hadn't been taken care of when I first became ill. I could only tell her that the cast had not been like the ones on earlier tours, and I had not made any friends except for Nelcha. She was the only one who knew or cared how sick I was.

There had been a girl in the chorus who was supposed to have been my under-study. Her mother traveled with her and I had the feeling she thought her daughter should have been the soloist.

The Fanchon & Marco office called and asked me to come to see Miss Fanchon. Mother was with me for what turned out to be an unpleasant interview. Miss Fanchon said she had been told I had left the show for an abortion. Mother was furious. She suggested I be taken to a doctor to show I had never been sexually active. She told her I had been given too much work to do. That was what caused my illness, certainly not a pregnancy. It was not a good meeting.

When I had been given good food, had rested, and had started to practice, we decided I should take lessons with Mr. Belcher, to get back in good shape.

In September 1931, Mr. Belcher asked if I would like to be in the dance production he was staging at the Hollywood Bowl for the festival "Symphony Under the Stars." I thought that would be wonderful and told him, "Yes." The professional class was rehearsing for the event. My friends Catherine and Eva were also in it. They had been the dancers in the act with Ed and me. When they heard I was going to be in the ballet, they said I could drive to the rehearsals with them. We all were awed when we rehearsed at the Hollywood Bowl; it was even larger than we had imagined. We were told we were the first ballet to perform there. It was becoming famous for the wonderful performances to be seen on the long wide stage nestled in a canyon.

Catherine and Eva were tall girls and had to portray men in the opening minuet. Their satin costumes were like the attire George Washington wore. I was more fortunate; after I put on a beautiful leotard I was helped into the middle of a huge hoop skirt. Ribbons from the waist of the leotard were attached to the skirt and it swung like a pendulum, and, oh yes, I had pantaloons. We all wore tall powdered white wigs.

Instead of a curtain, strong lights were shown into the audience so they could not see what was happening on the stage. When the performance started, the lights went off, the stage lights went on.

When the people saw the dancers posed for the minuet there was a murmur from them. Our formal dance was well received, but when we were revealed for the ballet there was a gasp! Sixty-four dancers dressed in classic pink tutus, two girls back to back posed in double lines, made the effect of a Degas picture. The gasp gave way to complete silence as though they were holding their breath, like we were. Then they began to applaud! I don't know how the other girls reacted but my knees turned to jelly! I was never as thrilled again. The symphony orchestra began to play and we danced as we had never danced before. I know I did not make a mistake and others said the same. We were truly inspired. I have always cherished the memory of that night.

Our ballet group was told to return to the Bowl for a filming of a short subject, "Beyond the Purple Pool." I have a copy of a page that was in "Pictorial California," a newspaper supplement. It shows us dancing in front of a pool of water, with a background of a fanciful castle. Too bad it was before color film. I never saw the short subject, but I understand the effect was quite remarkable considering we were actually dancing on a bare stage with the orchestra in the pit, down in front. A new invention called Process Camera had been used.

Mr. Belcher chose twenty-one dancers, including Catherine, Eva and me, for his "Corp de Ballet." He told us he had more difficult work for us. We were to perform with the Los Angeles Grand Opera Association. Gaetano Merola was the General Director, and Armando Agnini the Technical Director. I was mentioned as a soloist in the program because of my previous experience. We traveled back to Long Beach each night when we were in the Los Angeles operas.

After the operas finished there, we sailed on an ocean liner to San Francisco. It was late when we retired to our staterooms because we stayed on deck in our steamer chairs enjoying the novelty of being on the ocean. We had another solo dancer with us at the hotel and the four of us had a lot of fun when we were not working.

We were more involved with the operas in San Francisco. The opera "Marouf," a little known comic opera, went along very well on Thursday night September 10. We were in Act Three, in the Sultan's palace. The dance supposedly occurred before an upcoming marriage, and we were actually performing for a bachelor's party. When Mr. Belcher had instructed us in Los Angeles, it seemed odd to be working with our usually decorous British teacher doing very exotic movements.

Two days later "Aida" was performed. The aria, "Celeste Aida" had been a favorite of mine so it was quite an event for me to be dancing in the opera. The dance of the priestesses was stately and solemn. Many years later I choreographed this dance for dancers in the "Daughters of the Nile." I enjoyed it all over again.

On the 14th, we were pages in "Lohengren" without doing any dances. The wigs we wore were the color of my own hair. For a lark, I didn't put on the wig during the dress rehearsal. Instead I combed my hair to look like the wig.   Armondo Agnini, the technical director, passed by us in the corridor while we waited for our entrance. I received a classic double take and was told, "Go put on your wig." He remembered me when we were on stage, and I was given the task of unfastening the train from Elsa's wedding gown. He told me, "You reach under the train behind the shoulders, pull the tape that will be hanging there, and the train will drop." If I was being punished it worked. I was not allowed to untie the bow at rehearsal, and I agonized about pulling that tape more than I had ever worried about a new routine. The dreaded performance arrived. I did my part. The train was released. It was over. Phew! What a relief!

Before "Carmen," we had a few days off. All we had to do was have a good time. We went sight seeing: Golden Gate Park, Chinatown, North Beach, and sometimes we just rested, and we enjoyed that, too. We did our dance in "Carmen" and returned to southern California.

I did club dates and got accustomed to lots of smoke-filled rooms, noisy crowds, and make-do dressing rooms, but I still was working. Other dancers said I had more jobs than they did. When I had an opportunity to see them dance, I told Mother, "If they worked as hard as I do, they might have more work."

No one else did a hard Russian dance, or a difficult acrobatic dance. My toe and oriental dances were difficult because I added acrobatic work. I had a large assortment of routines and costumes, so I had return engagements at some of the clubs. I did have a few auditions at the studios resulting from Mr. Belcher's thoughtfulness. His secretary continued calling me for motion picture auditions. It was a long distance call from Los Angeles to Long Beach and not one that was made casually.

I stopped going after a few attempts. I didn't seem to fit the profile for a chorus dancer. I wondered why they had the audition in the first place. The ones chosen were mostly those that had already worked for the choreographer and were known by name. Frankly, I just did not fit in. It had nothing to do with my dance ability because we weren't asked to dance. Anatomy was more important, and I was rather undeveloped except for my legs. The few pictures I did work in were the ones Mr. Belcher choreographed.

I wish there were VCRs of the films I had performed in so that I could view them on my television. It is impossible because I do not even know the names of some of the pictures. They didn't keep all of the films because they were highly inflammable, and after some disastrous fires on studio lots, many films were not kept. Evidently only those they felt were important were kept.

I continued to live with Mother and Daddy in Long Beach, which meant long trips to any of the places that were booked out of Los Angeles, I was told, "too bad you don't live in Los Angeles, I could have more bookings for you." I was surprised when a call came from Fanchon & Marco, not from one of their agents who handled the little theaters, but from Alice. "Can you come in tomorrow morning for an audition?" I said I could. "Do you know where the new studio is in Hollywood?" I told her, "Yes, I'll be there." I remembered all too well the day Mother and I had our interview with Miss Fanchon in the new studio. I had never expected a call from the studio again. She had been so cold. Now I wondered what was in store for me.

Chapter 11

After arriving at the Hollywood studio, I went to the studio dressing room to change. No one else was there, and when I went into the rehearsal room, I was still alone. Alice had said to wear toe slippers, so after I put them on, I went to the barre to warm up. The door opened and Alice entered the room with a man who looked vaguely familiar. Alice beckoned to me, and introduced me to Leon Leonidoff. I recognized him from pictures I had seen in The Dance Magazine. He had produced shows at the Roxy Theater, in New York, for many years. It was wonderful that he was producing an "Idea" for Fanchon & Marco. If I was auditioning for him, I hoped he would like my work, but why weren't there other girls? I soon found out I wasn't the only one perplexed.

Mr. Leonidoff said he was surprised to find only one ballet dancer in the room. When he inquired why, Alice told him, "Miss Fanchon wants you to see Lucile's work. She has been in several of our 'Ideas.'" He looked doubtful, but after sitting down and using dance terminology, he began to tell me what to do. I was glad I had helped my dance teachers all those years and had learned the French names of dance steps. Typically, he gave me combinations he had used before, and I would do them. At first he seemed surprised, then we began to work together as a team. Alice, who had left the room, came back, and he told her he had not expected to find a ballet dancer who reminded him of Gambie. That was the nickname of Maria Gamberilla, his favorite soloist. The comparison to this wonderful dancer made me feel prouder than I had for a long time.

He said, "I am very pleased. I would like to see the acrobatic dancers now."

I thought perhaps we had finished earlier than expected, and I offered to go to the room where they might be waiting and tell them to come in. Instead Alice turned to me and said, "Lucile, show Mr. Leonidoff your acrobatic work."

While I changed my shoes, I explained my dance also contained ballet steps and I would do the dance first. When I had finished, he asked me to do several different acrobatic tricks. I wondered what he had in mind when he asked me to do walkovers from a crouched position. My knees and thighs responded because of my Russian squat steps, and I was able to follow his instructions.

Alice had remained in the room, and he told her, "You were right, Alice, when you said I would be happy with Lucile's work. I am amazed. She is the first dancer I have ever seen capable of doing both ballet and acrobatic work so well."

When he complimented me, he said he was looking forward to working with me. If Mr. Leonidoff was happy, I was on a fluffy pink cloud.

The next day he proved he was as different as night and day from the producer of the "Around the World Idea." The atmosphere in the room was more like a dance studio. The chorus girls had been rehearsing the production number I was to be in for several days, and Mr. Leonidoff was ready to stage my part. My dance was a difficult challenge. Every night I was worn out, but I was so happy I did not mind.

One night I was so tired I did something foolish, which could have led to serious consequences. We had worked later than usual, and I was afraid I would miss my 10:20 Red Car to Long Beach. It took sometime for the streetcars to go from Hollywood to downtown Los Angeles and the next Red Car to Long Beach would not leave until 11:00. Just as I came out of the entrance to the studio, the streetcar passed. It didn't stop at the corner. I must have looked dismayed because a sports car with the top down stopped in front of me. The young man driving leaned across the seat and asked me, "Would you like to catch that street car?" Without thinking I said, "Yes."

He told me, "Get in. I think we can catch up to it in a couple of blocks." This sounded good to me. I could imagine my brother, who was about the same age, offering to do the same thing.

Quickly taking the seat next to him, I explained why I had to catch this particular streetcar. After a few blocks we both realized it was hopeless. He turned to me and asked, "Where are you going?"

Instead of answering him I thanked him for trying to catch the streetcar and told him if he would just take me to the station it would help me. He asked again, "Where are you going?" I explained that I was on my way home to Long Beach and taking me to the station would mean I could get an earlier Red Car and get home sooner.

"That is not too far," he said. "It's such a nice night, could I drive you home? I was trying to make up my mind where I wanted to go, and I haven't been to Long Beach for awhile. How about it?"

I was tired. The 11:00 o'clock Red Car would get me to Long Beach much later, and I would not get much sleep before I would have to come back to Hollywood for the 8:00 o'clock rehearsal. Because I was comparing this young man to my brother I told him, "Yes."

It was a lovely ride to my home, and we talked all the way. In the back of my mind was the question, "Why can't I find some one to go out with like this nice young man? I never seem to meet anyone like him."

In front of my house he turned to me and said, "Don't you ever do this again. I could have taken you someplace and taken advantage of you. It happens all the time. Now, after talking to you for a few minutes, I realize you are a nice girl, and you were not looking for a pickup to have a good time. You probably would not have gone with me if you hadn't been so tired and it was so late." He lectured me for a few minutes and again said, "Don't ever do this again, even if you are reminded of your brother."

I promised him I wouldn't, thanked him for bringing me home safely, and went into the house and received more scolding. First Mother and then my brother scolded me and told me how lucky I had been because the man had been so decent. Mother suggested I ask if I could leave the rehearsals earlier. When I did, it was easier to make the Red Car in time.

The next production number was more sophisticated, and it made me wonder if I could cope with the different style of dancing in New York if I were to go there. Tap dancer, Jack Lester, was featured in a Harlem setting with an elaborate background. The girls made their entrance from a higher level, entering from the open mouth of a huge painted "Ubangi's" head, then going down stairs to the stage. Their dance was full of what was then called "snake hips." Their feathered costumes really exaggerated the movements of those hips. The movements fascinated me, and I practiced until I could do them just as well as the girls. When I got home, I showed Daddy my achievement, and he let me know he disapproved. He had not liked it when I proudly showed him how I could shimmy, a few years before, and he did not like what I was doing now any better.

The closing production number was in a sophisticated night club scene. This was to be my favorite production. The musical arrangement of "Manhattan Serenade" fit it perfectly. The girls were costumed in satin pajamas with panels of sequins in the pants legs. A chiffon top with full sleeves completed the costume and everything was the color of chartreuse-even the wigs they wore. Their dance was a precision kicking routine and before they finished, they circled off into the wings. Reappearing in a double line, they carried arched wreaths made of orchid net trimmed with artificial orchids. I entered between the arches they made. I wore a ballerina tutu made of chiffon velvet in a lovely shade that matched the orchids. Artificial orchids went from the left shoulder across and down onto the skirt. Between the girls traveling to center stage, I did releves on my left foot, (going from flat foot to toe point up and down), while kicking my right leg from a bent knee out to a straight leg. When the girls made a double circle with the wreaths, I did turns traveling under the arches they made. Luckily, I never did run into anyone.

They danced off the stage, and I did 16 fouette turns. After bourree's to the left side of the stage I traveled across the stage in a semi-backbend with tiny steps. It was more difficult in the larger theaters with stages which seemed to last forever. I had to control my breathing and just snatch what air I could while in the back-bend. I concluded the dance with rapid turns in a circle around the stage. The dance was similar to the solos the ballerinas do in ballets. Mr. Leonidoff told me he had not expect-ed to find such an experienced dancer on the West Coast and he was really satisfied with my work.

One day during rehearsals, Alice sent for me to sign my contract. I hoped I would get more money because of my unusually difficult solos. However, I found my pay was to be the same amount I had received in the "Orientale Idea," $55.00 less 5%. I protested but was told everyone was being cut because of the Depression. Unfortunately, I still didn't have any idea of how the different points of contracts should be discussed until both came to an agreement. I did try to explain that I was doing the work of two dancers and was an important part of the production. Alice told me I should be grateful to have this opportunity when so many dancers were "at liberty." In time, I was to realize that dancers were often very necessary for the success of a show but were generally underpaid.

There would be more money for me this time because I would not have to pay for any expenses for Mother. She said I should send her part of my salary every week so that she could save it for me. I agreed, thinking if she ever needed anything, the money would be there for her. Daddy would be supporting her, but I knew she would need more spending money. We agreed on a sum I could live on, and I would send the rest to her. I had been planning on saving money, enough for a trip to New York when the show closed in New Orleans.

Before we opened the show at the Loew's State, I was told that I should bleach my natural golden blonde hair to a platinum blonde shade. I said I did not want to start bleaching my hair, and my mother would not like that at all. I managed to keep my own color of hair for a month, but in Oakland I gave in. While I was near Mother, Alice couldn't change my mind. In Oakland I was tired of the continual demand and had my hair bleached. To complete the picture of the glamorous person I was supposed to be, I wore a suntan body make up. It was perfect with my orchid costume. I decided to try to have a natural tan. When it was possible, I would go to the roof of the hotel where we were staying and sunbathe. Suntan lotions were not common yet, so I followed somebody's suggestion and used olive oil and vinegar to keep from burning. I smelled like a salad dressing most of the time.

Later, when tights came in, body makeup on the legs was no longer necessary, but I still tried to tan my upper body. My dermatologist blames my profusion of moles on my sunbathing for years. Now I live in fear of skin cancer and get checked at least twice a year. If anything is suspicious, it is removed. Everyone now is warned about the danger of too much sun and people should pay attention. I regret that I did not stay with the body make up. Then my body would not now look like a speckled trout and I would not have to worry about skin cancer. I stay out of the sun as much as possible.

Before leaving Los Angeles, I went to see Mr. Belcher in his new Hollywood studio and he asked for a picture of me. I was proud of the picture I gave him, because

I had never seen anyone else do the pose in the photo. It was one of the publicity shots taken after the last show at Loew's State opening night and it was particularly difficult.

The photographer asked me to stand on one toe, then bring the other foot up to my head. I asked for someone to stand back of the curtain then put a hand next to where my hand was in the front. I had the edge of my hand and the little finger of my left hand pressed against this invisible hand and that was my only support to maintain for balance. After several shots that seemed to take a long time, he said, "All done." The picture was exceptional and appeared in most of the newspaper ads for the "Manhattan Idea" as we went across the country. I also used it for my own publicity for the rest of my theatrical career. For my next picture, I changed into my monkey costume. This time the photographer asked me to stand on my hands and place one foot on my head and extend the other upward. I asked for help again. I asked for someone to stand in front of me while I tried a handstand. My aide held her hand up so I could touch it with the upraised foot.   Gradually pulling back from her hand I was balanced. I managed to say I was ready. The photographer went to work. Finally, I was told I could come down. I didn't, and again he told me to come down. I started to giggle, but couldn't move. My back had locked, since this was basically the same position I had held for the previous pose.

I gasped, "Someone push my leg." Only then could I go into a walkover and stand upright. This picture was also shown in the papers for many years. Later, it would change my life.

Mr. Belcher sent the ballet photo with an article to London to a dance magazine. Not knowing what he had done, I was surprised when I received a copy of the magazine that mother sent to me. I was on the front page! The article reported I was planning on visiting England in the future. That was stretching the truth a little. That would have been wonderful, but New York was my first big desire, and the great Depression prevented me from going anyplace.

Fresno was more enjoyable this time. The local Mickey Mouse Club was celebrating a birthday and the reporters gave the "Monkey" lots of publicity. A reporter interviewed me and asked me what it felt like being a monkey? I told him it was fun. I did not see the connection with Mickey Mouse and my monkey, but I didn't mind the extra attention.

In San Francisco we played the new Fox Theater near the heart of the city. The theater had everything that was modern but never became a success and was destroyed to make way for more profitable buildings. But the Warfield is still going strong with special shows.

The motion picture for the Fox and Oakland was "His Woman," starring Gary Cooper and Claudette Colbert. The reviews were poor because of a bad vehicle but the stars certainly survived.

Walt Roesner led the orchestra in San Francisco and Hermie King in Oakland. Both were well known musical directors at the time. Orchestras were "hot" and enjoying great popularity.

On December 11, we opened at the Fox Paramount Theater in Portland, Oregon. On Saturday we were to do 6 shows because of a morning benefit. Early that morning I became ill. Evidently I had eaten something that did not agree with me. When the business day started I found a doctor who gave me some medicine. I went on to the theater to get ready for the first performance. It was to be one of my longest days. After the last curtain of the second show I had to be carried off the stage by a stagehand, who took me to a cot in the property room. That was the procedure for the rest of the six shows. At last, the day was done, and I feebly made my way to my hotel.

I was fine the next day, glad to be able to do the five regular shows. When you are at home, an illness is not of any consequence. In show business, it becomes a major problem when you are the principle dancer in a production. That is, when you learn the meaning of, "the show must go on." My favorite ballet picture was in the advertisement for the 5th Avenue Theater in Seattle. "Lissome Ballerina, Lucile Vercon." was the caption. I was confused at first, then I remembered when I was still rehearsing I had been asked to go to the publicity office. They had suggested I needed to have a Russian or French name. I was joking when I suggested the name, "Iversonoff." No, they didn't like that. I suggested "Vercon" which sounded French. I was still joking but here it was in the Seattle newspaper. It was changed, and I was relieved when my name was my own in the subsequent ads.

Soon after, the ads read, "Lucille, On Toes Of Gold." I rather liked the sound of that so didn't complain. It was continued in the ads for theaters across the United States. I was tired of asking people to spell my name with one "l", so I finally accepted either way.

Time went by quickly in this show, not at all like the last one. It was nearing Christmas when we arrived in Vancouver at the now familiar Strand Theater. Marilyn Miller was starring in the picture "Her Majesty's Love," and Gus Arnheim and his "Famous Coconut Grove Orchestra" were featured on the stage. The theater manager introduced me to a gentleman back stage. I was told the cast was invited to the man's yacht for a Christmas Dinner, and my help was needed. We went into the familiar Green Room to talk about his generous offer. He told me I was to arrange the transportation for everyone. The big day arrived, and we were taken by cars to the large beautiful yacht. We had a wonderful turkey dinner with all the trimmings including a piece of mince pie to take to the theater. We did full justice to the meal and spent some time on deck watching the setting sun sparkling on the little waves that made the yacht rock ever so gently. We thanked our host for his thoughtfulness, and after our brief motor boat trip to the shore, we were driven back to the theater to do our night shows. Our schedule had been arranged so we would have extra time for the dinner. This Christmas I wasn't homesick. I didn't have time!

In Milwaukee, there was an entrance to a restaurant across the alley from the backstage door of the theater. We could go there and have something to eat or drink between shows. I would take one of my constant companions, a book or a magazine, and relax while I ate my ice cream.

One night a young man sat down beside me. He asked what I was reading and began talking to me. I ignored him at first, but he seemed harmless, so we started to talk. It was very casual. The evening before our last night he said, "Be sure and come in tomorrow night to say goodbye."

The next night after I had finished my packing, I looked at my watch and decided I did have time for a soft drink and could say goodbye to my friend. Carrying my overnight case, my purse and magazine I went to the restaurant. He sat beside me and I told him I did not have much time. When I got up to leave, he helped me with my coat and belongings, shook my hand and wished me good luck.

I joined some of the girls in their cab to go to the station. Arriving there, I opened my purse for my share of the fare and found my wallet was gone! I knew I had it because I had just put my week's salary in it at the theater dressing room. I had been "set up" by my casual friend who had planned to rob me from the beginning.

My first impulse was to go back to the restaurant but the girls said, "You can't go back. It is time for the train to leave." I realized it would not make much difference anyhow; he would have left in a hurry. When I told our manager about my loss, he gave me an advance, and I sent Mother the usual amount of money from my salary. I did not want to worry her, and felt some shame at having been tricked.

A few nights previously, I had telephoned her and given her some really bad news. Our manager had told me the district manager had a lady friend with a talented daughter who was to take my role in the production finale when we opened in Chicago at the Chicago Theater.

My contract did not have any safeguards for me. There was nothing I could do but accept the change. I asked him, "Is this for the rest of the tour?" He said, "It will depend if his friend's daughter wants to stay with the show."

There had not been any warning, and I was in shock for a few minutes. My first thought was of giving my notice. Then I remembered how much trouble I had getting home the last time I left a show, and decided to think things over.

My Mother had written to my Uncle Clancy, who lived in Chicago. He had invited me to stay at his home while I was there. Considering my financial condition, I was happy about this lucky break. The last time I had seen Uncle Clancy was when he had come home to Minneapolis from the war. He had not been well because he had been one of many who had been gassed in World War I. I was just six or seven years old at that time, so I barely remembered him. I did remember he had a Polish bride who did not speak very much English, but was a pretty, sweet, gentle person. She certainly had become Americanized since I had first seen her. They met me at the station in Chicago and took my bags to their home after arranging to pick me up at the theater after the last show. I didn't have much time to visit with them because of my hours differing from theirs, but they did see to it that I had a hearty breakfast and a light lunch every night. My cousin and I were almost the same age and he did visit with me a little.

When I arrived at the Chicago Theater, I found a letter for me from New York. It was from Eddie, one of the men in the Arabic tumbler's act in the Long Beach Exposition.

The past summer we had encountered each other in agent's offices and become friends. Sometimes he had given me a lift in his car when we went from Los Angeles to

Hollywood. The trade paper Variety carried the names of cities where the shows were playing. That was how Ed had found where I would be.

Several times, we had worked at the same theaters, and it was at one of them that he told me he was thinking of going to New York where there were more vaudeville theaters. It was a strange coincidence for me to hear from him at this time. He wrote that he had found work, and he wanted to know my plans. Was I still hoping to come to New York after I closed in New Orleans? He had a male partner, and they wanted to add two girls to their act. They were rehearsing with a girl dancer, his partner's friend, and would work as a trio until I joined them. It would be a song and dance variety act. Would I be interested? I wrote him a letter that night and told him what had happened to me and that I might be at liberty sooner than I had thought. Then I phoned Mother to ask what she thought of the plan. She advised me to not do anything right away because things might change. She said, "practice." I would need to be ready for anything that might happen.

One of the chorus girls had been released and I took her place in the line for the Jack Lester sequence and the Manhattan production number. It was strange when I had to dance behind the new soloist. She was called a "Personality Dancer," and her dance was flirtatious, with few ballet steps. Evidently, she did not do acrobatics, so I still did my acrobatic routine dance with the organ grinders. I was practicing ballet between shows when one of the electricians, still working at his board, said, "You should be the solo dancer in the finale." I explained what had happened, and he was very surprised and sympathetic. He did not seem to think too much of the girl taking my place.

Later in the evening he said he wanted to talk to me. He told me there was going to be a big benefit show with acts from the theaters entertaining. Even stars from Hollywood were participating. Would I dance, if it were arranged?

I told him that I didn't have a costume with me. He said, "We will take care of that. Don't worry." The next day he handed me a note with the address of a place where I could rent a costume. He said the stage crew would pay any charges.

Everything worked out just as he had promised. I found a two piece costume, black velvet trunks decorated with many rhinestones and a turquoise chiffon blouse with billowy sleeves, also trimmed with rhinestones.

Between our two night shows, a bus drove us to a large building which usually housed professional sports where a temporary stage had been erected for the benefit. It was filled to capacity with people and was very noisy. Also, to my dismay, the air was filled with cigarette smoke. Inhaling second-hand smoke made my throat burn, and it was hard for me to breathe when I was dancing, which was one reason I preferred to dance in theaters.

When I found I was to follow a famous movie actress, I became nervous. When she left the stage to only perfunctory applause, I became even more nervous. Then I heard my introduction to "Stardust." I calmed down and climbed the stairs to the stage. At first, I was content just doing my familiar dance. The audience was quiet. Then my early tricks drew applause. When I ended my first chorus by jumping into the air and kicking my head with both feet, and doing it several times, they really began to applaud. They did not stop until the end of my dance. A chorus later, they were still applauding, and I kept on taking bows until I carefully went down the stairs in back of the stage. I was so excited my knees were rubbery. After all, I had practically stopped the show.

There were so many agents at the foot of the stairs; it was like a wonderful dream. All of them wanted to talk to me. It was like a scene in a movie musical where the understudy replaces the star and becomes an instant success.

Agents gave me cards and said, "Call me." There was not any time to talk because the bus was waiting to take us back to the theater for our last show.

Back at the theater, nothing had changed. My ego trip was just for me. No one else was aware of it, even the others who had performed at the benefit. They had been boarding the bus and hadn't seen my performance or known about my success. None of the agents thought of looking for me in the chorus at the Chicago Theater.

The next theater we played in Chicago was a long distance from my uncle's home, so I stayed with the girl with whom I had been rooming. Charley Chase was making a guest appearance at the theater. The picture was about Hawaii and the chorines were given grass skirts and wigs of long black hair for the short hula that we performed in front of a beach scene. We were setting the mood before the star's appearance. The black wig enhanced my green eyes and briefly I thought of dying my own hair. Then I remembered I didn't like touching up the roots of my platinum hair, and realized I would not like it any better with a different color.

Evidently my roommate and Charley Chase had become acquainted during the week. I didn't think that they had been dating because she had returned to the hotel with me every night. The closing night she said he had asked her to have a bite to eat with him before his train left. Later at the hotel, I heard them talking outside our door. Opening the door, I said, "Come in, I am still up."

We talked together for awhile, and then he said he would leave us and go to the station to wait for his train. He had checked out of his hotel before the first show. When we heard his train did not leave until 5:00 am, we suggested he could wait the remaining three hours with us. The conversation was lively for awhile, then all three of us began yawning. We finally lay down on the bed fully dressed after setting the alarm clock. It was crowded, but soon we were all asleep. When the alarm went off, he put on his shoes and coat, thanked us for our hospitality, picked up his bags and left. My roommate and I agreed we could always say we had slept with a Movie Star. Then we realized that no one would believe our innocent night and would probably distort it, so we kept it to ourselves. Whenever I hear shocking stories about movie stars, I wonder if they are as bad as they are made out to be. We went back to sleep and it seemed just a few minutes before it was time for us to take a cab to the Paradise Theater in another part of Chicago.

My uncle wanted me to stay with them again because the elevated trains would be convenient at both ends. I needed help to know how to reach the nearest station. One of the stage crew, Burt, had caught my eye because he was near my age. I told him my problem and he said, "I live in that direction and I would be happy to take you to your uncle's home in my car."

This was better than I had expected. I had not relished the idea of traveling so late on the elevated train again, and now I would have a safe ride to my uncle's home. We seemed to find many things to talk about. I began to look forward to the ride each night with him. It was cold in the car but not as cold as it would have been on the elevated train.

A few days after we opened at the Paradise Theater I heard loud voices coming from a room at the end of the hall. I was surprised when I recognized Mr. Leonidoff's accent. He had flown from New York to straighten out the damage to his show. He was furious. He said I was to be reinstated immediately. He was angry because no one had consulted him about the change he certainly would not have allowed. I knew I had my place back when he told them it was a terrible thing to do to Lucile, a brilliant dancer.

I was a happy girl when I heard him say that.

Eddie had sent his phone number to me, and when I phoned him and told him I was staying with the show, he was disappointed that I would not be joining him. He did hope that I would be able to come to New York at the conclusion of our tour. I hoped so, too.

Burt and I seemed to have many things to talk about as he drove me to my uncle's home that first night. We continued talking back stage the next day. In a few days, I was convinced I was in love. I had never felt this way before, even with Ronnie. There seemed to be an electric current between us whenever our eyes met. We talked together between shows.

One cold dark windy night, he drove me to a secluded spot instead of driving me to my uncle's home, and he stopped the car and kissed me. It was a brief kiss with a long embrace. His arm was around me and I leaned against him. He said, "I drove here so we could talk. There is something that I should have told you before." I shivered, and not only because of the icy wind coming off the lake. I had a premonition that he was going to tell me something I really did not want to know. I was surprised when he told me he was married and had been for several years. He continued, "My father and mother have been close friends with another couple for a long time. They were married about the same time and shortly after I was born, the other couple had a baby daughter. She and I grew up together and when we heard our parents discussing how nice it would be if we were to marry when we were older, we thought it was a good idea. We ran away and got married when we were 16, and we have two children. We get along just fine except now we are more like brother and sister than husband and wife. This never bothered me until a few days ago when I met you and realized what love was like."

The tears that had formed in my eyes began to run down my cheeks. I was in his arms again, and we were both crying. We agreed there was nothing to be done about our situation when we finally were composed enough to talk. He told me how he had joined his father in working at the theater as a stagehand, and the next day he took me to meet him. He was the property man who took care of everything backstage and was sitting at his desk. Burt left us alone, and his dad pulled up a chair for me to sit on. I wondered what he would have to say to me.

"Burt has told me about you two. There is so much talk back here that I already knew something unusual was happening"

His voice was sympathetic, and he reached over and patted my hand. He repeated the same story that Burt had told me about the two families and said the parents had been happy about the marriage at the time. Later, he had wondered whether it really was for the best.

He told me, "We are Catholic you know, so divorce is out of the question."

My throat was so choked it was hard for me to talk, but I explained to him that I would never cause a divorce. It would be against my principles. Also, my family was very strict, and would never understand. Obviously he was relieved, and we talked awhile about the things that can happen in a lifetime. There was no future for Burt and me, especially since he had two children. At the end of the week's engagement at the theater we said good-bye, and that was that. Only it wasn't. Burt wrote to me. He telephoned me and even came to see me in Toledo, Ohio, traveling through a heavy snowstorm. I told him I could not stand the emotional stress any longer, and we said our last good-bye. I never heard from him again. I don't know if it was unusual, but it seemed as though married men were attracted to me. After awhile, if I was asked for a date, I asked first, "Are you married?" I could not understand why so many men thought that did not make any difference.

One day in Cincinnati, I was unable to work. When I woke up that morning, I couldn't move my head because my neck was so stiff. My head leaned to the right, and my shoulder was pulled up almost to my ear. I managed to dress and went out to look for a doctor. The one I found said I had a wry neck, probably from a cold. He loaned me a heat lamp to use and told me to go to bed. I called our manager when I returned to the hotel. He came to my room and could see I was helpless. I stayed all day in bed with the lamp shining on my shoulder.

The manager told me they would try to get along with the new chorus girl they had hired in Chicago. She had said she was a toe dancer and was supposed to be my understudy. He hurried away to call her for a hasty rehearsal.

The manager had been confident all would be well, but after the first show, he came to me in consternation and told me, "The girl didn't do as well as we had hoped." I was really dismayed at his words. I had been hoping the girl would give a good performance and that I needn't worry.

He had intended to ask me if I could possibly dance. When he saw that even getting out of bed was difficult, he left shaking his head. The next day I was still in pain, but I could hold my shoulder down and I was able to do the Manhattan finale. The monkey act was shelved for a couple of days.

All went well except for the turns in my ballet routine. When dancers do turns, we do what is called "spotting." We have to look at one spot so we won't get dizzy. The head does not turn with the body until it has to, then snaps around quickly so we can look again at the same spot. If we were not turning we would look like we were moving our head rapidly from side to side saying, "No, no, no."

My neck hurt with each turn. In a few days, I became more flexible so that I could do my dance more easily and could be the monkey again.

The next star I met was Dorothy Mackail, one of the best comediennes in motion pictures. She was a real down to earth person. Talking to Miss Mackail was a thrill after I had watched her pictures from the wings so often. I would pass her room, going down the hall, and she would call out, "Hi, monkey. Come in and talk to me." Sometimes she would send her maid out for a snack for us, which made me feel pretty special. I was sorry when the week was over. The autographed photo that she gave me still brings back special memories.

We played the Metropolitan Theater in Boston. When I was there, the added attraction was the Mills Brothers. A wonderful act! It was the original quartet and they really did harmonize.

The theater is so beautiful they have renovated it. Big theatrical productions are staged there now. After the feature picture was shown, Fabian Sevitsky directed the large symphonic orchestra in an overture. Often I would get in my first costume and sit in the wings to watch and listen to the beautiful music before my first number. It was the first time I had watched a symphonic orchestra of accomplished musicians.

In high school, my favorite class had been music appreciation, and the excellent teacher taught us what to look for in the different instruments. When I traveled, my portable phonograph was with me with several large records of "Masterpieces of Music" packed in my trunk. Live music was so different that I did not miss many of the overtures that week.

Madame Sevitsky would be in Maestro Fabian's dressing room with the door open between shows. We smiled at each other, and in the evening of our opening day, she motioned for me to come in and talk to her. She had not been in the States very long and did not know much English. Between shows I would sit with her and we would sew together. She liked to embroider, too. We did manage to understand each other most of the time. The maestro was pleased and began to talk to me.

During one performance, I saw him watching from the wings. Afterwards, he complimented me on my toe dance, and said that I belonged in a ballet company. However, he told me I was too thin and did not eat enough. The next day he informed me he had made arrangements for me to eat my meals at a restaurant the rest of the week. He had ordered what I should eat. Although I knew no one dared to disagree with him, I told him I could not do that. I timidly explained that this would leave my room-mate eating alone (the only reason I could think of just then).

"Take her with you! That is even better. You should not eat alone."

So my roommate and I had wonderful meals that certainly cost more than we were accustomed to, and oh, how delicious! My only disappointment was that I did not dare eat any of the marvelous desserts that I could see other patrons enjoying. That would have been more than the "Monkey" could handle.

Madame and I had tears in our eyes when we said goodbye at the end of our week. She told me her husband wanted to see me. I found him in the orchestra room sorting out the orchestrations. He had presents for me! He gave me a large box of Whitman's candy, the largest bottle of Houbrigant's Quelques Fleurs cologne I had ever seen and several expensive magazines to take to the train. The gifts were wonderful, but what I had gained from their friendship was worth much more. I had another memory to cherish. Either Sevitsky went back to Europe or he stayed on the East Coast. I tried to follow his career, which should have been spectacular, but he just disappeared. Several years later, we met again, but that is another story.

Everything was changing with the declining economy. Many big stores had to close, and theaters were showing only motion pictures or closing. Crime was taking the front page with shootouts between bootleggers. One night, I accepted an invitation to visit a speakeasy. The stories I had heard from the other girls had made me curious. I had promised my father I would not drink bootleg liquor, and I was not going to drink any now. The smoke made me so uncomfortable that I went back to the hotel.

I cannot remember where or when, but I do remember one fun night. Two of the ushers asked my roommate and me for a date. We had talked with them when we were having our usual nightly repast at one of the popular White House eating-places (a forerunner of what are now called "fast food restaurants"). Their approach was different. They asked us if our hotel room had a big table. We said it did. Then they asked us if we would eat with them the next night. They would bring some food to our room at the hotel. When they arrived the next night, we were treated to a marvelous aroma. They were carrying a big bag of barbecued spareribs and a bundle of newspapers. We spread the newspapers on the table and feasted on the most wonderful ribs. They had also brought lots of napkins, a necessity because we had to eat with our hands. We ate until we almost burst. There was lots of laughter, too, because of the sauce that was smeared all over our faces. When we had cleaned those ribs thoroughly, the boys took the newspapers and scraps, and saying they had enjoyed themselves, bid us goodnight. We certainly had enjoyed ourselves with our unusual dates, and we talked about how nice they had been.

In Atlanta, I would be staying with my Aunt Mildred again. She was alone too much because Uncle Joe traveled all the time. Most of the time her only companion was her Pekingese, Kiki, and the maid who came in a few days of the week. Upon my arrival, I wasn't surprised when Mildred gave me a letter from Mother, but I could hardly believe what I read. Her letter gave me mixed feelings. Mother would be arriving the next day! I knew she would have had to use my money that I had been sending to her all this time. I had gone without so many things so I would have the money to go to New York after the tour ended. Would that be possible now? When the excitement of her arrival was over, she told me she would be traveling with me for the rest of the tour, so I had better make the travel arrangements right away. Not one word did she say about my plans, it seems she had never taken them seriously.

We found three "Ideas" were in Atlanta at the same time because of cancellations that had been made at theaters on the circuit. We had to wait until the current show left. I began to realize how the Depression would be affecting show business. It would never be the same again.

My aunt had a friend who had a summer home at a nearby lake, and Aunt Mildred and I went there one day to swim. My hostess asked about the "Ideas," and when

I told her how some were more or less stranded in Atlanta for the week, she said she would enjoy having the performers come for an afternoon. I did some telephoning and several did want to come, so we arranged time and transportation. The "Idea" that would be leaving in a few days had three teams of adagio dancers in the cast. They were all full of energy, and, following the usual behavior of dancers, they started to try different adagio tricks on the expansive lawn. The girls were thrown from one fellow to another. While they rested, they asked me to do some of my acrobatic work. Finally, I summoned enough courage to ask if I could do some of their trio tricks with them. I loved it. I remember one especially. One fellow took both my feet. The other took my hands, and I can only describe it by saying my body became a jump rope. Round and round I went. Then I showed them some of the tricks that Ed and I had done with one of the boys partnering me. Ed and I had been the only ones to do these tricks as far as I knew. They said they were glad to have new material. They were impressed when I told them I had been Ed's first partner. He and Ruth were enjoying a successful career in Europe. They told me after a divorce from El Rita, Ed had married Ruth, and they had started a family. We had a wonderful picnic dinner, and at twilight we lounged and sang for awhile. It had been a special day at this beautiful place by the lake.

Our show opened at the Fox Theater with the enormous stage, and I survived the strenuous crossing in my traveling backbend. My thoughts went back to the lovely birthday party. I wondered what had happened to my special friend, dear generous Bill. We had not been near New York City this time, so I had not been able to contact him.

Mother and I traveled alone to Miami, Oklahoma, to join the rest of the troupe who had gone there earlier. For the last leg of our trip, Mother and I transferred to a train pulled by an engine that was an antique, I am sure. It huffed and puffed along. We rode in the caboose with an old pot-bellied stove.

We went on to the big cities: Oklahoma City, San Antonio, and New Orleans for our final weeks. New Orleans was not only hot, but humid, too. Mother became so sick that I called a doctor. He tried to make her comfortable, but took me aside and told me she needed to be home in California as soon as possible. Until then I had hoped I could go to New York and join Eddie in his act. Instead, I took Mother home. I think my guardian angel was looking after me. Had I gone to New York, I might have ended up in a line waiting for an apple. There were many show people in those lines.

There were many sights I would not have been able to see if I had not traveled from coast to coast and border to border. Now I would return to going from agent to agent.

Arabasque in Toe Dance

Stardust Costume for Acrobatic Dance

They Called It My Double Head Kick

Picture for Agents and Publicity

More Pictures from Agents Folder

Indian Night, Lake Tahoe Night Club

My Mother Made My Only Abbreviated Costumes

More Pictures of My Friend Eva

Chapter 12

Whenever possible, I tried to go to classes at Belcher's Studio. That was where I met Chuck, a new student, who was looking for an adagio partner. One evening when I was practicing in the studio before class, he asked me to try some lifts with him. I soon realized he didn't have enough experience or strength, besides, I told him I wanted to continue working by myself. He asked me if he could come to see me some Sunday because his work involved traveling during the week, and he was only in town on weekends.

He phoned one Sunday morning. Mother said we were going to the beach and that he could join us. From then on, Chuck was with us each Sunday. Daddy liked Chuck and when we planned to go to La Jolla to see a total eclipse, he invited Chuck to join us.

Arriving there, we parked above the ocean on a tall cliff. An eerie experience began as the sky darkened and the sea gulls headed for their nests, making a big fuss about the twilight coming in the middle of the day. People were lowering their voices until they became silent, and all we could hear was the surf breaking on the rocks below. Daddy had pieces of black film for us, so we could watch the sun slowly disappearing without injuring our eyes. When the sun started to emerge on the other side, people cheered. Long ago, people had thought the world was coming to an end when the sun disappeared, and some of that superstition remained with us. We couldn't help feeling uneasy.

The sea gulls left their roosts and resumed their noisy hunting for food. We explored La Jolla and had our picnic lunch. After we took pictures, we returned to Long Beach.

When it rained, Chuck and I would go to a matinee. I was enjoying having a boyfriend, but did not know he was getting serious. I was surprised when one day he asked me to marry him. I told him I wanted to continue with my career. I was not ready to get married. I knew he did have a good position with a firm and could afford a wife, but I knew I was not in love with him. One rainy Sunday, after a matinee, Chuck parked the car by my home and again asked me to marry him. I said, "No, I am not ready for marriage."

When I started to open the door to leave the car, he frightened me when he grabbed me. When I pulled away from him, the sleeve of my velvet jacket ripped. Mother wanted to know why I was upset when I went into the house. When I showed her my jacket and told her the reason, she said it would be better if I were not to see Chuck again.

The next weekend, I was dancing on a variety bill at the West Coast Theater in Long Beach. On Sunday night, the stage doorman came to my dressing room and said there was a young man asking for me. Mother went to the stage door with me, and, seeing Chuck, she told him to leave. He said he wanted to apologize for his behavior. She told me I could talk with him but not leave with him.

His car was parked in the alley in the back of the theater. He got into the driver's seat. I stood outside on the passenger's side until a car drove behind his car, and the driver honked his horn. Chuck said, "Jump in and I'll go around the block."

I got in the car, but instead of going around the block, he started to drive along Ocean Boulevard. I told him, you promised not to drive away, but he continued driving until he turned the car into a short dead end street with the beach far below. I said, "I can't sit here, I have to get back to the theater." He turned the motor off, and grabbing me by the shoulders, he insisted that I agree to marry him. Again I told him I wanted to continue my dancing and wasn't ready to marry. I tried to get him to release me, and thought I had, but instead his hands went to my throat. I began to be frightened. I tried to break his hold, and when I couldn't, I started to claw at his face with my nails until he released me. We sat in silence for a few minutes, and I thought it was all over. He had other ideas.

He started the engine of the car and shouted, "We are going over the cliff. We will die together." I grabbed his arm when he started to put the car into gear and held on with all my strength. I kept pleading for him to stop the car, and after what seemed like ages, he did. Again we sat in silence. I was trying to make sense out of the whole thing. He had always been good humored, had never lost his temper with me, and I had never seen this side of his character. I knew I had to get back to the theater. Mother would be looking for me and would wonder what had happened. I said, as calmly as I could, "Please take me back to the theater."

To my immense relief, without a word, he backed the car out of the short street and drove me to the back of the theater. I got out of the car and had barely slammed the car door when he sped off. Sobbing, I ran by the bewildered doorman and went down the stairs to my dressing room. Mother was talking to the orchestra leader, Lloyd Skeels. When I had stopped crying, I told them what had happened. They both scolded me for getting in the car, I agreed they were right.

A few days later, Chuck's mother phoned and told me Chuck had been ill. She blamed me. Before I could ask how Chuck was, she told me what a wicked person I was. She blamed me for his being sick after my meeting with him. He had been found in Santa Barbara, a town up the coast where his family lived. One of Chuck's clients had come to open his store and, upon opening the back door to the alley, had found Chuck unconscious at the wheel of his car. He had been taken to a hospital and his parents notified. Her voice become abusive and she told me I was never to see her son again, accusing me of being a sexy showgirl, trying to snare her son. She would not listen to what I had to say and broke the connection when I called Mother to the phone to talk with her. Mother and I decided Chuck must have been drinking that night because it was the only way we could explain his change of character. Chuck did not come to the classes anymore and I did not hear from him again. A few years later, I heard he was a successful businessman, with a wife and children.

This year I would be home for Christmas. I enjoyed being at home to share in the festivities. It was fun trimming the tree, and helping fix Christmas dinner. New Year's Eve I danced at two places and, while Daddy and I were driving to the second one, we recalled a previous New Year's adventure. The "Idea" I had been in was playing at the Egyptian Theater in Hollywood. After our last show, the production number had to go to the Loew's State and perform. Daddy had come to drive me home. Instead, he had followed the bus that took the cast to Los Angeles. We had a police escort in the lead. It was a wild ride. I sat in the back of the bus so I could watch Daddy expertly following us. He said he had never had to drive like that before, and I doubted that he ever did it again.

I continued on with my one- or two-day performances, sometimes at a club and occasionally a weekend at a theater. On March 8, 1933 Mother, Daddy and I went to two basketball games, one at a junior high school, and the other at Poly High. On Friday the 9th, I left early in the morning for Los Angeles. There I met the act that drove me to Bakersfield where we were appearing at a theater for the weekend.

We only did three shows, so I went out to dinner between the matinee and the first night show. Just before I went into the theater, I heard newsboys calling out "Extra! Extra! Read all about it." I started to buy a paper but was stopped by my friends who told me I wouldn't have time to read it. I could get the paper after the last show.

When they brought a copy of the paper to me, I read that there had been a large earthquake in Long Beach. The headline said thousands of people were injured and hundreds dead. I sent a telegram when I could not reach home by the telephone; I was told the lines were down. My friends stayed with me for awhile until they thought I had calmed down enough to sleep. I thought I could, but my imagination would not let me. After a sleepless night, I went to the theater. There was a telegram for me that said my family was all right, and they were worried about me! The Los Angeles Times March 10th morning paper headline read, "Scores perish in Southland Quake." The story of the quake read, "More than thousand injured; damage totals millions as buildings fall, fire sweeps nearby towns. At midnight fifteen bodies were recovered in Long Beach and under the wreckage of buildings many more bodies may be buried." I read the rest of the story and could not find anything that would reassure me. I did not have my own transportation, so there was nothing for me to do but try to compose myself and wait until we finished the last show Sunday night.

We drove to a dark Long Beach. People were camping in their front yards with low campfires adding to the ghostly scene. Many of the California style homes looked strange because the porches were part way up the front of the structures. I had not known what to expect when we drove up to the front of my home. I had tried to telephone home many times without success. Each time, I was informed the lines were still inoperable. When the car arrived in front of the house, I gave a sigh of relief, because nothing had changed. The door opened, and my brother came out and held me tight. After thanking my friends, he took me inside the house.

"We are sleeping in the living room," he explained. His fiancée, Henrietta, was in a sleeping bag alongside his empty one on the floor. I kissed Mother, who was on the divan and then peeked in the door of the adjourning bedroom, and Daddy said, "Glad you are home safe and sound." I went to him for a big bear hug. There were still a few hours before dawn, so I snuggled in beside my brother. I felt a slight tremor, but it did not feel like much. I sat right up, but Mother said. "Get some sleep Lucile. We get up early."

I was still waiting to feel a quake in the morning when I sat down to eat my breakfast. As I was pulling the chair to the table, I again missed the jerky movement.

After breakfast, Alton and I drove to see Fred, a long time friend. His family was occupying a large tent in their front yard. We had just reached Fred's home and had joined him when I felt the earth move one way and then another. My stomach tried to keep up with the motion, and I said to my brother, "I see what you mean." I joined the rest of the town in dreading every tremor.

We drove around the town, and he showed me the schools where we had watched two different basketball games on Thursday night. The brick gymnasiums were in shambles. If the quake had occurred at the time a game was going, on there would have been hundreds of casualties.

We drove by Farnham's clothing store where Alton worked. The alley was full of bricks from the buildings on either side. Alton said, "After the first quake, I ran between the buildings to see what damage had been done. There were no bricks on the ground. I had no sooner stepped into the back door of the store, when the after shock came, and all those bricks which had been loosened fell down into the alley. Good thing I had reached that door in time." Many people had not been so fortunate and had been caught by falling bricks that killed them when the second quake hit.

When we returned home, I found my telegram had just arrived. It took from Friday night to Monday afternoon to be delivered.

Everyone had a story to tell. One couple was shopping in a grocery store after coming home from their honeymoon. When the quake hit, she grabbed his hand and ran to the entrance of the store. He tried to stop her, but she went out the door in front of him just in time to be caught under a barrage of bricks that killed her instantly. He was left standing in the doorway with his hand still outstretched.

A missing couple was found days later in their convertible car in front of their apartment house. The building had partially collapsed and bricks completely covered the car.

There were many stories and some of them were even humorous. There was the story of the man who was upstairs in his bathroom taking a bath. When the quake began, he did not even take time to grab a towel he was in such a hurry to get out of the confines of his small bathroom. He ran down the narrow staircase, and once on the street, he realized he was stark naked. Somebody brought him a robe to wear until he felt it was safe to return to his apartment. The small tremors continued. Then some weeks later, there was another sizable quake, but again I was out of town. My Guardian Angel was certainly watching over me.

Everything was getting back to normal, and I was practicing at the theater again. One day Lloyd Skeels, the orchestra leader, met me on the stage. He asked me if I would be interested in a revue he was hoping to stage. I told him, "I will have to ask Mother's opinion, and I know she will want to talk to you about it."

Later, Mr. Skeels explained to her, "My contract here will be expiring in a few weeks, and I think a variety show would do well in theaters in small towns in California, Oregon and Washington. I am preparing some acts to travel."

If I could join the show, Mr. Skeels assured her no harm would come to me. She worried about my traveling in cars. I would be living out of a suitcase, and I said it wouldn't be the first time. She finally gave her approval, helped me pack two suitcases, one for my costumes and makeup, the other for my personal wardrobe. The latter would have to hold warm and cold clothing. I knew the master of ceremonies, Vince Silk, a successful comedian who was well known in San Francisco and Hollywood. A phrase popular in show business was "Don't send out your laundry until after the first show." I'd heard Mr. Fountain jokingly say this to Vince. Mr. Fountain knew all those Iowans could be easily offended. Long Beach was for a time known as "Little Iowa." Vince had many jokes, and some were a bit risqué. Like most comedians, he was always under scrutiny. He stood behind a lectern and used a large artificial baloney for accenting his jokes. He wore a professor's robe and hat. His hair, heavy eyebrows, and mustache were also black. Dressed in this costume, he was impressive.

Comedian and eccentric dancer Lee Wilmot was on the show, too. They were so different they did not clash and were successful entertainers in their own way. A young lady, Mitzi Dale, accompanied Lee. She was the "straight man" for his jokes. They were not replicas of George Burns and Gracie Allen, but they did not have any trouble pleasing the audiences. She did a hula dance, which Lee then burlesqued. The audiences loved it.

Lenore Landrum, a coloratura soprano, pleased everyone because, not only did she have a wonderful voice, but, as the newspaper reviews said, "She was easy on the eyes as well." Lloyd Skeel's band of ten men completed the roster. He had chosen men who could sing and perform musical solos.

The performers and musicians who had cars drove the rest of us. I was lucky. I could sleep during the trips because I did not have to drive.

Even though we had our own musicians, a run through was necessary for the lights, curtains and everything that was done backstage. If it was a "one day stand," we did not check into a hotel. Once in awhile the theater would have both hot and cold running water in the dressing rooms. Taking the "spit" baths there was not so bad. Sleeping with my head on my crossed arms resting on the dressing table had become very easy, so I would nap between shows. After the last show we would load into the cars again and take off for the next town. Before long, I would fall asleep quickly and sleep until we arrived at our destination.

Shows like this would have an "advance man." He traveled ahead of us booking the show into the different places. The theater managers must have been shrewd. I noticed that if we were booked in for a percentage of the gross, we would have less attendance, mostly because of the lack of advance publicity. When we had sold out performances, it seemed we had been booked in for a set amount that was never enough. It was not many weeks before we were not receiving our full salary. Probably the reason we did not quit was the fact there was not too much to be found in the booking offices in Los Angeles and Hollywood. Then there is that old adage: The show must go on. We were lucky in having a troupe that had a sense of humor. We laughed a lot.

We drove into Coalinga, a very small town, and before going to the theater, we went to a restaurant nearby. The waitress was surprised to see so many of us and asked where we were going. "We are the members of the NRA Revue at the theater," we informed her. "What Revue?" she said. Vince explained the title meant National Recovery Administration. She informed us there had not been any advance publicity for the show. We had only a handful of people in the audience for the first show, which was quite discouraging. The second matinee was half full, and the two night shows were sold out. The manager of the theater could not apologize enough, and he made a good offer if we were to return to the theater when we were on our way back south. We did return later. This time the theater was full for every performance, and the dressing rooms were fit to be in, unlike our first visit. In their eagerness to have everything just right for us they had not only cleaned the stage but had oiled it!

My first dance was my Oriental dance. I did a split and my white skirt promptly became a black and white skirt. For the rest of the shows I used my alternate skirt of red chiffon. It did not show the oil quite as much. Each time I finished my acrobatic dance I looked as though I was in the middle of preparing for a black faced act! I was a mess. No hot water either!

The pictures of Coalinga after earthquake showed great damage. I felt sorry for the town because the people had been so nice to us. Unless one has experienced an earthquake it is hard to imagine how frightening it is.

The unsuccessful tour traveled to the San Francisco Bay area, and the show was closed. One good thing came from the show. Vince and I became friends and shared better times later.

When it was Thanksgiving time, I did not accept any bookings for the holiday. I wanted to be able to enjoy a good turkey dinner on Thanksgiving for a change. Alas, for the best of plans. West Coast Agency telephoned me early that morning, "Can you go to Glendale? Lee Wilmot's girl is too sick to work, and he suggested I call you to help him out." I asked for details and Daddy drove me to Glendale. He went home while I did my four shows. My Oriental dance was burlesqued by Lee, instead of the hula Dale usually did. I also did my acrobatic dance. When Mother and Daddy came after me, the turkey and trimmings they brought tasted much better than the turkey sandwich I had eaten at the corner drugstore.

I often played the Strand Theater in Long Beach when their agent Mrs. Meiklejon called me. Many times when she was in need of an act I would hear from her, often on the morning of the opening day. She knew I had many different dances and changes of costumes, and she could depend on me. I told her once, "The stage door automatically opens when I come down the alley. I am there so often." Evidently no one complained and I was glad to be in my hometown.

Going into the stage door one day, I bumped into a big man who held me for a moment to steady me. I looked up into boxing champion Jack Dempsey's face. He asked me if I was all right. He did not remember me from the show at the Water Carnival in Long Beach when I was much smaller, but I had never forgotten the night he had talked with me. He had made his mark in the sporting world as a boxer, and he had made a mark in my mind as a gentleman. Alton was envious when I told him about the first time I had met and talked with Mr. Dempsey, and he wished he could have talked to him this time. The champion appeared in many theaters, but I never bumped into him again.

In 1934, with prohibition repealed, another area opened up for my work. When an agent told me to see about a revue that was rehearsing for a nightclub, I thought, "Good, now I will get into something steady." The producer asked me to join the revue, and I rehearsed for two weeks. The rehearsal hall was in the same building as a nightclub and I was led to believe we were rehearsing to open there. The revue was whipped into shape and it was time for us to open. The day I went to rehearse with the orchestra I found it was an audition, not a rehearsal! The owner of the nightclub was not interested in anyone except for one dancer-me. I was given a contract for two weeks. The producer just disappeared. I never received compensation for my lost time and travel expenses, but I did have some work. Aunt Bea let me sleep on a couch in her apartment for the two weeks.

A few weeks later, I had the same experience. The producer's story was different. He was going to take his show traveling, and he claimed it was solidly booked. I was told I would be given the schedule of theaters at the next rehearsal on Monday. When I went there, the rehearsal hall was empty. Not wanting to waste the trip, I went to the agents lugging my rehearsal clothes. The trips had been costly. The agents were always sorry but that did not help my purse.

An agent sent me to see Carter De Haven, the well-known motion picture director in Hollywood. He owned two nightclubs, one in Venice called the Ship Cafe and the other in Burbank, the Airport Gardens. A rehearsal was being held at the latter, where I went to audition. Mr. de Haven, who was quite pleasant, liked my work and suggested I join the rehearsal for the next show. In it were three young excellent dancers, Don, Ernie and Dorothy, and we soon became friends. The trio was new to show business and it was refreshing to be with them. The policy of both nightclubs was to serve dinners for the employees. Everyone involved with the operation of the club would sit down at a long table in the kitchen area and could have their choice of the food that was prepared for serving to the patrons later. The success of the club was partially the result of the fine cuisine. The same cast was together for several weeks. One day while rehearsing for another show, we were introduced to Mrs. de Haven and her small daughter Gloria. She was dressed like a doll and was incredibly pretty. I was not surprised when she became a movie star years later.

The Airport Gardens was next to the Burbank Airport. One day after the morning rehearsal, I was crossing the field alongside the airport runway on the way to the street where I would catch a bus. I saw a young man coming toward me from the hangers, and when he reached me we began to talk. He said he was a pilot, Jimmy Doolittle. We talked until we arrived at the street, and after wishing each other good luck, we went our separate ways. Fortunately, he did have the good luck he would need for his adventurous career. I followed it in the newspapers and never forgot my brief encounter with him.

After two new shows at the Airport Gardens, the trio and I were transferred to the Ship Cafe in Venice. It was a small replica of an ocean liner, and inside was a complete nightclub.

I had been staying with Bea, but now Mother and I rented a small apartment on the beach front. It was a little vacation for Mother, and I enjoyed having her companionship. We had all day to amuse ourselves and to explore the small town.

We did not have to cook our dinners because Mother was invited to eat at the club. The musicians were always pulling tricks on each other so there was good laughter besides good food. The dressing rooms were up some wooden stairs from the kitchen to a space above the dining room. Coming down the stairs one night after changing into my Russian costume, I felt something greasy rub off on my hands as I held the railing. I did not have time to go wash my hands, and I thought nothing more about it. In my entrance step, I circled the dance floor with my arms crossed in front of my chest. Oh, what was that smell? I soon realized it was Limburger cheese and every time I brought my hands in front of my face, I got a strong whiff of it. The men in the band had thought of a new trick, putting cheese on the stair railing, and it was my luck to be the recipient.

When my routine was about to finish, I put my hands on the floor to do my "Wind the Clock" step. The cheese got on the floor. When I came to the final fast turns that had replaced the duck step, I tried to avoid that patch of cheese, but I stepped on it and went sailing across the room. I recovered before I ran into a table of guests. My heart was pounding harder than usual as I washed off that offending smelly cheese.

One night the trio of dancers and I decided to go to the amusement park, which was near the Ship Cafe. Dorothy and I wore the outfits we always wore between shows, forerunners of printed cotton jumpers that would become popular years later. They were not sold in stores; we purchased them from a lady who came backstage to sell them. Dorothy and I kept our make up on because of the limited time. We were out for fun. The roller coaster was famous, and I wanted to see how it compared with the coaster on the Pike in Long Beach, whose dips I knew by heart. This was a fun ride, too, and we did our share of screams. We had popcorn and watched the barkers showing off in front of the sideshows. Later in the week we returned just for the roller coaster.

The trio was doing a lovely waltz one night with Dorothy going from one partner to the other. After they exited, the boys doubled up with laughter. When they told Dorothy what they were laughing about, she was not amused. Her gown of black satin was trimmed with a white gardenia near the left shoulder. In twirling her around, Ernie accidentally pulled her dress until her breast was uncovered. When Don came to her side he thought, "I hadn't noticed the gardenia had a pink center. Oh no, it is her boob!" He quickly managed to straighten the gown. Of course the men of the orchestra had seen it, and they teased poor Dorothy about her extra "gardenia."

We were told to change our numbers for a new show. Two of my oriental costumes were of different types, so when I was asked for a new dance, I planned a new one that would not be as difficult. I got up early on rehearsal morning, caught the Red Car into Los Angeles and went to Sherman and Clay, a store that carried all types of music. I had been purchasing my orchestrations there for years, and when one of the salesmen recognized me, I told him what I needed.

He said, "There is a new song, "Love Songs of the Nile." I will play it for you." Luck was with me. I said, "I like it," The song never became a hit but suited me just fine. He played it several times until I said, "I have it set." After I bought the orchestration I hurried to get a Red Car back to Venice. On the trip, I found it was an easy to mark and did not require any cutting or pasting. Then in my mind I plotted the steps for the dance. The routine worked out perfectly with the music. I was to do that dance for many years without changing it.

When I closed at the Ship Cafe, Mother returned home.

An agent told me of a girl who wanted to share an apartment. When we met, she said she had a home in Los Angeles but thought it would be fun to live right in town. Glenda had long golden hair that fell in soft waves to her shoulders, pretty blue eyes and a complexion like cream. Her costumes were made of yards of flowing chiffon. I was reminded of my friend in junior high school who didn't dance very much but just floated around. Glenda had the same kind of hair and complexion, and from the amount of work the agents gave her, I think she did the same kind of dancing. She could have lived at home but was anxious to try living on her own. She didn't know how lucky she was when her mother would come to see her and always left her special food or some money.

The nightclub I was currently working in was really a large ballroom with the kind of slippery floor I hated. The owner manager was so strict the performers even had to punch a time clock. We had to remain in our dressing rooms between shows. We could not go out on an errand. That was one engagement I was glad to finish.

I was booked into Lobby # 2, a nightclub in Juarez, Mexico, just across the border from El Paso. A long bus ride took me to El Paso, and after crossing the bridge over the Rio Grande, I found the club close by. Juarez reminded me of Tijuana south of San Diego, but it was larger.

Entering the club I saw many slot machines and gaming tables. A girl who was making change for the customers led me to the dining room area where the orchestra was preparing to rehearse. I met Nina, another dancer, who had arrived earlier. She was petite with large black eyes and long black hair. She told me about her family who had a French restaurant in Hollywood. We decided to share a room in an old hotel in El Paso, which was not much to look at, but served our purpose. We would not spend much time there, and more important, we found a good place to eat nearby that was open late at night when we had our good meal.

Every day we walked across the international bridge to the club to practice. Afterwards, we would go into a little building next door that had a bar that served a small bottle of Cerveza beer. It cost five cents and, better still, there was a dip made of avocados called guacamole. We were alone in the place, and the owner refilled the bowls of chips and dips as soon as we emptied them. He usually fed us so well that we skipped the light lunch we would normally have had.

Everything was great until a cold left me with a cough that kept me awake at night. One evening after the first show, I almost collapsed from weakness brought on by coughing. Someone sent for Mr. Borland, the owner, and he came back to my dressing room to see me. He insisted I should go back to the hotel, go to bed and get some sleep, but I told him I could not sleep because of coughing all night. He got a pint of whiskey and told me to mix it with hot water and I'd get some sleep. Then his driver took me to my hotel.

Mother had doused our family with hot toddies when we had colds. Now, after I undressed, I turned back the covers of the bed, ran the water in the sink until it was hot, and made my drink. It tasted horrible! Without lemon, honey and cloves, it was not at all like Mother's toddies. I forced myself to swallow it and hurried into bed. Many minutes went by and I coughed and stayed awake. I went back to the sink and made another drink. I drank it and hurried back to bed. Nothing happened. So, I finished the bottle! I never knew when Nina came in. Next day, no cough! It was wonderful. My headache disappeared after breakfast, and we went on to practice. In a few days I was fully recovered. I never drank bourbon whiskey again.

The audiences were composed of Americans who enjoyed the reasonable food and the gambling. Mother and Daddy would have enjoyed it; although Mother did not drink, she would have liked the entertainment. After the two weeks had passed, Nina and I took the bus ride together back to Los Angeles.

"What can I do at a skating marathon?" I was talking to Bill Meiklejon in his office. He said, "You will dance several times. They have 'time outs' and then you go into a passageway under the rink, up to a stage in the center and perform."

It was a boring week. They could skate around and around for hours, with an occasional skirmish to change leadership. It did not take long for me to tire of watching them. I never understood the sport's popularity but the stands were always at least half filled in the afternoon and crowded at night.

When Bill Meiklejon came to the rink to pay me on the last afternoon, he asked me to have a soft drink with him at the lunch counter. He said, "Lucile, I am not going to pay you." I know I looked surprised. Then he said, "I have never seen you dance before, and I think anyone who enjoys dancing so much does not need to be paid, too." We talked for awhile and then he handed me my envelope and ended the suspense.

I hardly knew Bill Meiklejon because his mother had usually seen me in the office. Later he became the casting director of a major Hollywood studio. I think I was shy around him because he was so good looking.

Glenda moved back with her parents. So when I opened at the Montmartre in Hollywood, I rented a small nearby apartment. The club was popular, and I stayed there for several shows. There were not too many nights when we would become snow blind (no customers, just white table cloths). It was funny, but often when there were only one or two tables filled, the customers would talk and ignore the entertainment. The show must go on, and we performed, but it was difficult under the circumstances.

I was invited to a party held in one of the cottages of the famous "Garden of Allah." I went out of curiosity to see a place I had heard of for years. The movie stars favored the "Garden" for different reasons, and I think many a star's future career was decided there. There were a number of couples at the party (I never did figure out who the host or hostess were). Having nothing else to do, I kept busy in the minuscule kitchen, pouring drinks, rinsing glasses, and passing hors d'oeuvres. Then the inevitable happened-all the couples disappeared into different rooms, and I was alone. I found my coat and left, deciding I did not like Hollywood parties if they were like this one.

I gave up my Hollywood apartment when I started working at the Italian Village in Los Angeles, right in the business part of town. There was a hotel located above the café, and they gave the performers special rates to stay there. I would go to the stairs in back of the kitchen cafe, go to the first floor to my room, and make my costume changes. Their Italian food was wonderful, and the cafe was well patronized. The schedule was confining because we did a luncheon show besides two nightly performances. Many of the customers were there daily, and their faces became familiar.

The young girl singer insisted I dance in one of the costumes from her dancing days. When our show changed after two weeks, I thought the costume suited my jazz toe dance perfectly. It was a good fit, but I asked her if it was safe, because instead of having the usual two straps going over the shoulders, the top of the bodice ended in a point at the base of my throat with a ribbon which tied in back of my neck. I was right in being concerned because at the matinee I had barely started my dance when the ribbon broke. I quickly held the bodice up with my hands or I would have been bare to the waist. The guests and the orchestra enjoyed my efforts to remain modest. I laughed along with them and gratefully accepted the larger than usual applause.

I become acquainted with one of the customers who would always occupy the booth opposite the swinging doors from the kitchen. Sometimes I would talk with him a little while until he returned to his work with the telephone company. One day after the matinee, he offered me a cigarette because he had forgotten I did not smoke. I playfully took the cigarette just as the swinging doors opened.

Mother stood there, took one look at the cigarette, turned and left. I ran after her. I knew I was in trouble from the expression on her face. We reached my room at the same time, and we did not leave it until we went out to dinner. She scolded me continually. She had often stayed overnight with me and usually I enjoyed her visits, but this night was one I never forgot. From the time we entered the room after the matinee until the small hours of the morning she scolded me. I was accused of doing horrendous things since I had been on my own. I could not convince her that I didn't smoke, drink or do any of the things she accused me of. To get away from her, I locked myself in the bathroom and she finally said, "We will go to bed and discuss this in the morning."

The next morning she had calmed down, forgiven me, and told me she believed me. I was deeply hurt because I had always tried to be everything she wanted me to be, and I could not believe she didn't have more faith in me. She should have known my addiction was a good book and a candy bar. Besides, I never met anyone I wanted to go out with. Frankly, I was not asked too often. I had a reputation as being a goody two shoes.

The next club I was to work for was out in a neighborhood area in Los Angeles. The agent said it would take some doing, but I could open there the same night I closed at the Village. The agent talked to the owners who agreed to the arrangement. My two night performances at the Village would not change, but the new club would start his night show upon my arrival. That was easy because the rest of the show was composed of only a singer. When I finished my last night show at the Village, I said a quick goodbye and dashed back to the new club in a cab. It went smoothly, but I was really tired when I finally took a cab to my apartment.

Without the luncheon shows, I thought it would be easier, but the second night when I finished my first show, the owner told me I was to sit at a table with a dozen men. I explained, "I never mix with the customers." He replied, "You do here. It is part of your job." The agent had put me in an awkward position. I said, "I'll try for one night." It did not work out. I had hardly taken a seat in between two of the men when the one on my left put his hand on my thigh. He laughed at me when I said, "Stop that,"

"What's the matter, aren't you my girl tonight?"

I said, "No. I'm not," and left the table. The owner came to me for an explanation.

"I am a dancer, and I have never mixed with the customers, and I am not going to begin now. You will have to get a new dancer because I am leaving if you expect me to sit with the customers."

After the last show I asked for my two night's pay and went to the phone to call a cab. A man who worked at the club came to me and said he would take me to my hotel. We had talked several times, and he had been just friendly. I had the heavy suitcases and my make up case, so I could not ride the streetcar. He would be saving me another cab fare, so I told him I would appreciate the ride.

When he parked in front of the apartment building, he insisted he should carry my suitcases. Once in the apartment, he looked around and said, "You are ready to turn in I see." Before leaving for work, I had lowered the wall bed in the living room.

Suddenly he grabbed me and pushed me back onto the bed and got on top of me, while trying to kiss me. Recovering from my surprise, I tried to get away from him. He was strong, but I was stronger. I got enough space between us to bite him on the arm as hard as I could. He cursed and sat up as I scrambled to my feet.

"What did you do that for?" he asked.

"You wouldn't let me go so I had to do something."

He was not wearing a coat and I saw his arm was bleeding through the shirt. I took him into the bathroom, put peroxide on his arm and a bandage. He left without another word, and I thought I was lucky he had not turned on me when I bit him. I wondered again why there were so many men who seemed to be so nice and yet could not to be trusted. I also wondered when I would stop making the mistake of trusting people.

I enjoyed working at the Gay Paree and was lucky to be asked there several times. It was on the second floor, with large windows overlooking Westlake Park. We did matinees, and Merle Carson's orchestra played for ballroom dancing before and after the entertainment. I sometimes had an early dinner after the matinee performance, and I would watch the ballroom dancers with envy. Movie star Caeser Romero was a frequent visitor. He was an excellent dancer, and I was envious of his lucky partners.

I was booked to perform on "The Monte Carlo," a gambling ship three miles off the coast. There were launches to take the guests to the ship. I enjoyed the sea breeze on my face when we went to the ship more than I enjoyed the uneven ballroom floor when the ship rolled and my feet never knew where the floor was going to be. The acrobatic dance was especially challenging. I was given a return engagement with six girls I trained, so I enjoyed the high seas for several weeks.

The ship was later destroyed on New Year's Eve, 1936. There had been festivities as usual, but after guests from the Coronado Hotel had left, a heavy gale hit the ship and tore her loose from her moorings. She sank after hitting the rocks south of the resort hotel. For years when the tides were extremely low, this blackened twisted hull could be seen.

My life was not exactly like I had thought it was going to be. I was relieved when Mother called and told me there was a possibility I could work at a nightclub in Long Beach. The club would not be ready for several weeks, and she would let me know when the producer would like to talk to me.

Chapter 13

Mother's phone call telling me there was going to be a production of "The Drunkard" in Long Beach with a possible part for me could not have come at a better time. My career was at a standstill. It was 1934, I was 22 years old, and I felt that I needed to make a change.

Mr. Fountain would stop by to see me when he came to Los Angeles to book pictures. He told me about his habit of every morning starting the day with bills and putting his change at night in a sock in a drawer. He gave me the coins, which helped me more than he realized. It bought me more food than I would have had otherwise. I never forgot his generosity during those hard times.

If I didn't work, I would not have any money. I used every cent wisely but the small salaries did not last long. I could never allow myself time between engagements and would close in one club and open in another the next night. I was persistent in looking for work. If I was not staying any longer at a club, I would go to the agents until I found work for the next week.

Without a car I had to ride streetcars, and because the last show at a night-club would sometimes not even begin until 2:00 in the morning, I had to live in a place that was within walking distance. This meant moving often from one little apartment to another. My arms were strong from my acrobatic work, but carrying heavy suitcases all the time kept my muscles toned up, too.

The small clubs were paying fifteen dollars a week, less ten percent for the agent. A welcome change was playing a theater for a weekend, giving me ten dollars a day. Then I would have the rest of the week so I could take lessons or go to Long Beach to see Mother.

Cooking in my small apartments kept expenses down, especially when I found there were many ways of cooking hamburger. Making popcorn in a tiny frying pan was my only treat.

The local agents kept me busy, but my salary never changed because I was not booked into the higher priced nightclubs. Their talent was booked in from the New York agencies, and they brought in new faces from the east or Europe.

I was told I could audition for work at the Cotton Club, one of the larger clubs. When I walked into the room, I almost turned and walked out again, when I realized I was to audition for the man who had produced the "Idea" I had to leave in Utica, New York. During my audition, I fell when I was doing my final spotters in my acrobatic routine. I was either nervous or the floor was too slippery. I never worked the Cotton Club. I walked out after I had dressed in my street clothes. I would never work there as long as he was the producer of the shows.

I registered with a new young agent, who had just opened an office, and we would talk about how hard it was to make a name for oneself. Occasionally we would go to an inexpensive restaurant and it would be "Dutch treat." He arranged a meeting with the producer of the floorshows at one of the leading hotels. The man's attitude told me he thought I was the agent's girl friend. Our talk terminated when he told me I would need a new wardrobe, much more abbreviated than the costumes shown in my picture folio. The idea of dancing in close proximity to the audience with nothing but a tiny bra and G-string for my attire did not appeal to me. He had not even asked me to audition for him. My body, not my talent, obviously was to be the attraction. When I told him I would never change to the type of attire he asked for, I never heard from him.

There was one booking office representing a well-known New York agency that I had not registered with, so I decided to take my pictures there. The only one in the reception room was the attractive secretary who said the agent would see me. When I entered his office, all the leather furniture and the massive desk impressed me. The large, well-dressed man held out his hand for my pictures and motioned for me to sit in a large upholstered chair opposite his desk.

I told him I was a dancer and gave him a brief resume of where I had worked. I began to get uneasy because of the way he was looking me over as he asked me questions. I pulled my skirt down over my knees, as far down as it would go. He listened intently as I told him about my work with Fanchon & Marco and other theatrical work until he left his desk and went behind my chair. When he came from behind my chair, he was displaying himself, and I heard him say, "Be a nice girl..." I didn't hear any more. I jumped to my feet and ran from the room, past the secretary and down the stairs. I didn't need work that badly. I never went back for my pictures; I didn't want to see that office again.

I did have one friend I had known since we had worked together in the NRA Revue. Vince and I would meet for a Dutch treat lunch and matinee once in awhile. He wasn't doing too well either and was talking about going home to San Francisco. He did leave and I really missed him because he had been such fun to be with. Vince had been the only one I knew in Los Angeles besides the agents.

Mother's suggestion that I call the man in Long Beach seemed logical. I phoned the producer of "The Drunkard" and he told me I had been so highly recommended I did not need to audition. He wanted to know if I was interested in taking part in the play. I would not have any lines; the part would be the hero's half-wit sister. She was a mute, so I would just memorize the entrances and exits and pantomime her part. He explained "The Drunkard" was an old time drama that had successfully played in Hollywood for years. The setting was a small stage with a roll up curtain and old fashioned footlights. The audience sat at small tables, ate peanuts and threw the shells on the floor. They booed the villain, and cheered the hero and heroine. The drama would be seen once a night and there would be dancing and two floor shows, I was to dance inthe floor shows. He offered me twenty-five dollars a week, without taking out ten percent for an agent fee.

When I moved in with Mother and Alton, I realized how unhappy I had been. I hadn't known how much I missed my family. It was the first time I had lived at home since my parent's separation, and I missed my Daddy. Papers for a divorce had not been filed, but there was not much doubt that the marriage was over. I had mixed feelings. My Daddy and I had always understood each other without saying much. When I had dinner with him one evening I was relieved to find that he did not consider my dancing a factor in their divorce. Incompatible was a new popular reason for a divorce, and they had been incompatible for many years.

On the day of the first rehearsal, I was given the script. It was a story of an orphaned young woman and her brother who owed the villain money. The villain had dishonorable intentions towards the young, innocent woman, who was in love with a gallant young fellow. His half-wit sister had little to do. I was to mime fear of the villain whenever we were in the same scene. My lover was missing and my big scene occurred when I was wandering in the dark forest by myself. I came upon the body of my lover, who had been slain, and I screamed. I had never screamed and wanted to try it first when I was alone. One morning, I was vacuuming the upstairs bedroom in the front of the house. Mother was downstairs in the backyard talking with Edna, the lady who lived downstairs with her husband. I thought the vacuum would be loud enough to cover the sound if I tried a scream. I took a big breath and did it! Immediately, Mother and Edna rushed up the stairs and came to me. "Are you all right? What happened?" I explained I was just rehearsing my scream for the play. They said I certainly did not have to worry about being heard. That afternoon, at the rehearsal, I screamed. The director was impressed and said, "Good!" That worry was behind me.

The performances were a success and enjoyed a long run. The part I played was not very demanding, but I gave it my best. My costume was a long dress of a drab material. I tried different kinds of make up and decided a pale face with the slightest of shadows under my eyes made me look sad. If I looked downcast, without any expression in my face, and did not smile, I felt I interpreted the role. Mostly I kept close to my brother, the hero of the piece. For my big scene, the spotlight followed my slow walk across the stage, in front of a curtain depicting a dark forest. The audience made sad oooh sounds. My scream startled the audience every show.

There was a long bar at the side of the cabaret room. It was partitioned off, except for a small archway with a curtain strung across the opening. Without fail, every night when I screamed, someone's head would pop around the curtain to see what had happened.

It was late after the second floor show, so my biggest problem was transportation. The last bus of the night took me to where I could transfer to the last streetcar. When I got off the streetcar I had several blocks to walk on the dark streets to our duplex.

Sometimes Alton would come to take me home. One night, he came after the last floorshow had started, and I was performing when he came into the room. When I finished my dance, I did my usual "get dressed fast and catch my bus routine." Shortly after I arrived home, the telephone rang and I answered it. It was Alton.

"What are you doing home? Why didn't you come to me so I could take you home?" I told him, I didn't know he was there.

"You looked right at me and smiled." He had not realized I could not see him with the spotlight in my eyes, and I was glad my smile looked so personal.

I told him, "Next time, come backstage after I finish my dance."

Mother was washing clothes one morning while I was making the bed in the front bedroom. I thought I heard her call my name and hurried to the back door that was at the top of the steps. She was sitting on the bottom step holding her right foot. She had broken her ankle. Now it was my turn to take care of her.

One morning, several weeks later, Mother said I had a long distance call from Vince in San Francisco. He told me he was working at the Embassy Nightclub and suggested that I come there and audition. They changed their show every three weeks, and they sometimes held the dancer for a second show. He felt sure I would be there for six weeks. I loved San Francisco and told Mother I'd like to go.

Mother said, "You can go, but I want to stay here because I'm enjoying my work at the drug store."

She was a cashier and was making friends and seeing people she had not seen for awhile. It was her first experience earning a salary and she wanted to continue to support herself. I told her to stay, but she could have a home with me anytime.

The call had come at a good time. Two nights before, a notice had been posted backstage that the show was going to close. I called Vince and told him I was going to be at liberty-show biz parlance for out of work. I told him I would be happy to come to San Francisco.

Vince arranged a room for me at his hotel, which was convenient to the cable car I would use. The line ended a block from the Embassy Club. The cable car was then driven onto a turntable so that the men could push it around to go back to Market Street.

The evening after I arrived in San Francisco, I went to the club for my audition. Walking toward the club from the cable car, I could see the celebrated Fisherman's Wharf a block farther down the street. Before I reached the wharf I saw an awning marked "Embassy Club" in front of a flight of stairs. At the top, the Maitre D' approached me and I told him that I was going to audition.

He led me to the side of the band area and pulled a curtain aside. He then told me to go up the stairs. Vince was in the hallway at the top. He introduced me to the girls in the dressing room, where I changed. After giving my music to the leader, I prepared for my dance at the end of the next intermission. Because of the excellent dinners served here, there were early diners, so I had a sizable audience to please. When the intermission was over, I was ready. Before coming down the stairs I had put some water on the tips of my toe slippers. If they were damp, I might be able to avoid slipping on the dance floor. Vince explained to the audience, that they were to see a guest artist. The introduction to my music, "Tales of the Vienna Woods," started. As I did my first step, I knew I was in trouble! The floor was suitable for ballroom dancing, but not for a toe dance. When I finished my dance with turns, I did a double pirouette but, hitting a good balance this time, I went around for a third turn. My foot, slipped, and suddenly I was down on the floor on my derriere. Oh well. I crossed my arms in front of me and made like a Russian dancer, shooting my feet out in front of me. The leader called out for the Hungarian Dance music and that wonderful group of musicians played it with gusto. The audience laughed with me as I scrambled to my feet.

Later in the show, I was to do the Stardust routine. I asked Vince if I was still doing it. He said not to worry. My little comedy act had taken care of the fall. Asking for some water from a waiter, I made a little puddle of it in a corner and stood in it so the soles of my ballet slippers would be damp. The Embassy audience was unusually appreciative for Stardust, which I was to find out later was typical. There were so many regulars, they really seemed to take pride in the performer's work. When I had finished dressing into my street clothes, I went down to meet Vince, who was waiting for me at the foot of the stairs. He took me to the office of

Mr. Spohn, one of the club's owners. After Mr. Spohn had complimented me, he got right down to business.

"Will you be able to be in the next show? Your salary will be thirty-five dollars a week. Each show lasts three weeks. You may be asked to be in the next show. Dancers can only be in two shows, our rule. You will do three shows a night, seven nights a week. We do not have room for a separate dressing room, so you will dress with the girls."

When I said I would be happy to work at the club, Spoonie, as everyone called him, seemed bored. When he started to look at some papers on his desk, I knew I was being dismissed. Vince had left after introducing us. I made my way back to his dressing room, and I told him I was hired and he asked me what I thought of Spoonie. I told him I did not have an opportunity to even thank him. "Sounds just like him, a man of few words," Vince said, as he took me to a back table to watch the second show. I did not tell him Spoonie made me think of a moving picture gangster. I never talked to the other owner. I saw him, but his appearance and manner really intimidated me. They turned out to be the best owners I had ever worked for, and as far as I knew, their only interest was the club.

When I had come to my first rehearsal, Dottie Dobson had made room for me to sit next to her at the long make-up table. The Dobson sisters had been choreographing the production numbers for a long time. Dottie was interested in my knowledge of many different types of dancing.

I was asked to stay for the next show. I offered to help the sisters with the dances for the new show. Dottie told Spoonie she would like to feature me in the production numbers. We worked so well together, I was asked to stay for another show, then another. My engagement not only lasted more than two shows, but I was there for two years! Fisherman's Wharf was a popular tourist attraction and the club was a favorite place to visit. Visitors went to the Embassy, not only for the excellent food, but also for the fine entertainment.

On many occasions, before the last show, a waiter would come to the dressing room, give me a 20 dollar bill, and tell me someone was requesting Star Dust for the late show. That $20 was like a $100 now. The tip was from customers who had missed the second show when I did my acrobatic dance and had told their visiting friends about the girl that kicked her head with both feet! So I did Stardust again in the third show.

Soon after I became a steady at the Embassy, I had a long distance telephone call from my Aunt Bea. She had been one of the casualties of the Depression. The bank in Los Angeles where she had worked for so many years had fired many of the old staff and employed new people at lower salaries. Those newly unemployed were to suffer the most in the depression. Fortunately, she had saved some money and this helped for awhile, but then she was in the position of having to take anything she could.

Mother had told me that Bea had been given work as a secretary that entailed traveling. Bea was calling me to tell me she had to leave her employer because he wanted more than her secretarial work. She was in Oregon and asked if she could join me. Of course I said yes, and a week later we moved into an apartment. After two or three months, she went to work in a department store selling dresses. When the buyer went to another more exclusive store, she took Bea with her. Bea made friends and soon she was enjoying life again.

Vince was busy with the AGVA, the American Guild of Variety Artists. It was a new Union in San Francisco and Vince was instrumental in getting it started.

I had resumed my friendships with Brownie and Barney, two friends of several years. I knew them when I had worked in San Francisco before. Vince knew them, too, and we started to have games of pinochle after the night's work was done. He and the fellows would bring beer and I would prepare a night snack for us. Bea would go to sleep earlier on our pull down wall bed, and when I came home, she would dress and join us. We would play cards until the early hours, and she would have time for a catnap before she went to work. With steady work, good friends, an apartment where I could cook what I wanted, I was happier than I had ever been.

Before our card game one night, I was trying to make the avocado dip I had enjoyed so much in Juarez. As usual, cutting the onions made my eyes water. Bea and I began to laugh when I began to emote like a dramatic actress weeping.

We heard a man's voice coming up from a window, a few floors below us. "Quiet down up there. Some people have to sleep." We didn't think we were making that much noise. When the fellows arrived we told them we would have to be especially quiet. We thought we were, but our downstairs person still objected, calling out, "Quiet up there."

Later on we heard the sound of someone in the hallway walking very quietly. We were next to the stairway, and we could hear that door being opened and closed very carefully. We were all sitting holding our breath trying to decide what was going on when there was a knock at our door. I went to the door and could see the outline of a uniformed man through the frosted window. I opened the door, and a tall police officer looked down at me. I was much smaller than he was because, as usual, I was barefoot. I felt like a little kid. I invited this officer and a young policeman, obviously a rookie, to come into the brief hallway of our apartment. In a gruff voice, the officer said, "What is going on here?"

Vince came to us and explained we were playing pinochle and wouldn't the men come in and have a beer? They came into the tiny kitchen area, and the older man accepted a beer while the rookie, reluctantly I thought, refused. Vince offered them some crackers and guacamole.

"Try this and perhaps you can tell us what is missing. We know it needs something, but what?" They took crackers and dipped into the guacamole. "Umm. Do you have any garlic in this?"

The officer had turned to me. "No, I never have used it." I said. He suggested, "Try it. I think that's all it needs." Then he continued, "One of the tenants called the police to complain about a wild party, but we had trouble finding it."

I said, "It was you in the hallway!"

"Yes, it was. We'll go downstairs and check with the manager." I offered to go with him, but he said that I was not the problem.

The next day the manager informed me the tenant had been asked to leave. "He had no business calling the police, and I don't want it to happen again." She smiled at me and that was that.

Oh yes! I went to North Beach, the Italian section, and bought garlic. I've never been without it since.

I continued to keep "Stardust" in the nine o'clock show, besides doing the production number. No problem. I changed my costumes often because Mother had made several for the dance. I did not change the music because it had become associated with me.

The first and last shows were the same. I did one group number and one of my other dances. They had to be changed every three weeks. I did many types of dances: Russian, Oriental, Spanish, Hawaiian, Rumba, Tap, and also my different toe dances, Jazz and Classical, including a sophisticated dance to "Mood Indigo" that was a forerunner of the modern jazz dance popular today.

Having to use only one of these dances every three weeks made it easy. Helping with the choreography and making up a new dance for the production number was fun for me. I helped design the costumes. I didn't have to choose music or mark the orchestrations. No wonder I had good health.

After seven nights a week for a year, without any days off, I approached Spoonie in his office one night. I told him I loved working at the Embassy Club but did not want to lose my enthusiasm. Could I miss a show? I had refused several offers to dance at the Edgewater Beach Club, and I wanted to try it. It would be to a different clientele. To my relief, Spoonie gave me the time off with the stipulation that I would rehearse for the following show.

The Edgewater Beach Club was a rambling white building situated on the long avenue fronting the ocean. The dining room where I performed was large. Alongside the orchestra was a curving staircase to a balcony. My dressing room, including a bathroom, was located up the stairs to the balcony. Between shows, I had the quiet times I missed at the Embassy because the girls were always talking.

Unless I was reading or embroidering, I would go out on the balcony to watch the scene below. The view to the dining room below looked like something from a motion picture set with crystal chandeliers, snowy white tablecloths and all the correct table settings. Ladies in beautiful gowns and gentlemen in tuxedos were reflected in the immense windows on the ocean side, and when I danced, they were polite and receptive. It was a pleasure to dance for them.

One night the orchestra played a trick on me. I am sure the drummer instigated it because I had fun tripping him up by changing my acrobatic dance so he had to be alert to make the proper percussion sounds for my kicks. I was finishing my Oriental dance, doing the turns I had used in the "Screenland Melodies Idea," hopping on one foot with the other foot extended while I turned rapidly, ending with a circle of turns. I sank to the floor, assuming the exotic pose that signified the end of the dance. The audience, as usual, had started their applause on my turns. Holding my pose, I realized the musicians had continued to play! Evidently they were doing a sixteen bar repeat! Rising to my feet, I repeated the last steps, finishing with another circle of turns and my pose. The audience gamely started to applaud again. Thank goodness the music ended properly and the dance was over. I laughed along with the men, then sped up the stairs for my costume change.

Practicing was still important even though I was working. I would go to the club earlier in the day and work out. The bartenders would be practicing, too. One of the house specialties was Pousse-Cafe. For this a small elegant thin glass is filled with several layers of liquor. It is difficult to do this without letting the different liquors mix. When the men found out I had a sweet tooth, they would call me over to the bar and give me a Pousse-Cafe they had practiced on. They could not be made until they were ordered and cost more because they took so much time to make. The alcohol content was low. It just tasted good. Because it was a sweet after dinner drink, I doubt if anyone had more than one.

Soon I started rehearsals for the next show at the Embassy, and then I was back to the old stand. Needless to say, other dancers in town envied me because a long engagement at one place was very unusual.

One night Vince introduced me to an elderly man who informed me he would like to invite the people on the show to have dinner on his yacht in the harbor. Would I arrange for two groups on two nights, one for the principals and one for the girls? When I told him about having arranged this kind of dinner in Vancouver, he was delighted and hoped I would do the same for him. One afternoon, I met the girls at the yacht club and we went to the yacht in a trim motor boat. A few days later, I did the same for the acts. Lucky me! I was a guest twice. To see the lights reflected on the water was wonderful, and I loved the gentle rocking of the boat. He had made a lovely gesture and one we all enjoyed.

In show business, we could work for many months without a night off, and our schedule was always the same. Our energy was high after our performances, and it took awhile to relax. We would be hungry, so went out to eat, and when we were seen having fun together, we were often censured and thought to be "wild." Our conversation and laughter was never louder than people who were having dinner at 6:00 in the evening, but our dinner was at two in the morning.

Vince would ask me to join him and his friends. Quite often I would be the only girl with three or four men. I enjoyed their talk about politics and business, or just listened to them trying to top each other's jokes.

I remembered Daddy's advice; "Never take a second drink until you know the effect the first one is going to have on you." Our family always had liquor in the house, but no one ever drank heavily. I liked the taste of some liquor but stopped if I began to feel any effect of it. I wanted to be in control of all my actions at all times. Anyway, I was in the bar for the company of my friends, not for the liquor. I could make one drink last for a long time.

I asked Vince if he thought I dared ask Spoonie for time off again. My wish was granted, and again he told me I still had a place in the next show. After a week of rest, I was booked for two weeks into a club across the bay in Oakland. The manager of the club asked me to represent his club at the annual President Roosevelt birthday party.

There were big benefits for the March of Dimes in order to provide more money for research for the dreaded disease Polio. The nightclubs and theaters furnished the entertainment with movie stars donating their time. The manager had given the Oakland Tribune the picture of me as a monkey in a handstand to publicize. The following night, one of the waiters knocked on my dressing room door, and said a reporter was asking for me. He introduced me to Walter Cochrane. He asked me to have a drink with him. I told him I would like a soft drink. He ordered a Scotch for himself and a Coca-Cola for me. Then he said, "I want to apologize for the error in the first edition."

"I was not aware there was an error," I said.

He unfolded the paper he was carrying and showed me my monkey picture upside down. It certainly looked funny with my hands up on the ceiling and my body hanging down into space. We talked for awhile, and he gave me the paper for my scrapbook. I was saying thank you for the picture and good night when he asked if I would have dinner with him at the club the next night. I started to say no, but then I thought a dinner at the club should be safe, so I said yes. The next night we did not talk about show business. He told me about some of his experiences as a newspaper reporter. I was able to talk to him about current events, which was a novelty for me. I found him extremely interesting. He was so different that I guess I was intrigued. We started to see each other often. He was of average height with dark blond hair that had a wave in it like my brother's, and blue eyes. He was not handsome, but then he was not bad looking either. He was eleven years my senior, and he drank more than I had ever seen anyone drink, although he never seemed to get high. After I went back to the Embassy Club, he would visit me there. His best friend was the photographer who went with him on assignments. The photographer's wife and I became friends, and Sundays were generally spent with them.

Walter's heavy drinking bothered me, and Bea agreed with me when I decided I had better stop seeing him. Walter's friends, the Dennisons, especially Denny, talked me into keeping the relationship going. He told me I had been a good influence on Walter, and he knew Walter cared for me.

A few months later my brother wrote to me telling me of his approaching marriage to Henrietta. When I told Walter I was flying down to Long Beach for the wedding and coming back the same day, he said he would like to go with me. I thought perhaps it would be a good idea for him to meet my family, so I consented.

Spoonie let me have the night off, and we both flew off to Long Beach. Alton was too busy getting married to Henrietta to see much of Walter, but Mother was with us most of the afternoon. She showed disapproval of Walter when she and I were alone for a few minutes before we left.

On the plane on the way home, Walter surprised me, saying, "Let's get married as soon as we can get a license."

I did not think it was a good idea, but he persuaded me we belonged together. I was foolish enough to think he would not drink so much if we were married. I began to feel I was becoming an old maid. Many of the girls around me were already married. I was 23 and still single! I thought the feeling I had for Walter was enough for marriage. I was sure by then no one was ever going to make me feel like I had felt about Burt in Chicago.

We had a civil ceremony on the following Saturday, with our friends the Dennisons as our witnesses. It was two weeks before I called Mother and told her. Fortunately, Alton was home because she almost fainted, and I had to call them back. Alton was also upset, but they did give me their blessings.

My new husband and I found the perfect apartment across from picturesque Merritt Lake. It was a corner apartment with a large kitchen, dining room, and corner living room all tastefully furnished. There was just one bedroom, but it had a sunroom next to it with a couch, small table and a chair.

We had been married in the morning, and I worked that night. Between shows we sat at a table and enjoyed being fussed over by my co-workers. I was a married woman now with a few drinks of champagne, and when he put his arm around me in the cab on the way to our new home, I kissed him more fervently than before.

To my surprise he pushed me away, and in an angry voice said, "I wondered how you would be with a man if you had been drinking." That rather dampened my enthusiasm, and our marriage was off to a poor beginning.

When I cooked all of our meals, Walter was amazed. He didn't think showgirls knew how to cook. I was to find out he thought all dancers fit in one category and did not realize that the girl he married had been raised by a strict mother and had never been far away from her influence. I think he thought I had more experience with men, too.

One of the girls at the Embassy said she had a surprise for me. Her Father had been hunting and had given her a package containing a dove, and two ducks. She knew I was familiar with wild fowl because in the dressing room between shows we had talked about cooking. She did not know how to cook them, and she thought I would know.

Walter said, "What are you going to do with them?"

I told him, "Wait and see."

When he sat down to my meal of roasted birds, complete with stuffing, mashed potatoes and giblet gravy, he really was surprised.

It was not easy working at the Embassy in San Francisco and living in Oakland. After the last show, I had to take a taxi from the club to the Ferry building at the end of Market Street. The last passenger ferry had left but I could make the 2:00am automobile ferry. It was against the law to walk onto it, so I joined others in the same predicament. All that was necessary was to walk alongside the cars waiting in line and wait for someone to ask if you needed a ride. (I would not do that nowadays.) I was lucky in getting rides with couples returning from a night on the town or going home from work. My favorite driver drove the Examiner truck that was taking a load of newspapers to Oakland. The driver tried to get there in time, because he worried about my hitching rides, but most of the time I had to do just that.

After arriving in Oakland I would ask my benefactor to take me to a corner a couple of blocks from home. Our home was practically in the center of town, so it was not dark and there were always people on the street. If I did ride with a single man, the ride from the ferry was so short there was not enough time to get personal. Conversation came easily because I would tell them where I had been and where I was going. To most people show business is glamorous, and there were always questions. I always refused any offers to go and have coffee.

When I arrived home after my ferry ride, Walter would be in bed. At first, I would think he was asleep, but finally I realized he hurried to be in bed each night before I got home and was only faking sleep. He spent his time and money in bars. Consequently, I never knew what kind of a mood he would be in. I never said anything to him about his drinking. I knew it would lead to an argument, something I was not good at.

One night I had quietly taken my place beside him in bed. By then we had been married about three months. I had just gone to sleep when I was suddenly kicked out of bed.

"Why?" I asked.

His answer totally amazed me. "How many agents have you slept with before we were married?"

He was furious and drunk. I began to think I had made a dreadful mistake. My husband was a jealous man with a wild imagination. I was married to a man with whom I only spent time on Sundays and in the evenings at the club. Our working hours had been so different. My foolish idea that our marriage would make a change in his drinking habits had been a fruitless desire. He probably was disappointed, too, because instead of a hot little number, he had married a dancer who did not have much energy left to make love after working hard. His breath was enough to discourage me anyhow.

I was worn out from the work, commuting, and doing my daily chores as a housewife. It was not strange that one morning I awoke with a horrible sore throat. I could not swallow, and I had a high fever. I made an appointment with a doctor, and after examining my throat he told me I had strep throat, which could be dangerous if I did not take care of it.

He told me to go home, take my medicine, and stay in bed, because I was really sick. I was as weak as a baby. Going to work was out of the question. The pain was intense. I could not swallow anything, but sucked on ice for moisture. I went home after getting my prescription filled, and called the Embassy Club. When I told Spoonie I was sick, he said not to worry. He would get a temporary replacement for me. When Mother learned I was sick, she came to take care of me. She slept on the couch in the sunroom. Under Mother's care, I gradually improved.

I had just recovered when Alton called to tell me my father had passed away. I went alone to the funeral because Mother did not want to go. She said she would stay and take care of Walter and the apartment. I decided to take the bus to Long Beach. I went by the Greyhound bus line and tried their new nighttime bus, with sleeping accommodations. They had built a few busses with compartments that converted to a bunk with curtains just like the Pullman cars on the trains. I found it comfortable but I spent most of the night looking out the window. When Alton took me to the funeral parlor, I saw Daddy looking as though he had just gone to sleep for awhile. I wished I could have told him how much I loved him and how sorry I was that we had grown so far apart. I never had a chance to know him after I had grown up. He had given me so much as a child, showing me how to do practical things that other girls did not know. A few years later, I realized even more how much he had taught me.

Mother went back to her job in Long Beach and left Walter and me alone. They were so different, they had not become very friendly.

Walter had decided I should not continue with my work but should stay at home and be a housewife. My illness had taken my strength so I was agreeable to the idea. Without my salary, we no longer could afford the lovely apartment. We moved into a much smaller place. It had a tiny breakfast room that was part of the kitchen and a small living room that became our bedroom when the wall bed was pulled down. We were still by Lake Merritt. It only took me one morning to move after Walter went to work, we had so few possessions. When he came home that evening, everything was in place and dinner was ready. He did not have to move a finger and just said everything looked fine. We did not have a car. He had had a bad car wreck he told me, and since then had not driven. He never explained, but his nicotine-stained fingers were gnarled with scar tissue from being burned. He could still punch the keys of a typewriter rapidly with his two forefingers. If he had not spent so much money on cigarettes and liquor we could have afforded a car, but I was the only one who thought so. It later appeared to me that perhaps he was not allowed to have a license.

I persuaded the custodian to let me plant some pretty flowers beside the driveway to the garages. He asked the other tenants to drive carefully so they would not run over them. I had a few plants in the apartment, too.

Every day Walter would call and tell me to meet him at the bar in the Tribune building. What an education I received then! He did not mind my hearing the stories the fellows told, and some were really wild. Show business jokes were pretty awful but did not hold a candle to the stories I heard while waiting for my husband to say it was time to go home.

He began to take me to his favorite places now that we had time together, and often we went to Izzy Gomez's bar in San Francisco, one of the newspaper reporter's hangouts. The specialty of the house was a Ramos Fizz. The place was reminiscent of Barbary Coast days, and Izzy himself was quite a character. I preferred the place that had a long bar, peanut shells on the floor, and every kind of beer that you could think of. There were always other reporters there, and I would listen fascinated with the stories they would tell.

We had planned a vacation, and just a few nights before we left, the custodian told us his Cocker Spaniel had a litter of pups and asked us if we wanted to see them. I had played with the dog and was anxious to see her babies. One puppy liked me, and I fell in love with him. Before we left on our trip we bought him and reluctantly left him with his mother.

Our trip to Susanville, California, was a welcome break because we stayed with friends who drank moderately. They took us to see how a huge lumber sawmill operated in the forest, and we spent the week either sightseeing or just resting and talking. It was a new experience for me, and I really enjoyed it. Walter was nicer when he was not drinking and our relationship improved.

When we returned home I found a very sick puppy with pneumonia, and I was told he might die. After some TLC, he recovered fully. We did not know what to call him until one evening Walter remarked that he had a good scoop on a story that day. The word scoop made my small Cocker Spaniel run to Walter, and from then on he was called Scoop. We took walks part way around Lake Merritt and my strength returned.

One evening I told my husband I thought I might be pregnant. I was thrilled, because I had always dreamed of having a family someday. Instead of joy, his face showed consternation. I thought he was concerned for my health because he said, "We will have to find a Doctor."

"Not yet," I said.

Then he really shocked me when he said, "You will have to have an abortion. I don't want a bastard! In the Catholic religion I am still married to my first wife. The divorce meant nothing. You and I had a civil marriage."

Fortunately, I was not pregnant. But I couldn't forget his reaction. It was so humiliating to realize that in his mind we were not married but just living together.

Walter had an offer to work for another newspaper, the Times in Los Angeles. We packed our personal clothes and, not having any furniture, moving south was easy. We found an apartment in the Silver Lake district. The apartment had a theatrical air, built to look like a Moorish home. Scoop and I were alone afternoons and evenings because Walter worked the night shift. Scoop was a good companion for me. He would not let me out of his sight and followed me when I cleaned the rooms as if he were trying to help me. I decided to train him.

"Hector and his Pups" was an animal act that I had liked when we were on the same bill at theaters. His dogs were all breeds, and I never saw him mistreat them. When they did all their tricks, they got a loving pat or a tasty treat as a reward. When I decided my well-mannered dog should learn to do some tricks, he thrived on the extra attention. His daily food would be placed on the floor, and he would not touch it until I said, "All right." When I left the room and did not return for a few minutes, he would wait patiently by his dish until I returned to give him permission to eat. He would sit up or lie down and stay until I said the magic word, "all right." He even said his prayers. I would place a morsel of food on the seat of a chair. He would go to the chair and sit up with his paws on the edge of it, placing his head on his paws in a prayerful position.

Scoop was a sad dog on the Sundays when I would go alone to see Mother in Long Beach. She had that day off from her position as cashier in the drug store. At first I would always leave at the same time. Then I had to vary the time because my suspicious husband thought I was cheating with the conductor of the streetcar. That was funny! Then I had to stop going to the same butcher shop all the time because he accused me of having an affair with the butcher! I was beginning to be afraid to talk to anyone.

The living room of the apartment was large, so I started to practice. Unfortunately, just when I began to feel I was in shape again, I caught a bad cold and Mother insisted I see her doctor in Long Beach. He told her I was not getting better because he thought I did not care about living very much. He said I was an unhappy person. He was not far wrong. Walter said we had to move to a cheaper apartment. We moved to a smaller apartment over a garage in back of the owner's home. The soles of my shoes were so thin I inserted cardboard in order to keep my feet off the ground.

Walter started to come home later and later. Many nights I would make myself as attractive as I could and try and keep awake for him. I never complained but just tried harder to make our marriage work. One day, he came into the kitchen and stood behind me. I hadn't heard him, and when he touched me, I screamed. I was not doing so well.

Because I still had a bad cough from my cold, Mother insisted I see her doctor again. Riding in the Red Car on the way to an appointment, I looked out the window and said to myself, "What am I going to do?"

A voice said to me. "You do not have to stay with him."

There was no one next to me, but I distinctly heard a voice! At the same time, a peaceful feeling came over me, and suddenly I knew what I had to do. Mother was waiting for me. "Lucile, what happened?"

I told her about the voice. "I've decided I am going to leave Walter."

She hugged me and said, "It must have been your Guardian angel. It's about time you came to your senses." She had never approved of the marriage, but had never interfered.

There was not too much to do in leaving the furnished apartment. When my two bags were packed, I was sad to see that the apartment did not look any different. The only money I had spent since our marriage was on groceries and what I needed to keep the house clean. I was too frightened to tell Walter of my decision. After he left for work one day, I wrote a note, then hugged Scoop and cried. He was the only thing I would miss. I had nothing to show for my two years of marriage. The only wedding presents I had were a blanket and the gift we had received from Mr. Fountain, a beautiful cut glass pitcher set. I had plenty of room for them in my bag because there was not much personal clothing.

Alton came to take me home. A week later, I packed the costumes, makeup and shoes Mother had been saving for me, and I returned to San Francisco to the apartment with Bea.

Mother wrote and told me Walter had phoned and said he wanted to talk to me. He had asked, "Is Lucile ready to come home yet?" He was dumbfounded when he heard that, instead of waiting for his call, I was back in San Francisco looking for work.

Chapter 14

Bea and I moved into an apartment on Leavenworth Street on Nob Hill, but not a part of the ritzy Nob Hill district. It was close to the cable car line so we had easy transportation to downtown for both of us. She could go to work and I could go to the clubs.

The living room and dining rooms were separated by double sliding doors. We each had a wall bed with a long closet behind it. Doors went into the little hallway, with the kitchen on one side and the bathroom on the other. Large windows had similar views of the brick walls of the adjoining apartment houses. The curtains hid that uninviting scene. In San Francisco, apartments rarely had an outside view. Divorce was not on my mind. I would have to save money until I could obtain one. I was told that Walter had started seeing a woman reporter soon after we moved to Los Angeles. I had believed him when he said he was working late or just out with the boys. This also accounted for the money that had gone. I had not missed him very much, and I felt easier about leaving him when I learned about his infidelity.

My reputation from my long session at the Embassy Club helped me to find work. Before I could start working, I had to join the American Guild of Variety Artists. Since I had left the Embassy and gone to Los Angeles, the union had become stronger. It was easy to join, and when that was taken care of, I was booked for two weeks in

Vallejo, California. I was glad to work outside of town until I was in better condition.

The club was far from the town and hotels. I was offered living quarters in the motel on the same property. It was close to the club, and I was able to do the practicing I needed every day. My unit had a bedroom with a double bed and an enclosed screen porch with a single bed. I decided to sleep there.

I needed music for the new dance I was working on. On Saturday I took the bus into San Francisco to buy the orchestration. When I got back to my room, I stopped in surprise when I opened the door. I had been told that I would be having a roommate, but not a man. Masculine gear was on the bureau, loafer shoes were on the floor, and a shirt and slacks were on a chair. I went to the club to protest. The first person I saw was a good-looking man, or was it a man? No, it was a good looking woman dressed like a man.

She came to me and said, "I am the new M.C. My name is Roberta, and you must be my roommate, Lucile? I am sorry I left things lying around, but I didn't have much time. I'll go over between shows and put my clothes away."

After the last show, we returned to our place. She took the bed, and I said I would continue to sleep on the porch. Still nervous, I did not go to sleep until I knew she was asleep. The next day I was relieved when I was told I could move into another place by myself. Roberta was expecting a "friend," so we were each given a place with a bedroom, bath and kitchen facility.

After my initial shock, Roberta and I would have many laughs together between shows. She found I had a wealth of stories from my days of listening to the reporters at the Oakland Tribune. I had not told them before, but I remembered them as I started to relate them to her. She loved them. It was the first and last time I ever told most of the jokes. They definitely were not parlor stories. Two nights after her young girlfriend arrived, I heard a dreadful commotion. The next day, I found out the fight was about me, and I decided to stay away from Roberta.

I was introduced to a good looking young man, tan and physically fit, obviously an outdoorsman. He said he spent a lot of time with his sailboat and asked me to go sailing with him on the bay. It sounded like fun, so I set the time to go sailing with him. It was a beautiful, sunny day with a little breeze. He was expert in handling the sails and told me how I could help. It was such a frail craft, I was nervous. If I had known how to swim, I would have enjoyed it more. That water looked deep! I didn't want to go sailing again, so I never saw him after that.

I refused the offer to stay for another two weeks. The morning I was to leave, I packed and left my baggage behind the curtains in the makeshift closet. I checked out at the office, had some breakfast at the coffee shop, and went back to my room for my bags before I caught the bus to San Francisco. I opened the door and heard a scream. I found that not only had the room been rented, but the bed was occupied! Keeping my eyes straight ahead of me, I hastily went to the curtains, picked up my bags and left. The maid had not seen my luggage while cleaning the room and evidently had reported the room was available.

Two things I made clear with the agents when I went to them. I did not do "smokers," the shows that had strip dancers, and I did not mix with the customers. More than ever, I appreciated my two years at the Embassy club.

One of my favorite clubs was the 365 Club on Market; I worked there more than once. They had an unusual attraction: "The Girl in the Fishbowl." She wore nude-colored body tights and looked like she was swimming in a large fish bowl. I believe she was actually downstairs, and the illusion was done with mirrors. She could converse with the customers, and there was always someone at the bowl when she was performing. While I was working at the 365 Club, I attended a union meeting. The topic under discussion was "B" girls, girls who sat with customers. I asked to be recognized and gave my opinion about the situation.

One girl said, "I meet men that way."

I told her, "I am working in clubs to make my living as a dancer, certainly not to meet men."

From the murmur of voices I knew I was not the only one who felt that way. I had never talked to a large group before and was surprised that I could do it. When the next election of officers took place, I was nominated to be on the advisory board. Again I was surprised when I was elected.

Vince, an officer of the board of directors, was happy when I showed an interest in the union. I doubt if I had much influence, but when it came to benefits, I was in favor of performers being paid. That was a subject I felt strongly about. We achieved minimum pay for anyone who worked at a benefit. Rules were made about "B" girls, but some of the girls made their own rules and continued to mix.

One agent, Sam Rosy, asked me if I would like to go to Lake Tahoe. It was summer time, and I agreed to go to the State Line Country Club. It was on the lower edge of Lake Tahoe on the Nevada and California state line. It looked like a private estate. Behind the main building were small log cabins housing the employees. The cabin I shared with one of the office girls was composed of a room big enough for twin beds, a pot-bellied wood stove, and a chair. The bathroom and closet were at one end of the room. My roommate spent her spare time with her friends in the offices, so I had the place to myself. It was ideal. She worked in the daytime and I worked at night. We both were neat, so it was almost like living alone.

A triangle was sounded to summon us to the large room next to the kitchen. A long table held the same delicious food that was on the menu of the club. Breakfast had stacks of tender pancakes, eggs any style, ham, sausages and bacon piled high with my favorite, hash brown potatoes. Large bowls of the soup of the day were served for lunch and dinner and were within easy reach. Big platters of steaks, roasted meats, different styles of potatoes and vegetables were served liberally. Fried chicken with all the trimmings always disappeared fast. The deserts, if you had room for them, were obviously made by a French chef. Dinner was early so I could eat as much as I wanted.

The large dining room behind a spacious gaming room had a good-sized dance floor. Eddie Oliver led an excellent orchestra. Male and female vocalists sang the popular songs of the day. While I was practicing in the ballroom one day, two of the musicians offered to show me the sights of Tahoe. Without a car, I had been confined to the area, so I gladly accepted their offer. A pier extended into the lake and boats were moored there. The water was too cold for swimming, and I never saw a hardy soul braving the depths. There was no descending beach. The water was deep close to shore. We drove on the dirt road around most of the lake, and I saw secluded spots I walked to later. I sat and read, watched the birds and squirrels, and took pictures. It was like a vacation, except I was getting paid. Now there are tall hotels with casinos occupying the same spot. A highway goes around the lake and there are many beautiful homes in the area. Nothing is the same.

In my photo album there is a snapshot of me perched on a low pole holding a sign saying "State Line." A white sun suit set off my tanned skin. There was not any need for me to wear body makeup, because I had a great tan in a few days.

The guests were in the mood to enjoy themselves, especially on costume night. I wore my Indian costume; it fit in with all the other Indians, cowboys, sheriffs and bandits.

A dance team and I comprised the floorshow, and I only saw them at show time. I assumed they drove in each night from Reno. We had two shows a night and only one number a show. After I had finished my second show, I would go into a small bar nearby. The owner was friendly, and we would talk. He would pour a brandy for me in a slender glass. I nursed that drink until I left to go to my cabin. Two dances a night, one at nine and the other at eleven, gave me time for myself. I read the books and magazines in the lounge by the immense fireplace and never gambled. The three weeks passed too soon, and I returned to San Francisco. Bea exclaimed over how healthy I looked.

In November 1937 I was at a nightclub in Marysville, California. The owner, Mr. Clement, and I were having a problem. He wanted me to "mix" with the customers. His wife had seen my rehearsal and had told him that my dancing would be a real treat for the customers, but that I was too nice a girl to mix. He gave in and I was able to stay in my dressing room between shows.

One evening, I went to the bar for a drink of water. The good-looking blond man I stood next to suggested I have a drink with him. I said, "Thank you, but I will be returning to my dressing room."

The bartender had heard my refusal and said, "Lucile, Frank has been coming here for a long time attending to his father's business. I think you two should know each other."

He introduced us, and we talked until my next show. After the show, I joined him at a table, and we talked some more. We had something in common. My new friend had been separated from his wife for several months, and they were getting a divorce. She was looking for a lawyer. A couple of nights later he asked me if I liked to picnic. I said yes. The next day, we drove to a place near the river and had lunch. We had delectable food from a hamper and enjoyed music from his large portable radio. It was to be the first of several pleasant afternoons when he did not have business meetings.

Between shows one night, I had a long distance call from Walter. Mother had told him where I was. He wanted me to meet him in Sacramento to discuss a divorce. We set a time and place and I arose early one morning to take an early bus to Sacramento and met him in a restaurant. He told me he wanted to marry his reporter girlfriend and would pay all the expenses for me if I would go to Reno, Nevada. He would arrange for me to stay at one of the ranches that were popular for divorcees and would send some money every week.

"When?" I asked.

He said that, if I agreed, he could make the arrangements right away and I would be home for Christmas. To have my expenses paid for six weeks plus not having to pay for the divorce would be easier than if I had to pay for everything myself. He looked relieved when I consented.

Returning to Marysville, I gave my notice. Frank was disappointed about my leaving, and asked, "May I drive to Reno to see you while you are there?" It seemed to be a great distance to drive but I said I would inform him of my address and telephone number. I liked Frank very much and I knew he liked me, but I wasn't ready for a relationship or wouldn't be until I had my divorce.

The morning I was to catch the bus for Reno, I stopped at my favorite restaurant for breakfast. When the waitress heard where I was bound for she said, "A salesman who comes here often is going to Reno today. Maybe he is still here." She returned almost immediately with him. We talked and he was looking me over as carefully as I was checking him out. After awhile he made up his mind and said, "If we are going to Reno today, we had better start." I was at ease with him and thought this would certainly be better than riding the bus, which would take longer. His car was comfortable and he was the sort of person who did not have to talk all the time. It was starting out to be a pleasant trip.

The weather had stayed nice for November until we reached the mountains. Snow started falling, which became heavier the higher we climbed. When we reached Truckee, we were informed that the road ahead was closed. There was not any question about it; we were going to have to stay in a hotel. We finally found a vacant sign but the clerk told us there was only one room available. After a stunned silence, we had a quick conference. Neither one of us wanted to spend the freezing night in the car, and it was the only vacancy sign we had seen. We took the room. After we had dinner in the coffee shop, we sat in front of the fireplace in the lobby and talked. He asked me if we could leave our luggage in the car in order to make an earlier start. I agreed that would be a good idea. After going to our room he said,

"Which side do you like to sleep on?"

I replied, "I always sleep on my Mother's right."

He said, "That is fine with me."

He went into the bathroom and in a few minutes he came out in his tee shirt and shorts and quickly slid into the left side of the bed. For a minute I stood alongside the bed, then I took off my dress and in my modest petticoat I slid into the bed staying well over on my side. I found the girl in the restaurant had been right. He was a nice person. Before long he was asleep, and after a thank you prayer, I was too.

When I awoke in the early morning, I was disoriented for a moment. Then I again gave my thanks to the good Lord for having taken such good care of me. After a quick breakfast we continued our trip to Reno on the newly cleared road. Traveling through the pine trees that were covered with snow was like becoming part of a Christmas card. He was evidently accustomed to driving on icy roads, and he drove carefully. We arrived in Reno, and he left me at the Golden Hotel. I never saw this unusual gentleman again.

Entering the hotel, the first person I saw was Louise, a friend from previous days in Oakland. Her husband Eddie, had been one of the reporters on the Oakland Tribune. Louise was just as happy to see me as I was to see her. She was a part-time operator at the hotel switchboard and was supporting herself and Eddie, who could not find any work.

I left my bags at the hotel when I went to see my lawyer. He was the father of a lawyer who practiced in Susanville, California, and Walter had known him previously. The son would come from Susanville to go to court with me in six weeks. The lawyer knew nothing about any ranch for me. He had received some money from Walter, and he gave it to me. When I added it to what I had in my purse the total was $70.00. This is what I lived on for the next seven weeks. In the following weeks, the lawyer said he did not receive any more money, and there were never any letters for me from Walter at general delivery, where I had been told to go. Neither of the lawyers contacted Walter, although they said they were trying to do so. It never occurred to me to return to San Francisco because I kept expecting to have more money from Walter, but my trips to the post office were in vain. I decided I should try to make the best of it. If I did go back to San Francisco, I would not have a divorce. I spent two nights at the hotel, then I found a rooming house where I could have meals and a room that was less expensive.

The room contained antiques, not because they were an attraction. They were just old. My bed had springs and a mattress that looked like a sway-backed horse. If I had walked in a U shape when I arose, I would not have been surprised. My sink was an old-fashioned pitcher and bowl with towels folded neatly alongside. Otherwise, I made trips down the hall. The food was the best part, and I looked forward to sitting down with the other boarders and listening to them talk while we ate.

Reno was still a small town and was divided between the residents and the gambling crowd. The residents kept to themselves and more or less ignored the gambling in town.

Louise and I thought it would help both of us if I would move in with them. Her landlady gave her consent and gave us a cot for me. The rooms were on the top floor of an old house. The ceiling was uneven because of the shape of the roof. If you were not careful, you would receive a bump on the head walking from one room to another. I developed a continuous stoop. The kitchen had a large iron stove, and we kept a pot on it to hold the vegetables left from our meals. Every other day, we had soup. We ate mostly vegetables, cheap then. I cooked ground meat in the many ways I had done in Los Angeles. Wieners were not expensive and we boiled, fried and also cooked them in sauerkraut for various meals. We all liked popcorn, so that was our evening treat when we became hungry again.

The foot of my bed was next to a window in the kitchen. When it snowed, I had snow on the sill right outside the window at my feet. I slept curled up into a ball because the blankets were thin.

I went to the nightclubs to find work, but they had their entertainment booked ahead, and the answer was "No." When I looked for work in the department stores, I was informed the college girls had applied long before their winter semester break. Never having used a cash register, it probably would have scared me to death, but I would have tried.

I met a former acquaintance on the street one day, a dealer I had met at the community dinners at the State Line Country Club. After I told him I was looking for work, he had an offer. He suggested I move in with him and keep house for him. I thanked him and told him I was helping friends. I was not interested in the kind of "house keeping" that his tone had implied. (There is such a thing as a leer!)

During the day, I took walks or read while sitting on a bench in the small park in front of the library. I took pieces of bread and fed the pigeons or watched the turbulent Truckee River. A bridge next to the Riverside Hotel was where new divorcees purportedly threw their wedding rings into the water. Walter had told me he was the reporter who had started that story! Perhaps he did.

One Sunday, Eddie took an overdose of sleeping pills, on purpose or not, I'll never know. I sat behind him on their bed with my legs around him to keep him erect and Louise and I managed to force a bottle of Citric of Magnesia down him. Then we gave him cups of coffee, and I walked him around the apartment until he was awake. It was all we could think of doing, since there was no money for a doctor. We were relieved when he recovered, pale and weak, but O.K.

Frank and I had been corresponding and he visited me once. Two weeks later, he asked me to meet him in Sacramento for a few hours. If I left on the midnight train that passed through Reno en route to the coast, I could return on a train that would arrive in Reno before midnight. He had heard this was done legally and would I please do it?

Louise and Eddie persuaded me to go; they thought I needed some fun for a change. I made the arrangements.

Everything would have gone smoothly except for a winter storm that was passing through. The train tracks went along the Truckee River and it was a sight. Trees and debris of all kinds were being swept along with the rushing "white water." It was interesting and exciting too. Again I was held up in Truckee. The train stayed there because of the floodwaters in the valley below. What a relief it was, when Frank found me and tucked me into his car. Many others had come to rescue the other passengers in the same fix. In Sacramento we enjoyed a good dinner, a movie and the few hours together. He asked me to marry him when we both had our divorces. He said we could have several months for a honeymoon and would drive around the United Sates. He told me there was a new vehicle they called a Teardrop that was towed in back of the car. It held a bed, and sometimes we could camp out instead of going to a hotel. I loved the plan and told him I would like to think about it. I was a little overwhelmed at the thought of getting married again. We didn't have too much time to talk about everything. It was time to go to the station. I boarded the train, which fortunately was on schedule and landed in Reno safe and sound, with time to spare.

My divorce hearing was to be on Friday, the 24th of December. The elder lawyer informed me his son would take me to dinner the night before, and we would discuss the procedures. Thursday night, the son drove me to the Riverside Hotel Dining room and we talked about the next day's plans. He drank most of his dinner then told me it would be easier if I were to spend the night with him! When I disagreed with him, he reluctantly took me back to the apartment and left in a bad mood.

Next morning, I waited in vain at the courthouse for my lawyer, who never came. When I called his father on the telephone, he apologized for his son who had become drunk the night before and was indisposed. He told me the appointment was rescheduled for Monday, the twenty-seventh, at ten in the morning......Merry Christmas!

Louise and Eddie had left to spend the holiday weekend with friends at the lake. I was alone and unhappy. My purse held the ticket for the bus ride to Long Beach and a little over ten dollars. I had scrimped for the seven weeks so I would have enough money to go home to Mother. She was unaware of my financial situation because, as usual, I felt it was my problem and had never told her just how bad it was for me. My independence was my biggest fault.

No one else seemed to be in the big house, and I went to bed early that Christmas Eve. Next morning was cold, with no heat coming into the rooms. Finally, I undressed and took a bath, a long bath. The water was hot, so I would keep the temperature warm by running hot water in the tub. There was a book in the bookcase, Sorrel and Son. For hours, I sat in the tub and tried to get interested in the driest book I had ever encountered. My fingers were wrinkled when I got out, and I felt wrinkled all over.

I went to the Riverside Coffee shop for a turkey dinner. There was a table by the window, and, as I had my $1.00 dinner, I watched the snow gently coming down. I went to a movie where it was warm and did not cost much. There was still five dollars in my purse.

I saw and will always remember Dorothy Lamour in "The Hurricane." She wore her first sarong, but certainly not her last. The song she sang, "The Moon of Montecorra," always brought back the memory of that lonely Christmas.

I still had Sunday to fill in somehow. It was warm enough for a walk. I looked at the store windows, then sat in the park on my favorite bench. People were dressed in their new Christmas clothes, their children playing with their shiny bright bicycles and wagons. The girls held their new dolls so they could be admired. When I went back to the apartment, I was relieved to find the heat had been turned on again. I ate anything edible in the kitchen.

On Monday, the time it took to obtain my divorce was shorter than our wedding ceremony had been two years before. My lawyer was aloof, and I was colder to him than my room had been all weekend.

On December 27, 1937, I received my divorce from Walter, and I hurried to the bus station where I had checked my bags earlier. I had eaten some scraps of food at the apartment that morning, and I still had enough money for a sandwich and a glass of milk. I spent some of my precious money on two Hershey bars to eat on the trip. The five dollars stretched much further than it would now.

When I arrived home, Mother and I had a late Christmas of our own. My gifts for my family had been very carefully planned. I had purchased pink satin material along with some lace. Then I had bought a bottle of powdered sachet. I embroidered the material and made two lingerie cases for Alton's wife, Henrietta, and for Bea. Mother received a four by five picture that had been taken in front of the library in Reno. A passing stranger had been kind enough to take a picture of me sitting on the steps with a stray dog. I gave Mr. Fountain a duplicate. Both were in very cheap frames, but they each said they liked them.

Mother had a surprise for me. Frank had phoned and said he would be arriving the next day. When she met him, she liked him immediately and approved when I told her she might be having a son-in-law. But the news that Frank told me was to change everything.

The only time he had driven to Reno to see me, his wife had gone to his apartment and managed to get his mail out of the box. She read a letter I had sent, and showed it to his father. He had detectives investigate, and Frank was informed he would be disinherited if he did not stop seeing the showgirl with whom he was involved. I knew from his attire, car, and the money that he so casually spent that he was not at all poor, but I had not known his father was a millionaire. Frank told me that his wife had changed her mind and would not give him a divorce. She even threatened to sue me for alienation of affections.

This was the news Frank had for me, and I was stunned. I told him we could not see each other any more. I did not want to be involved in a scandal. I shuddered when I considered the possible headlines. "Show girl has romance with millionaire's son!" Just the type of juicy news the editors loved. Gone were our plans of a happy ever after marriage. Instead he went back to San Francisco, and a few days later I joined Bea. It was not over that easily. Frank would come to see me even though he knew he was being tailed. I did not know what he was thinking of and I refused to talk to him.

Mother decided to come to live with Bea and me. She did the cooking and housework, and Bea and I were the breadwinners. In February I had a lucky break. I was asked to audition six girls for a new floorshow at The Baghdad. Our show opened on the 9th of February. For the choreography and my own solos, I received $75.00 a week. Things were picking up!

On opening night Mother and I were in my dressing room talking about how the dance numbers had been received during the first show. A waitress came to my dressing room and said, "Dr. Houseman would like you to come to his table." I told her that I do not visit with customers. She told me he was one of the owners, so I agreed to meet him.

She took me to his table, and a tall gray haired man asked me my name. I told him and was perplexed when he wanted to know if that were my real name. I said "yes" again and asked him if he would like to talk to my mother. He did not answer me but turned to the waitress who was still with us. "Ask her mother to come here." The girl left and returned with Mother. "What is the matter?" Mother asked me.

"He does not believe that my name is Lucile Iverson."

Dr. Houseman introduced himself and with a questioning tone in his voice said, "Your name is Iverson?" "

"Yes," Mother answered, in a tone that said, "You had better not question me!"

He said, "I apologize, I thought someone was staging a bad joke. Would you and Lucile please sit down and have a drink with us. I'll try to explain."

Mother said she did not drink, and I said the same. It was settled we should have a soft drink. Then we looked at him and waited for him to tell us what it was all about. He explained. He had lost his wife to leukemia several months before and her maiden name had been Iverson. Our name was not too common, and he had drawn the wrong conclusion. It seemed there were three owners who had merged to buy this club, and they were accustomed to playing jokes on each other. He thought he had been the object of their humor and apologized for his mistake. We were introduced to his guests and answered their questions about my dancing career. Mother really enjoyed talking about that. I stayed at the table until I left for the second show. Mother did not come back to the dressing room after the show, so I rejoined them. Dr. Houseman told me Mother had agreed to allow his driver to take her home, and he personally would take me home after the last show. When Mother left, I excused myself because I wanted to talk to my dancers. After the last show he escorted me to his Cadillac and took me to my apartment. We had finished our light conversation when he turned to me, and said, "Do you, or don't you?"

I did not understand what he meant for a moment, and when I did, I said, "I certainly do not."

"Well that is all right. We will just be friends." And that was what we were to become. He escorted me to the apartment door and told me, "I will take you home after the show every night. Tell your mother." With that he left.

I told Mother, and we agreed he probably was old enough to be my father. True to his word, he did take me home every night. When he realized that I liked to eat after the performances, we went each night to the same Greek restaurant. It had a long counter with high chairs and a few tables along the wall. The food was excellent, and I ordered a huge artichoke almost every night. It was cooked with so many good flavors that I did not need to dip my leaves into any dressing. I found if I cooked my artichokes with French salad dressing plus garlic, I could almost get the same flavor.

Gabe, his driver, was usually with us, and I concluded he was a friend and bodyguard because Dr. Houseman carried a large sum of money with him. There was some talk about card games that I assumed were for high stakes in poker. He invited me to come to see him in his office whenever I was downtown. He would escort me to the cable car.

It was raining heavily one day, and while waiting for the cable car, we stood in the entrance to a lingerie shop. "Why don't we go in and see if there is something you would like?" He laughed at my embarrassment when I said, "No!"

One night as he was driving me home, he told me about the lady he went to see after he took me home each night. She was elderly and an invalid after a stroke. Before he went to his own home, he would spend some time with her. One night he said I was to tell Mother I would be home later than usual the next night. Mrs. Black wanted to meet me. The next night we drove to an imposing home near Golden Gate Park. When he opened the door and we went into the hallway towards the stairway, I could see there was beautiful furniture in the living room. When I first walked into the bedroom, I could hardly see Mrs. Black. She was so tiny she hardly made a mound in the bed. She extended a frail hand to me, and I was almost afraid to touch her because she looked so fragile. I sat beside her bed in a chair. That night started an unusual friendship with a dear elderly lady who could barely talk, but somehow we managed to communicate. It took me a little time to learn how to communicate with her when Dr. Housman or Gabe were not in the room. She was able to make signs with her hands which helped a lot.

Dr. Houseman would disappear sometimes for a short time but Gabe was always present. He liked to tease me, and one night when Mrs. Black had found I liked oysters, he was told to prepare some for me. They were tiny oysters that had been flown from the East Coast. Crackers and a big bowl of oysters were set in front of me. I knew I was to dip them in the sauce that accompanied them. What I didn't know was that you shouldn't eat too many of them. I kept eating until they seemed to grow inside my stomach. Gabe had known he was giving me too many oysters and thought it a funny joke. I did not think it was so funny. I had been brought up to always finish what was on my plate. This was one time when I should have broken the rule.

One night Mrs. Black pointed to a chest of drawers. I went to it. She pointed again, this time to a certain drawer. I opened it and found there were rolls of silk material. She nodded her head slightly so I took out the rolls and put the rolls on the bed. I could tell she wanted me to choose one them. They were of beautiful colors and, with difficulty, I chose one roll. They had been brought from China long ago. I thanked her, and Mother made dresses for Henrietta and me from the yards of beautiful material. The room had many Chinese figurines, and she watched me admiring them, and that seemed to delight her. I told her about my collection of Netuskes and she nodded her head. We would enjoy sharing a small bottle of Champagne, so she had Gabe bring a case to the apartment. He also brought roasts of filets, and Mother, Bea and I enjoyed her gifts.

Mrs. Black and I would often just sit in silence, and I would hold her hand. If she could have talked I knew she would have had some wonderful experiences to tell me because she had traveled extensively. When I heard she had passed away, I hoped she was now happy with the handsome man who had preceded her in death. I had seen a picture of him near her bedside, and I saw her looking at it with eyes full of love.

Dr. Houseman always seemed to have a table full of guests at the club, and he would often ask me to sit with them. Once he asked me to join him when he was dining with one lady. We had been talking awhile when he asked her if she thought I would fit in with her establishment. She said she did not think so. When he said she was a "Madam," they laughed at my reaction.

In San Francisco doctors kept check on the health of "the girls," and evidently, he had been taking care of hers for a long time. She had a wonderful sense of humor and a personality that went with it, but I soon excused myself and went to my dressing room. When I would see her later, I would say "Hello" and then go on my way. Experience had taught me dancers in show business had enough trouble keeping a good reputation, and I did not need to be seen with a woman who was in the "sporting" business.

When the Transbay Bridge was opened, the city celebrated with "Western Days." Everyone was asked by the city to dress in appropriate attire. Downtown San Francisco looked as though the cattle would be driven through the city streets at any time. My dancers and I put together western type costumes and added a tap dance to a melody of western songs.

The Transbay Bridge between Oakland and San Francisco never received the publicity the Golden Gate Bridge did, but I thought it was wonderful. When I was traveling on the ferryboats, I had watched the progress as they erected the bridge. There were caissons placed where the towers would be, and at night it was interesting to see men working under the illumination of enormous lights. They looked diminutive inside the immense caissons. When they spun the cables, it was fascinating to watch. After the bridge was finished, it was the demise of the ferryboats and many shared my sorrow at the loss of one of San Francisco's best attractions.

The costume Mother made for me for the "Western Days" had a satin shirt and a little vest and skirt, both fringed. They were selling inexpensive broad brimmed hats, so, of course, I had one. The ensemble was black, which set off my blonde hair. Boots were too expensive, but when Dr. Houseman lent me a pearl handled gun I felt like a western cowgirl. When he and Gabe brought the gun and holster to me, the doctor said, "Did you check to see if it is empty?"

Gabe said, "Yes."

I took Gabe's word for it. The gun was small, and the belt and holster fit neatly around my hips. I heard gunshots during the festivities, but I left my gun in its holster and did not even make believe I would shoot it.

The audience approved of my girl's western type routine and my Indian dance. The step the Indian in Minneapolis had taught me was the only authentic step in the dance. The headdress was one we had found in the children's toy department, and the bra and trunks were fringed. It was the most abbreviated costume Mother had ever made for me, and I applied my brown colored Wheatcroft body makeup liberally.

When the doctor and Gabe came after the gun, Gabe aimed it at the floor and pulled the trigger. The resulting shot shocked all of us. Gabe and I ran down the stairs to the apartment below and rang the doorbell. The lady there said nothing unusual had happened, so we returned upstairs. Gabe received some harsh words that I felt he deserved. Thank goodness my Daddy had taught me to respect a gun. He had told me never to point it at anyone and pull the trigger.

When the club started to pay us each night I knew something was wrong. Then I heard they had declared bankruptcy. One morning Doctor Houseman called and told me to go to the club and collect my belongings because the Baghdad Club had closed. He said, "Come to my office, too." He insisted on giving me $50.00 dollars and told me if I needed more to tell him.

After I left his office, I went to the agents to let them know I was at liberty. I was given a contract to work at Matteonis in Stockton. Mother did not go with me but joined me on my second week. It was during my first week that I saw Frank for the last time. In San Francisco, he had come to the Baghdad two times, and each time I had told him goodbye and asked him not to come again. Late one morning, I was surprised when I answered a knock on my hotel room door and saw Frank standing there. He wanted to talk.

I said, "There is nothing to talk about. Please leave."
I shut the door, and, thinking he had gone, I threw myself on my bed and cried. I didn't know that instead of leaving he was still standing outside my door. He heard me sobbing. He finally realized what he was doing to me and telephoned me from the lobby downstairs. He promised never to follow me again.

While I was working at the Baghdad, mother had made a colorful rumba costume for me. It was of a red and white flowered cotton print, and the bra had big ruffled sleeves. The skirt was more like a train and was also heavily ruffled. I had some lessons so I could do a good rumba. I was ready to try the number in a club. The second week at Mateonis, I put the rumba in the first show.
Mrs. Matteoni, who had been friendly with mother and me, came to my dressing room after the show and said, "Lucile, that dance is not you. You did it very well, but I can't see you shaking your shoulders and using your hips like that. Have you another dance you can do?"

Mother and I could not see anything wrong with the dance, but I did another one in the last show. I still shudder when I recall one hot sultry night in Stockton.

I was doing spotters in Stardust, the acrobatic routine. I was too limber, and when my hands were still on the floor my foot went over my head and came down on one hand. My body was in a tight circle. I managed to release the foot enough to free my hand. My heart beat faster for a few minutes. It was scary, and I was thankful it only happened one time.

While I was working there, a doctor was introduced to me. He was interested in knowing how much energy I used while I was performing my acrobatic dance. I allowed him to take my blood pressure, temperature, and pulse before I did my dance and again immediately after. He then told me I used as much energy in my routine as a laborer would all day. I realized why I was so tired every night. Going to sleep was never a problem. He also said I worked as hard as any athlete, but I found that hard to believe.

Mother asked me where we were going next, and I told her I didn't have a booking. She insisted I write to the agents, including one that I had not even visited. The agent telephoned me and asked me to go to Monterey to work at a club there. We took a bus. When I reached the bus station, I went to the man in the ticket window and asked if there was a hotel near the club where I was going to dance. He looked at me kind of funny but gave me the name of a hotel. I left Mother there to unpack and rest, and I took a taxi to the club. When I saw it I understood the ticket man's reaction. Instead of the lovely place I had expected, it was a store which had been converted to a nightclub. The orchestra was ready, so I started to rehearse.

I usually just marked the routines when I rehearsed, but if I were not comfortable about the state of the floor, I would do my dance. This time I did the toe dance first. Then I gave the leader "Stardust," the Spanish waltz and the Russian dance music. The front door opened just as I had finished. A lady came to me immediately and started to question me. She wanted know if I "mixed." She said she had been told on the phone what a good dancer I was and realized I was not the type of girl she needed. The lady was obviously upset and told me I could do the night show, then she would have someone else finish the weekend. The customers were from the nearby army camp, and she needed a girl that would sit with the soldiers.

Mother and I noticed that there were elaborate dresses hanging on hooks on the wall when we were first sitting in the dressing room. After knocking on the door, a female impersonator entered and spoke rapidly with a decided lisp. He told me, "We share the dressing room because it is the only one. If you don't mind waiting outside for just a few minutes, I'll slip into one of my gowns. I will wear it all evening so I won't be bothering you again." We left the room.

We found he did mix, and the men bought him drink after drink. Besides being the M.C., he sang risqué songs that made the fellows roar with laughter. The two of us were the floorshow. Before the last show the owner came to the dressing room and said, "The boys like your dancing so much I'll make an exception, and you can stay for the weekend. Then I will drive you to San Francisco, and we both will see the agent."

After an uncomfortable ride to San Francisco, I went into the agent's private office and introduced myself. Then I asked why she had sent me to that club in Monterey. She said she knew that I had worked for Mr.Clement in Marysville, more than once. He only had dancers who did drink with the customers. I enlightened her.

"Mr. Clements was always nice to me, but he never asked for me to mix."

I thought I would never hear from the agent, but a few months later she did call me.

As soon as I could, I went to see Dr. Houseman and returned the $50.00 he had given me. He wanted me to keep it, but I put it on his desk and left. We remained friends, and I would go to his office once in awhile and talk if he were not busy.

The last time I saw him was at Christmas when Bea and I had an open house. He brought me a bottle of Caron's Tobac Blond perfume. I bought more of it when my bottle was empty and continued using it until they stopped making it. I treasure the little bottle I have left because it reminds me of my days in San Francisco and the good friend I had there.

One club occupied two floors in a large building in the center of town. Dinners were served on the top floor and the bar was one floor below. The third show was at two in the morning. It was lucky there was a pianist whom I had worked with before. He was concerned about my walking up the hill on Leavenworth Street alone in the middle of the night. Each night he escorted me to my apartment. Marvin was practicing to become a concert pianist and practiced several hours each day. He said he needed the exercise.

I received an invitation to a piano recital in the mail one day. It was from Marvin. I was free that night, and I was able to attend and enjoyed myself immensely. I kept on working steadily, mostly at different nightclubs. Occasionally there would be an engagement for one or two days at a theater. I had danced most of my life for clubs like the Elks or the Masons and now I was doing it again. Some of them were in small towns, and I would drive to them with the other acts.

I felt I needed some lessons, and I didn't take any bookings for a few weeks. I went to the Christianson Ballet School and was placed in the advanced class. The air became cooler when it was discovered I was a nightclub dancer. A young teacher informed me I was not in an acrobatic class when I kicked a little higher than the others at the barre.

Ballet has changed. Now I see the legs in a perfect split in leaps and in arabesques.

I took my acrobatic performances back to the nightclubs after three weeks of ballet. Mother said I was ahead of my time, and 50 years later, I realized how true her words were.

Chapter 15

Mother received a letter from Mrs. Alexander with a newspaper clipping telling about her daughter Eva's wonderful opportunity. She was en route to Yokohama with a show that was scheduled to tour Japan, China, India, Burma, Siam and Java. Eva was my high-kicking friend who had been in my vaudeville act back when we were both in our teens. She had graduated from high school in 1931 and had entered show business when it was starting downhill for dancers. Eva had worked around Los Angeles for years, so a chance to travel probably had appealed to her. Her mother sent a clipping from Japan showing Eva's picture on a huge banner on the wall of a building. Because she was so much taller than the average Japanese female, she was enjoying a lot of publicity.

One day a letter from Mrs. Alexander brought us bad news. Eva was in a hospital in Calcutta, India, ill with typhoid fever. After touring with the Rex Story Dance Company for a year, she had been one of twenty tourists who had been stricken with typhoid in a crowded Calcutta hotel.

At first, it was reported her condition was not unduly serious. That was reassuring until we received another letter. Eva had passed away. A cable from the American Consul in Calcutta had informed her parents of her death. An Englishman, who had stayed at the same hotel, had also succumbed to the dread disease. Eva had been alone because the company had continued their tour into the interior of India to fill other engagements. I recalled how I had felt when I had been alone in the Grace Hospital in Detroit for ten days without any family or friends, and I grieved all the more for what poor Eva had endured.

A few months later when we were visiting in Long Beach, we wanted to call on Eva's mother. However, our mutual friend Catherine told us we could not see Mrs. Alexander because Eva's grief-stricken father would not let his wife see any of Eva's former dance friends. Eva was an only child who had been his pride and joy. Now he was full of bitterness. Later, in San Francisco a package came to me from Long Beach. Eva's mother had sent Eva's Bible to me. There wasn't a note of explanation in the package. The notes of reference to certain verses in Eva's hand writing made it special to me. I hoped she had the same relationship I had always felt with a guardian angel.

Mother and I realized how fortunate I had been to start dancing with Fanchon & and Marco when I did. When a booking came for two weeks in Sacramento, Mother decided to accompany me. She wanted to see the city again. That was when we met Roy, or rather Mother met Roy. She had been in the audience watching the show, and the two of them had struck up a conversation. She thought we might like each other and brought him backstage to introduce us. The three of us were to become good friends.

A curious situation prevented Roy and me from having a romance. He told us about his marriage several years earlier to a woman who was his wife in name only. They had married when his best friend was killed in an automobile accident. The woman was his fiancée and was pregnant. Roy told us that, after the accident, he offered to marry her so that the child would not be illegitimate. We never did meet his wife, and he never mentioned her or the child again.

Roy was tall and slender, always kind and considerate, and was especially nice to my mother. He treated me like a sister. We were to enjoy his friendship for years. When my engagements took me anywhere near Sacramento, Roy and I would go fishing, and one time we even went hunting for deer. I trudged alongside Roy after we parked the car in the woods. I was hoping we would not see any deer. We didn't until we came back to the car, and there was a beautiful buck standing right in front of the car! It took flight as soon as it saw us. Roy could not fire because it was too close to the car. To my relief, he did not shoot a deer that day.

One time we went to the sloughs that were near Sacramento. He tossed bottles and cans as far as he could into the water, and I would shoot them with his .22 rifle. I had been doing quite well at bringing them down. Then he gave me his pistol and threw a bottle farther than he had before. I had never been able to shoot well with a pistol because I always pulled my hand down when I pulled the trigger. I held a bead on the bottle and pulled the trigger. Bullseye! Down went the bottle. I felt terrible! I think I was more disappointed than he was when none of the remaining tosses went as far.

Another time, when I was working in Sacramento, we drove to a mountain stream. He tried to teach me how to fly cast, but I could only snag the branches of the trees. I was working in a nightclub at that time, so had not had enough sleep. I took a nap while he continued casting. A wonderful smell awakened me. He had quietly built a small campfire and was roasting trout on branches of wood. Ummm! That was the best trout I ever tasted.

Sometimes on Saturday, he would drive to see us in San Francisco and would take mother to the theater while I was working at a club. On Sunday, the three of us would take in the sights of the town. He seemed to be trying to spoil us and succeeded pretty well. We were to lose contact with him, and I often wondered about the young man who treated me like a sister--well almost. We did share a few kisses.

One day, to my surprise, I received a call from the agent who had booked me in Monterey. When I went to her office, she offered me a booking of ten weeks at the big Lido Club. A young man had been experimenting with the new fluorescent lights and had costumes that were decorated with a special paint. With a special "black light," the unpainted portion of the costume did not show. She had recalled I could do a wide variety of dances and asked me if I could choreograph dances for all the costumes. I was delighted and signed the contract, and it was one of my best engagements.

The skeleton became an acrobat because the white bones were painted on a black body suit. The dance I choreographed for the Burmese costume was the hardest to set and the easiest dance I had ever done. The long tight dress had a split along one leg or I would not have been able to move at all. Elbow length white gloves had painted fingernails glued to the tips of the fingers at least an inch past my own nails. While in front of a mirror, I practiced a dance that was mostly a series of slow moves from one posture to another. Some of my ideas came from newsreels I had seen of Burmese Temple dancers.

The Lido was a favorite of Italians, and most nights there would be a wedding party, with long tables laden with steak dinners and many bottles of wine. The waiters would come to my downstairs dressing room with a complete dinner for me. Some of the guests of the wedding parties would be too busy toasting everyone to eat. I protested, but was told the food had not been touched, and it would be a shame to waste it. Sometimes when I left to go home they would give me a bag containing half-filled bottles of red wine.

A member of the San Francisco Symphony Orchestra called and asked me to dance for a highly publicized charity ball. He warned me that there wouldn't be a rehearsal, and that my music should be in good condition. The director was very strict. I remembered that the music for my Russian dance was old and tattered. This was a special event, and I felt honored, to have been asked to perform, so I bought a new orchestration and prepared it for the big day. I wanted everything to be just right.

I will never forget that performance! With my best smile I started my Russian Cossack dance. First step just fine, then catastrophe hit. The musicians were all playing different music. Well, it wasn't really music. I kept to my routine, and finally they were together again. This was one time when I did not laugh over a mishap. We finished together, thank goodness, but I could not look at anyone as I went to my dressing room to change for my reliable "Stardust." After the show my friend gave me my music and showed me what I had done. After the first eight bars of music I had pasted the next sixteen bars upside down on the sheet for the trumpet player who was to carry the melody. They had no one to follow. It was one of the most embarrassing moments of my life. My friend had recommended me, and I had let him down. I was most contrite, but I lost a friend. I doubt if anyone in the audience had noticed unless they were familiar with the music. The director gave my friend a bad time, and I certainly understood why. I had not received any pay for the benefit but I had certainly learned a lesson.

The Golden Gate National World's Fair was held between 1939 and 1940.

Yerba Buena Island was in the bay between San Francisco and Oakland, and the San Francisco Oakland Bay Bridge tunneled right through it. An artificial island, Treasure Island, was built by bringing loads and loads of soil next to Yerba Buena. That was where the fair was held. On Sundays, Mother, Bea and I would take a ferry that took us to the island.

Many of the splendid buildings representing different countries had pools of water in front of them. At night, the water reflected the buildings, which were decorated with many colored lights, resulting in a spectacular effect. Waterfalls and statues were scattered throughout the grounds, making it a fairyland. From the San Francisco waterfront, the island looked like a mirage floating on the water when the fog came in.

Swimmer and movie star Esther Williams was featured in Billy Rose's Aquacade, a synchronized water ballet with a bevy of beautiful girls. Another favorite, besides the Aquacade, was the Palace of Fine Arts, because of the rare treasures that were shown there. It had masterpiece paintings, statuary, and more objects than we could absorb in one visit, so we went many times.

In February 1940, Ella Weston, an agent I had seldom worked for, called me and asked me to come to her office the following day. It was crowded with people when I arrived. I was introduced to Mr. Stutz, who explained he and his partner were producing a show to travel to cities in the Northwest. Although the traveling would be by car, I was interested because we would be performing in theaters. I was grateful to be able to earn a living for Mother and myself in nightclubs, but the idea of dancing again for people who came solely to be entertained was enticing. Also, I liked the idea that I would be working for several weeks with a steady income. Two girls younger than I were also being interviewed. My age, plus a good reputation, must have impressed the mothers of the girls. They said that Dorothy and Sandra could join the show if I were to be in it. After discussing salaries and hearing the plans for the show, we signed our contracts. I was to receive $45.00 dollars a week.

We drove to Elko, Nevada, for the opening of our tour. I would have preferred someplace closer to San Francisco, but because of Mrs. Weston's reassurance, I was not worried. On our drive to Elko, Sandra said she preferred to be called Sandy, and Dorothy asked us to call her Dottie. They asked if I had a nickname but,

I said I didn't. Sandy was short and her body was plump like a baby's. Not fat, just plump. She was an acrobatic dancer, too, which never caused either of us any trouble. Our friendship lasted for many years. After I left San Francisco, we exchanged Christmas cards with letters until I received a letter from her husband, informing me of her death in 1998.

We were to find that we were not the only dancers in the "World's Fair Follies." There were two fairly young women who had been performing on the midway at the fair. Their dances were the same they had done to entice people into the sideshows. Their boyfriends drove the automobiles that provided transportation for the acts. The men also helped with the odd jobs needed for the production.

It was a good cast for a variety show. There were two splendid male tap dancers and a ventriloquist. Dottie was a tap dancer and did a really good tap dance on her toes. Her slippers had metal tips on the toes, and she used them with expertise. She had a slender body, pretty, dark hair, and had a crush on the good-looking singer on the show. Another good-looking fellow was a medalist who had just been in an athletic competition performing on a horizontal bar. He and his wife left the show after the opening week. It was a smart move.

The one night stand in Elko was a disappointment. The theater was barely half full for the performances. We were promised we would be paid in Salt Lake City, our next destination. Mr. Stutz said his partner and his wife would join us there, and she would dance in the show, too.

When I saw her the next morning at the theater, I was curious. During the first matinee, I stood in the wings to watch her dance. Her makeup looked like a mask on her aged face, and her costume reminded me of pictures I had seen of burlesque dancers. To my dismay, her dance was a burlesque dance, too. Towards the end of her exhibition, she sashayed over to the side curtain and held it while lowering her voluptuous body. Then on the way up, she gave a tremendous bump. The theater chandelier I had admired years before must have trembled from the shock. She did not perform in the next show, and I heard she left town that evening.

My friends and I gave the producers our notice. We wanted our wages from the Capital Theater and fares to return to San Francisco. At the end of the week we did not get any money for our fares and did not receive all our promised salary.

Without the money, we had to stay with the show. We should have written home asking for money to return because we never did receive a full salary. We received promises that the show would be doing better instead. Money was doled out to us and usually it was just enough for our food and hotels. Because of traveling at night there were many times we did not go to a hotel. The problem was the same we had when I had toured with Lloyd Skeels. The advance man, the partner, would always make a wrong deal.

There were five in our car. A dancer, Nola, and Charlie, her boyfriend, who was our driver, were in the front seat. I was in the middle of the back seat with Sandy and Dottie, who rested their heads on my shoulders while they slept. Nola would talk until she fell asleep. I kept awake because I wanted to be certain that Charlie did not doze off, too. He was a careful driver, but I still kept awake.

There was only one time that I was frightened. In the middle of the night in Idaho, we were traveling on a very narrow road. The moon was not shining, and it was dark except for the pair of headlights coming towards us from a distance. I watched those lights as though I was mesmerized, and I dreaded the moment when we would pass. It reached us and passed so close I felt the pressure of air in our vehicle.

I thought, "This is it." I heard myself call out to my Mother. Charlie said, "That was close!" I agreed. When I talked to Mother, a few nights later on one of my rare phone calls, she asked me if I was all right. She told me she had been awakened in the middle of her sleep a couple of nights previously by my voice calling to her. I told her of the experience, and she was relieved to find that nothing had occurred. We both were amazed that she had been awakened at the same time I had called out. It reminded us of the time I had heard her call my name when she fell and broke her ankle and I was some distance away. We also both remembered the night that my grandmother had been struck by a car in front of her home in Minneapolis. Mother and I had heard a knock at our door, but Daddy didn't. All incidents that made us wonder.

We were to have a touch of drama following the matinee one afternoon. Dottie, Sandy and I were taking off our makeup because we had some time before the first night show. One of the older dancers came into our dressing room and said, "Lucile, get dressed quickly and go to the hotel."

"Why?" I said, thinking it was a joke.

Then she told me. "Mrs. Stutz has come to join her husband, and she is looking for you with a gun in her hand. She has been drinking and thinks you are the logical girl for her husband to be fooling around with. It seems he has always had a girlfriend in his previous shows. Sandy and Dottie are too young, so she is looking for you. We think you could be an innocent victim if you don't hurry up and get to your hotel room."

We followed her advice and were happy to have done so when we found the story was true. We were relieved the next morning when Mrs. Stutz was safely on a train bound for home. Very foolishly, I accosted Mr. Stutz in his room later to tell him the girls and I were serious about leaving the show and to ask him to give us enough money to go home. I left in a hurry because he misunderstood the reason for my coming to his room and tried to kiss me.

We had traveled to Eureka, California, and the girls and I were walking towards the stairway of the hotel when they stopped at a room and knocked. The door opened to reveal part of the cast crowded into the room, singing "Happy Birthday Lucile." I blew out the candles they had placed on cupcakes, and we all enjoyed the special treat that they had prepared for my twenty-eighth birthday.

During the overnight trip from Wenatchee, Washington, and Portland, Oregon, I began to feel ill. My back hurt so much I could not find a comfortable position. "The Three Graces," the name they were calling us, found an apartment that was advertised on the theater bulletin board. When the girls left for the rehearsal, I went to bed. I had a high fever and the theater house doctor came to see me. He gave the girls a prescription and said I was to stay in bed. I was too sick to care. When I could not keep the medicine down and was getting worse instead of better, I called Mother. She took a bus and came to me right away. Two days after she arrived, she had me on my feet again in time for me to go to Seattle with the show. Reluctantly, she went back home.

In Seattle, we were to open at a large popular nightclub. During the orchestra rehearsal, Sandy and I were limbering up in the audience area when I heard her fall. I went to her and found her chin was bleeding. When I looked at it closely, I saw it was split open. She had hit one of the heavy chairs when she fell.

"We have to get you to a doctor right away," I told her. She said, "No" and insisted I could do whatever was needed. After arguing without success I said, "I'll do what I can."

Sometimes I was called "Doc Iverson" because I had quite an assortment of medical supplies in my suitcase. My mother had taught me what to do for problems that were not serious enough for a doctor. I had helped fellow performers for years. For Sandy, I made a neat little "butterfly" and brought the open flesh together after cleaning the cut. We covered the small white patch that went over it with make-up so it was not noticeable.

When she healed, all she had was a tiny scar in the same place where I had a scar. She thought it was great that we had matching scars. I was just glad they were under our chins, and she had not hurt herself very much from the fall.

Instead of taking it easy the week after my illness, I worked harder than ever. Sandy, Dottie, and I were the only dancers. The other dancers were not allowed to perform because their type of dancing was considered too suggestive. I had to do three numbers a show instead of two to help fill out the program. Fortunately, after a day or so, I was back to my usual strength in spite of the hard work. It was the last week for the "World's Fair Follies Show." Sandy, Dottie, and I were to remember many shared experiences and laughs.

A theater manager had asked me to work the next week at his theater in Seattle. I was happy to have some money and did not have to ask Mother to send me some. I was also able to take the train home and didn't have to ride back in a car.

I returned to San Francisco, and I went to see Mrs. Weston. She said she had not realized that the "Follies" managers had not known how to book the show. The advance man had failed miserably. I will never know if Mr. Stutz had also been taken in by his partner or perhaps the man himself thought he was more capable than he turned out to be. Personally, I was owed about $300, and some on the show were owed more.

My two "one night stand" shows, the "World's Fair Follies," and the "NRA Revue" were certainly not successful, but I was to hear the same story from other show people during the Depression. Several years later, through the union, I finally received the money owed to me. Mr. Stutz was trying to put together another show, but he could not do so until "The World's Fair Follies" cast had been paid. He could not make up for all the hardships we had experienced, but, fortunately, the funny memories are usually the ones we remember.

Back home again, I was booked in a club in San Jose with a south sea décor, with floor to ceiling windows that looked out on a tropical garden. I did my Hawaiian dance that I had learned earlier from a teacher who was a Hawaiian native. He had taught me the correct way to use my arms and hands. For the first time, I felt confident with my arm movements in my different types of dancing. As a blonde, I didn't look the part, but I was told I did a real hula, and I was happy to have an easy dance to add to my repertoire.

Attendance always dropped in the Spring in the night clubs so I asked for bookings in the smaller northern towns. This gave me an opportunity to practice new routines, and once I even sewed a costume for myself by hand. Beside my customary baggage, I had a large suitcase containing a paisley bed spread that was light to carry. This went on the hotel bed. At the foot of the bed I placed the suitcase on the provided support, making a table. I covered the suitcase with a colored cloth and I had a light plate that would hold fruit. Sometimes I would place wildflowers in a glass beside my books or magazines on my table. The bag also contained supplies for breakfast in my room. I had a sterno stove on which I could brew my tea. I used a contraption that looked like a pyramid for making toast. Sugar, salt and pepper were in small containers. A cereal bowl and plate, along with my fork, knives, spoons and a can opener, completed my supplies. This was my home away from home and I was content to come to it after the day was done for my evening snack. The maids were agreeable to my arrangements because my room was always clean and pleasant.

I was working in Chico, California, and two boys in the orchestra told me they were going horseback riding. They asked the girl singer and me to join them. They told us the stable was located in the area where "Robin Hood" had been filmed and the forest was very beautiful.

My acquaintance with horses had been very limited. There had been grand-mother's Molly that had pulled the buggy back in Minneapolis. Then there had been the time, when I was about 14, that Alton and two daughters of our friends rented horses and went for a ride. I couldn't go with them because Mother said I was too young, and it would not be good for my dancing. So I watched them wistfully

270

as they went off to ride. When they returned, Alton put me on the gentle horse one of the girls had ridden. Mother had consented to my having a little ride if Alton walked alongside. The horse, knowing it had a novice rider, suddenly decided he wanted to return to the stables and ran off in that direction. I was holding on as I had been told. Alton quickly remounted his horse and tried to catch up to my steed. He was worried when he saw that my horse was going to cross a small creek on a bridge that everyone had been told not to use. Not knowing the bridge was unsafe, I was having the time of my life! This was closer to flying than anything I had ever experienced. When we reached the stable, I reluctantly allowed myself to be taken down. Since that time, I watched how people mounted a horse and their riding posture. I had made up my mind that I was going to ride someday and now was my chance.

I purchased male trousers. Unfortunately, they were not made of a soft material. Slacks for girls were not yet fashionable. When we reached the stable, the girl singer received all the instructions. The stable boy thought I knew what I was doing because I mounted the horse correctly. I knew nothing about having a saddle that was right for my size and mine was too broad. Stirrups? Well my feet were in them, so I thought they must be all right.

We took off on our ride. When my horse decided to go a different direction from the others, I was alone. The trail my horse took me on must have been his favorite. As I looked around, I understood why "Robin Hood" had been filmed there. It was like a Sherwood Forest. Everything was so quiet that I began to feel uneasy and turned my horse around towards the stable, hoping I might find the others and join them. My horse evidently thought if we were going home, we might as well get there as soon as possible. His trot turned into a gallop. My "Whoa" fell on deaf ears. This time I was on my own, so I held on tight with my legs and hoped for the best. The ride was soon over and the stable boy came and assisted me to land on terra firma.

"Did you have a good ride?" he asked me.

"Yes, but I think I had better not overdo it." I told him, I thought maybe some riding lessons would be in order if I were to go riding again.

For the remainder of the week I had to dance in costumes that covered my legs. The rough material of my pants had rubbed the inside of my legs, causing large sores. In addition, I was bruised half way down my legs, beautiful colors, but not suitable for display. When the M.C. introduced me and I entered the dance floor, the orchestra would play "Horses, Horses, Horses, Crazy over Horses." It was a popular song and everyone recognized it.

Another year I was in Chico again, where the club was in a hotel. The town was not a good place for me. One of the girls from the dining room said, "My boyfriend and I are going out to eat after the show. Would you like to join us?" I agreed, but was surprised when a fellow I did not know joined us. He did not seem to be interested in me, and he and the boyfriend were talking about a fishing trip they had been on recently. Evidently, they took it for granted I would be agreeable to any of their plans because they decided to visit this fellow's room, which was over some nearby stores.

When they proposed a drink before we were to go to eat, I accepted one drink. Because it was raining, I thought they were being considerate when the waitress and her boyfriend said they would go out for sandwiches for us. When my host offered to freshen my drink I said, "No thanks." We tried to hold a conversation, though we could not seem to find anything we both cared to talk about. Some time passed and I said, "I think they have decided not to come back, so I am leaving."

After putting on my coat, I approached the door. He went to the door to open it for me, I thought, so I was completely relaxed. Then he turned to me and, without warning, struck me on the left jaw with his fist. My knees buckled and I fell to the floor, but I was not unconscious. My mind raced. "What is going on?" I acted as though he had knocked me out. I was afraid that if I were to get up he would knock me down again. When I didn't move, he half dragged and half carried me to a chair and then went to the wall bed and lowered it. Then he put me on the bed and took off my coat, shoes and dress. I was down to my slip, and I began to think it was time to stop my acting. He left me and I dared open my eyes enough to see what he was doing. He took off his shoes and lay down on the bed on the other side, and I braced myself to give him a good fight. Fortunately, I did not need to. He passed out as soon as his head touched the pillow.

After what seemed an eternity, I tried to bring myself to a sitting position as quietly as I could. Then I stood up, put on my dress and coat, and carried my shoes to the door where my purse was on the floor. I picked it up and opened the door without a sound. When I got into the hallway, I softly closed the door, put on my shoes and left. It was still raining as I hurried down the deserted street to my hotel.

When I was safely in my room, I started to cry harder than I ever had in my life. My face, where he had hit me hurt, but that was not the reason I was crying. I was filled with rage and wanted to retaliate. I thought I would call my brother and have him bring friends and beat this guy up. No. That would not do. I did not want to go to the police. They would ask what I was doing in this man's room in the first place. Finally I went to sleep after deciding there was really nothing I could do. I thought I would never go into a man's room again.

The next evening I told the waitress what had happened after they had left me in the room. She tried to explain why they had not returned. Her boyfriend said it was too late, so without giving me a thought, they had changed their plans and gone home. She telephoned the man that had hit me. Then she came to me and told me his alibi. It seems he had recently been engaged to a blonde girl who had persuaded him to open a joint bank account, combining their money. Then she had skipped town with all the money. In his mind I became that girl when he had too much to drink. I was in the dining room when he came to me and apologized. I couldn't say anything because I was still so angry, and he left. My chin had a bruise, which I covered with makeup, but my neck was stiff for several days from the blow that had forced my head to the side. Later I heard he had been a professional boxer. Maybe my acting had saved me from a severe beating.

I was booked into the club in Vallejo again. On several evenings, a large table was set up for several young officers from the Naval Station at Vallejo. They asked me if I would sit with them between shows, and, because they were young, good looking, and really nice, I did. They were from a submarine that was being worked on at the base. They could see there was an attraction between one of their fellow officers and myself, and they did their best to foster the relationship. Why? It seemed they had decided I would be a good wife to have at the home base because I would be a good hostess! They completely ignored the fact that this man was already engaged to a girl back home.

We did talk and exchanged stories of our lives that could not have been more different. We certainly would not have had any chance for a future. It would have been the story of the wealthy young man and the showgirl all over again.

One Sunday afternoon, they invited me to have dinner with them at the base. Before dinner they took me to the room where there were guns and targets and instructed a sailor to give me a choice of guns and to set up targets for me. They knew I liked to shoot and were giving me a chance to enjoy myself. That I did.

For once I could fire from a standing, sitting, or prone position and did not have to worry about ammunition. I did not hit the bull's eye each time, but I did not do too shabbily either. After awhile they came for me, and we had dinner. It was a fun time. We had a few more evenings together, and then it was time for me to go back to San Francisco. I was misty eyed when I told them goodbye. It had been wonderful for me to associate with young men close to my own age who treated me with respect. My friend came to see me in San Francisco, and we went to see the "Ice Follies." Bea went with us and the three of us, had a great time. We were late arriving at the ice rink. Because there were no seats available and, I guess, because he was wearing an officer's uniform, they gave us a box seat in the front end of the rink. People were wondering who we were because the ice skaters gave us a special bow at the conclusion of their numbers. We thought it very funny, but really enjoyed the attention.

My Christmas holidays had been all over the country, but my last Christmas in the northwest was the strangest. I told Mother that Dinty had phoned and told me that he had a booking for me in Elko, Nevada. It was for a show on Christmas and New Year's.

She said, "If you want to do it, we could have our own Christmas before you go."

Dinty had been with the Horace Height group and had become a booking agent when he retired from the orchestra. His wife and Bea had worked together, so we knew each other fairly well. I called Dinty and asked for particulars. Tommy Lynne would be the only person I would know-we had been on several shows together. He wore his tuxedo better than anyone I had ever seen, except Fred Astaire, and Tommy even danced like his idol. I would not feel so alone on Christmas with him, so I said yes, I would go. Also on the show would be a magician and his wife. Tommy and I would be driving with them.

Mother, Bea and I had our Christmas dinner the night before I left, and we exchanged our presents. Leaving early on Christmas Eve day, our group started on our journey to the Elko Hotel. It was cold and foggy when they came to my apartment. I was waiting at the curb, and Tommy helped me with my luggage. When I was settled in the back seat with him, he gave me a package and asked me to hold it for him. I adjusted the lap robe around me and thought I might get some sleep.

Instead the magician said, "Would you like to hold our rabbit for us?" So I put Tommy's package between the window and myself and put the little creature in my lap. He was perfectly at home under the lap robe and curled up into a little ball. When I stroked him he just looked at me with his big eyes then went to sleep.

It did not get any warmer on our trip, especially in the mountains where there was snow on the ground. We talked about how pretty it was until I suddenly let out a different exclamation. "Oh! The rabbit just wet on me." Everyone laughed but me. The idea of it wetting on a very personal place did not amuse me at all. We stopped at the next gas station, but the pipes were frozen. After what seemed like ages, we arrived at the Elko Hotel. It had been built during more prosperous days and was a historical landmark. Modernization had not taken away any of its beauty. The owner was giving the townspeople a special treat for the holidays.

Tommy had been told he would be sharing a room with the magician's assistant, who had brought the equipment for the illusions in his car. A shared bathroom connected their room with mine. They understood when I said I was going to take a shower immediately. When I was going to put the package in Tommy's room, he told me to take care of it.

The fellows had work to do for the magician, and since I was feeling much better after my shower, I decided to go out and shop. A grocery store had some Christmas trees, and I found a perfect small tree. I bought some tiny ornaments and goodies to eat after the last show. The town was clothed in snow and icicles, so I walked very carefully because the sidewalks were icy. The boys were still helping the magician set up, so I went to work on the tree. I wrapped the base in a snowy white towel. The ornaments and the canes looked good, but it needed something. I added bits of cotton and made snow on the branches. My efforts were well rewarded, and the boys said the tree almost made up for not being at home.

"Where is the package?" Tommy was looking at the tree that had replaced the package on the desk. I gave it to him, and he placed it under the tree. It was rehearsal time and we dashed out to the small but good orchestra. We met the singer and the M.C., who was also the comedian. It was an agreeable group that had an excellent dinner in the coffee shop after the rehearsal. We used our hotel rooms to put on our make up and costumes because of the lack of dressing rooms. Nothing was like we were accustomed to, but everyone tried to make us feel at home.

We did a dinner show for an enthusiastic audience and were very complacent when we returned to our rooms. The feelings did not last long. The telephone rang. It was Dinty with bad news. The owner had called him and said he was canceling the show! He said we were good, but he wanted a really funny show, not just good performers. Outside of our M.C., who had a monologue, and a few comedy lines from the magician, we were not funny.

Dinty was of course upset and said it was not our fault, but could we do anything about the situation? I told him, that for many years I had wanted to ham up my toe and Oriental dances.

"Can you do that? he asked.

"I'd love to. What about the acrobatic dance?"

"That was good. He liked it, so keep it in. I'll call you back in a few minutes."

Tommy told Dinty he had an eccentric tap dance. The musicians would already know the popular music he used. The magician said he could use all of us in a finale. He would teach us some simple tricks that we wouldn't have any trouble learning. The M.C. had some funny material he could add.

Dinty called and said we were to be given a chance, and after practicing the tricks the magician showed us for the finale, we were ready for the second show.

The owner was surprised at the transformation and said we could stay on. We celebrated our success and Christmas Eve with my cookies and soft drinks. It was well after midnight when Tommy said, "I know you don't open your packages until Christmas morning, but I think it is that now."

He reached for the package and with an elaborate bow, he presented it to me.

"You made me carry my own gift?" I made believe to hit him.

"I hope you like it," was all he said.

I loved it. It was a Raggedy Ann doll! I was so pleased. It traveled with me and always reminded me of that crazy engagement in Elko. Our show was a success. The owner was pleased. Dinty was pleased, and we had fun being magicians. Funny, but I never did figure out my trick, although it always worked when I followed the instructions.

I would have liked to continue with the comedy routines but it was still too early for dancers to do more than one type of dancing. One day I was practicing in a dance studio that rented space to dancers. When I saw they had a good gymnastic mat, on an impulse I decided I would do a front walkover without my hands. I had never used the difficult trick in my routine, but I didn't want to forget how to do it. This time I fell, landing hard on the mat. It did not hurt particularly, so I continued to practice, and then went home. I did not experience any problem with my back that night.

The next day was a Sunday, and I was booked at a theatre, in Eureka. My Oriental dance was first. I slid into my split and found I could not get out of it. My legs would not move. I got to my feet in a different way than usual and managed to go on with the routine. In my dressing room, I quickly changed into my costume for my acrobatic dance and found a spot to limber up more. I thought perhaps the long ride that had started in the middle of the night had somehow affected my muscles. My back did hurt, but then it had hurt off and on since Ed had dropped me so many years ago. I was able to continue that day by changing my routines so I could still dance but my movements were limited. The hardest part to handle was the fear that I would repeat the split episode and not be able to get up. Something had to be done, but what?

1955

Opening Oct. 1st

Lucille Iverson Dance Studio

7297 University Ave.

- Tap
- Ballet
- Acrobatic
- Baton
- Ballroom
- Stage Training

Enroll Now

HO9-7515

14 Years of Teaching in San Diego

Pres. Associated Dancing Teachers of Southern Calif.

Class or Private Lessons

CY5-9458

THEATERS

SATURDAY MORNING, SEPTEMBER 17, 1955

a-15

Dancers Elect Miss Iverson

Lucille Iverson of San Diego is the new president of the Associated Dancing Teachers of Southern California. She was installed at a meeting of the organization in Los Angeles. She previously was first vice president. Miss Iverson has been teaching here since 1941. She is the second San Diego dancing teacher to hold the association presidency. Gladys Bowen was president in 1951.

Miss Iverson

I'm at the Barre, in my First Dance Studio

A Picture of Myself in my Studio

MC at USO Show, Florence Richard is my Accompanist

Left to Right - My Friend, Catherine Adams, Myself, Ernest Belcher & Margaret Otero

Tom Sheey Presents Gold Tap Shoes to Ginger Rogers at DMA Banquet. I look on.

DANCE MASTERS OF AMERICA
74th ANNUAL CONVENTION
Lafayette Hotel ☆ Long Beach, California
August 11th — 15th, 1958
Photo by Kickbush • Tujunga, Calif.

I was Miss Hollywood!

I am Demonstrating with Judy at a D.M.A. Workshop

The Newspaper sent a Photographer
to get pictures of me for Ginger Roger's
Bond Show at the Orpheum Theatre
in San Diego, California.

Featured Dance at the Paris Inn, San Diego, California

Another Performance at the Paris Inn

My Brother, Alton Iverson when he was in his Thirties

Myself, when I was in my Thirties

Mr. Fountain, My Friend from Childhood On

Mr. Fountain, and Myself

Chapter 16

Monday morning, Mother and I discussed my back problem. She wanted to know if I was in pain, but I told her I only had trouble when I was doing acrobatic work. I was also worried that I might have the same problem coming out of a split that I had experienced the day before. There hadn't been any warning and that frightened me.

She said, "Maybe it is time you become the dance teacher you have always wanted to be." She showed me the paper she had been reading the day before. An advertisement told about a building that had possibilities for a dance studio. It was in Burlingame, a town down the peninsula. We had not thought of having a dance studio in the bay area because we always talked of having one in Long Beach. We decided to investigate, and I made an appointment with the agent. The next day we took the train to Burlingame.

This pretty suburb is south of the big city and at that time was mostly residential, with morning and night commuters who took the train to work in San Francisco. Arriving at the address, I had my first doubts because it was on the main street, and the homes appeared to be large and expensive. The agent told us the Women's Club had vacated the place when they had moved to their new residence. The brown rambling building had a large dance floor and many rooms, and we loved it immediately. We did not think we could afford the building, but we let the agent show us the separate meeting rooms and a kitchen. Mother whispered to me. "We could make a livable apartment here." When we heard how much they were asking for the lease, we thanked him for his trouble and took the bus back home.

Mother and I had always been thrifty. Any extra money was put into the bank. While we did have some treats once in while, we saved for the future when I would have a dance studio. I had always admired my dance teachers. Before I became a professional dancer, teaching was my goal. I wanted to know all the types of dances so I could teach them. I never gave up my dream but hoped I would make enough money being a professional dancer so I could open the school of my dreams. It would be a real academy with live-in students and academic teachers. The Depression had taken my dream from me. Everything fell apart when the theaters started to drop stage shows. From then on, it was a hard struggle to just make a living.

A dancer's performing life is short. I had been working steadily for fifteen years and had been dancing seriously since I was eleven years old. Mother and I had had a good life, but there was never enough money to really put away a good sum.

In early 1941, my long time friend, Catherine, called me from San Diego, where she was now living with her husband and little boy Kenny. She had been shopping in town, and had stopped to talk to the husband of a dance teacher. He asked if she knew of anyone who would be interested in working in his wife's branch studio. He said it would be full time. It was located on the other side of town from her studio.

Catherine had sold her studio in Long Beach before moving to San Diego. She had not known I would have been interested in buying it. She had heard from Mrs. Alexander that I was looking for a studio and thinking this might be right for me, she telephoned me.

I asked her to make an appointment with the teacher, and Catherine invited me to stay with her. I was venturing into new territory, and I prayed I was doing what was right.   When it was time to leave, I took my ride to the station in a cab because of my luggage, but I would have preferred a cable car. How I would miss them. But there was no use looking back. I had to move on to the next stage of my life.

Catherine met me at the station in San Diego, and we drove to Sunset Cliffs.

Her home was on the side of a hill, three blocks from the ocean. The cliffs reminded me of Long Beach, and I could hear the waves breaking on the shore.

Harry, Catherine's husband, was enthusiastic about his position as skipper of a yacht. If he was not away on a voyage, he would be on board supervising the crew who were taking care of the trim luxurious yacht. Since it had been transferred to San Diego by its owner, it was moored in the bay at the Kona Kai Club, which fit in with the surrounding South Sea look.

The sound of the surf lulled me to sleep, and I woke up the next morning feeling refreshed, and eager to meet the dance teacher. After a hearty breakfast, we drove over the hill to the Normal Heights area branch studio where I met Gladys. She did not ask many questions about my dance experience, but showed me the single studio room with a curtain drawn across the back. She explained I could live in the studio and sleep on the cot behind the curtain. This was more of an opportunity for an advanced student to start teaching and was out of the question for me. I told her I was not interested, thanked her, and left.

I wondered why Catherine had put me to this trouble. I was to find out very soon when she divulged what she really had in mind. On the way back to her home I found she had other plans for me. She said I should have my own dance studio. She said she knew of a good location in the shopping area of Ocean Beach, which was adjacent to Sunset Cliffs, and said that I should see it.

The vacant store she showed me was located in the same building as a Safeway store, a bakery and the Ocean Beach News. It was smaller than the one I had seen that morning. I was not enthusiastic about teaching in a store, even if it was in a good location.

We looked into the front windows and I wondered what she saw that made it feasible. She said we should at least look inside. A telephone number was posted in one window, and we called from the newspaper office. The owner answered and in a short time she was showing us the place. The store had two partitions, and the front room, as we had surmised, had been an office. A doorway in the first partition led into a large room that probably measured 35 by 20 feet. Another partition had a door that led into a space about 5 feet deep, which had an adjoining bathroom, composed of a sink and lavatory. So far, the only thing I liked was the price of the lease, $35 dollars a month. I said I did not like the concrete floor and Catherine said that tile would make a good covering. She continued telling me the advantages. A desk and some chairs would make a good reception room in front, and the back area would have plenty space for a dressing room.

She told me the place was as big as her studio had been in Long Beach. I had visualized her studio as bigger because I knew she always had a large enrollment. Catherine, I was to find out, had a way of persuading people, and I was not the first or last to have my life changed by her. To this day, I do not know how it happened so quickly. I made two telephone calls. One was to Mother asking her to pack our belongings and join me. The other was to Mr. Fountain to ask him for a loan of $500.00. He said he would send the money right away so I could get started. The next day, I signed a three-year lease and was the owner of a dance studio!

When the tile salesman arrived, he barely looked at the floor before he said, "It would be out of the question to put tile down here. With the ocean just one block away there would be too much moisture for tiles to last." I was not too disappointed. Having danced on tile over concrete, I knew it was very hard on the feet. A wood floor would be much better. When we returned to Catherine's home, I looked in the telephone book for contractors. After three calls, I knew I was in trouble, because their estimates were around a $1,000 dollars to install a floor. I knew that my budget would not possibly allow me to spend that amount.

When I had worked with Daddy when he was a contractor building homes, together we had frequently figured how much lumber he would need for his buildings. After some calculating, I called lumberyards and located one that had prices within my reach. I ordered some lumber to be delivered the next day. There would not be very much left of my loan from Mr. Fountain, but I believed I knew what I was doing.

I had telephoned a man after reading his ad in the Ocean Beach News, and he watched with me when they brought the lumber. When it was in front of the store on the street, he said he could install the floor and could start that day. I was glad he was eager to get the floor done because I was going to pay him by the hour. He was not so eager to work fast after he started.

Two days later when it was half done, two young men who were working at Convair, where they built planes, asked me how much he was charging. When I told them I was paying him by the hour they offered to put the floor down the next morning, which was a Saturday. They said they would divide the money, and one of them said part of his could go for lessons for his daughter. They gave me a fair price, and I hired them. When they finished at noon, as promised, the father brought a piece of pine flooring about a yard long to me.

He asked, "Who ordered your lumber? He did a good job because this is all that is left." When I told him I had, he wanted to know how I did it. I told him about Daddy who had been a contractor, and how I had worked with him when he was designing homes. When I helped him figure how much lumber was needed, he said it would help me with my arithmetic. Years later, I realized I had received more schooling than Daddy had ever had, and it was a question of who was helping whom? But now I was profiting from the experience. My hard worker asked, "Who is going to finish the floor?"

I told him I was going to try, and I did. It meant filling the cracks, then sanding it, which I did with only one tiny dig into the wood. When the floor was ready all I needed was barres for the ballet exercises.

After explaining my need to my new friend, he said he would try to make them. I described them, and he made a good set of barres. After he installed a large mirror on one wall, the result was a nice compact dance studio. He did all this for credit for dance lessons for his daughter, which certainly helped because I was running out of cash.

Mr. Fountain's loan had disappeared, and the money Mother and I had saved was dwindling. I went to the bank to ask for a loan. I was refused. I didn't know what to do until Mother said, "I'll ask for a loan." Mother was given it because of her credit record, which was excellent. And I had been paying for almost everything for her since I was sixteen years old! Later we had a good laugh about that. I had asked my former carpenter if he could paint, and when he said he could, I told him to start painting around the front windows. Again I was to pay him by the hour. He was so slow that I dismissed him, and I finished the painting myself.

I laid the linoleum for the reception room and dressing rooms. Where I needed more light, I used extension cords for the light fixtures, so I would not get into trouble with hidden wiring. The local lumberyard cut some lengths of wood for me to install in my two store windows facing the sidewalk. I fastened my theatrical

8 x 10 photos to the boards so passersby might see them.

San Diego was filling with aircraft workers, and housing was getting scarce and expensive. There were apartment houses, but they were too expensive for us without going further into debt. We decided to live in the studio for awhile. It would not be like the studio in Burlingame, but we would make it do.

Heavy lining on the drapes for the two store-type windows gave privacy. My sign, "Ocean Beach Dance Studio" was painted on the door, and the rest of the glass was painted so that it was opaque.

We planned what furniture was needed and where it was to go. The first thing was a couch that opened to a bed for us. One of the few things I had wanted from my family was a small cabinet my Daddy had made years before. Now I had a place for it. Mother and I congratulated each other because our place looked like a miniature studio apartment. Mother transferred her accounts from the department stores in Long Beach. I soon established my credit with stores with Mother as co-signer. I knew that I could establish a good credit record now that I was in business.

Show people had difficulty establishing credit, I suppose because they traveled so much. Then there are always the people who made it hard on others because they would leave town owing money.

Mr. & Mrs. Hartvigson, who owned the paper, had become our friends, and they helped me with an ad and printed it. The Ocean Beach Dance Studio opened on Memorial Day, 1941, and because it was a holiday, the streets were full of casual shoppers besides the people who had been enjoying the beach. They stopped and looked at the pictures in the window. We had the door open and soon Mother became busy enrolling students. We had already made the price and schedule lists. That evening, Mother and I took a walk, and after we had gone a block and all the store windows were dark, we started to laugh. What in the world were we doing in this small suburb where the lights went out and "the streets were rolled up by eight?" Certainly it was not like San Francisco. We returned to our new home and we both agreed that, although it was not a palace, it was cozy, and better still, ours.

Now we knew where we would be for years into the future and could settle down and make friends.

We started to relax after the first month when our new adventure went well.

Catherine suggested I charge $5 a month for two class lessons a week. A loaf of bread just cost a dime, so our prices were right.

Before long, I had different grades of classes from preschool to high school. Tuesday and Thursday filled up, then I added Monday and Wednesday. Private lessons came in on Friday. At first I started from 10;00 am to 5:00 pm, then it became 9:00 am to hours after dinner.

I still remembered helping my teachers with the younger students, and now the knowledge came in handy. I taught Mr. Belcher's barre work and his floor combinations, and enjoyed making my own ideas come true. My training from different teachers in tap dancing helped. I realized I needed a mat for my acrobatic work.

A mattress factory was listed in the telephone book, and I called and asked the owner for an acrobatic mat. Neither of us knew what I wanted. I was in strange territory so I gave him a width and length and he gave me a price. When he delivered it to the studio, I thought, how am I going to manage such a huge mat? I was not the only surprised one. He said he would not go back on his quoted price, but I certainly was receiving a bargain. Rolled out, it reached 2/3 of the studio floor's length and a 1/3 of its width. It was so thick it could have been used as a gigantic bed! Just rolling it out and back again was great exercise. That turned out to be a minor problem, but the children had fun opening it out and rolling it back in place again.

I had not been around little ones for years. In the 20's, children were taught to be seen and not heard, and the classes were really disciplined. Those days were gone forever, I found out. Mother and I exchanged amazed looks when we heard the mothers say, "What do you want to do now? Go shopping with Mommy or go home?" Then they would do what the child wanted!

This behavior showed in other ways. If I suggested something pertaining to the lessons, it was the child who made the decision. There were exceptions of course, but it did not seem to occur often.

My method of immediately establishing that they were to give me their full attention worked well. They found I meant what I said and they behaved, and I relaxed. Then the classes were not only instructive, but fun too.

We could not tell if the students were addressing Mrs. Iverson or Miss Iverson, so Mother suggested I should be called Miss Lucile. It worked, but I always felt like making a curtsy, like a southern belle. I was nice though, and I never said, "You all come, you heah?" It was a good solution to our problem, and I am still being called Miss Lucile by former students who are now parents....and grandparents!

Before long, I was asked to teach private ballroom lessons. The men working at the airplane plants were earning good pay, and because ballroom dancing was popular, they wanted lessons. When I told Mother I had not planned on teaching ballroom, she reminded me I had taught my brother's girlfriends and also had taught ballroom dancing in the music conservatory when I was in high school. Once I overcame a little shyness, I enjoyed giving the lessons. The private ballroom lessons were given in the evenings, and a few came in early in the morning. It depended on what shift they were working. Before long, I had a ballroom class coming in one night a week. Each month brought more students, and because of the small studio, I limited my size of classes, which meant more of them.

I opened an account with Thearle's Music Company and purchased a good record player. Mother and I did not quite agree on how many records I needed, but finally she realized I had to have ballroom, tap, and ballet music, which had to come from classical records. It was a pleasure to be able to go into one of Thearle's small rooms with a phonograph and hear the records before I bought any. Then I could add it to my account without any worry.

We soon became adjusted to our new life style in the little suburb. We enjoyed getting to know people in the stores and area. The owner of the drug store, Mr. Kraft, was our state senator and sometimes I was asked to join a group of friends and employees when he entertained at a Chinese restaurant. I had never seen so many different dishes of food before, and I really enjoyed them.

Our front door had a transom over it and we kept it open most of the time for ventilation. At night, with the drapes closed, it did not look like the place was occupied. We would be talking or reading and would hear the remarks of the people passing by when they looked at the photo display.

There was a theater nearby and couples would stop to see my pictures as they walked by. My favorite overheard remark was from a young woman to her escort who was admiring my pictures. She said, "I have seen her and those pictures really make her look a lot better than she really is." She was probably right. The photos were not too recent and her indignant tone made Mother and me laugh. Fortunately, or unfortunately, I could not peek to see who was talking.

The first time we took the city bus into town, the other passengers stared at us. Attired in our San Francisco style clothing, with hats and gloves, we looked different. Mother gave up the gloves finally, but she always out-dressed everyone. Skirts and sweaters were my favorites, so I fit in better. I loved hats, but soon stopped wearing them. It did take a long time before Mother's and my style of dress became more casual. On that first trip into town we had a surprise when the bus went by the main dance studio of the teacher who had interviewed me. Catherine had driven into San Diego proper by a different route. She had not told me that I would be fairly close to Gladys's studio. I was dismayed, but it was too late to make any changes. I don't think either of us suffered from the proximity.

Two theatrical agents were happy to take my resume and pictures. They called me for club dates occasionally. Busses were convenient for transportation, and it was a nice change from my new routine. I was to remember one particular night at the Officer's Club on Rosecranz Avenue where the Navy base was located. There was talk of war, but mostly everyone was intent on having a good time, drinking and dancing after the dinner and show.

The next morning was Sunday, and I went to the Kraft drug store for the Sunday paper. When I entered the store I was told of the Pearl Harbor raid by the Japanese. I ran to the studio and turned on my portable radio. Mother was fixing breakfast and came and listened. It was hard to believe the news we heard that morning, December 7, 1941. We had been led to believe there would not be anything to fear from Japan.

Like everyone else, we were in shock. Everything moved fast, not only for the military, but for civilians as well. We were acquainted with the area air warden, a young man who took his duties of looking for anything unusual seriously. We told him our telephone would be available to him at all hours. Also, we walked around the neighborhood and reported to him anyone who was not complying with blackout orders. We put up blackout curtains, which gave us even more privacy when we put them next to the front windows. When they were testing the Sirens, all lights were supposed to be extinguished.

The shortages of almost everything increased. One almost forgot silk hosiery ever existed, they were so scarce. My first pair of nylon hosiery lasted for months. Then they changed, and they lasted only a trifle longer than silk hose. It was not profitable to have hosiery that lasted forever.

We had ration stamps, but that did not mean all food was available. The alley close by led to the back of the Safeway store. Mother watched, and when the trucks went by, she waited a few minutes and then went to buy the items that would be gone in an hour.

The area between the dance floor and the back had become our kitchen and dressing room. For our kitchen we had a tiny ice box, plus a two burner electric stove that was used for cooking our meals. It also heated the water for the galvanized tub we used for our baths. Our kitchen furniture consisted of a small table, two chairs, and a diminutive cupboard. The other side of this small space was our dressing room. I had installed a pole across the end and Mother had made a curtain for our closet. Our dresses and coats we placed there, and the rest was stored in a dresser. She also made colorful curtains for the two door openings. My portable sewing machine certainly came in handy.

The two stores on each side of us took up part of our space. All three rest rooms were in a row. Theirs extended into our space and, because their ceilings were lower than the rest of the studio, there was a ledge for us to store the boxes of odds and ends we had. I would climb a ladder to reach this plateau.

We did not have a back exit, which perplexed me. I thought the inspectors would have objected to the fact that all we had was a large window in the bathroom and no back door.

Mother laughed at my antics when I tried out the galvanized tub for the first time. She accepted the offer of a distant cousin who lived nearby and would walk there for a good old-fashioned tub bath. I occasionally went there for a shower but used our tub most of the time because I wanted to bathe at night.

Catherine had been right when she had told me a dance studio was needed in Ocean Beach. That year I paid my first Income Tax, on $500! With Mr. Fountain repaid we began to spend money on ourselves. Mother loved to dress well. She felt she could spend more because she was helping to run the studio. She was there on morning class days, but at other times, she would take the bus into town and look around and shop. Now she had her own money and could shop all she wanted. I encouraged her to go to matinees, and occasionally on weekends we both went into town to see a show and have dinner.

The best part of teaching was making up dances. The next year, I was asked if I had some dancers for the local Fourth of July celebration. I sent my more advanced pupils, and they danced better than even I expected. From then on I was asked frequently for dancers for different functions. It became more like a revue as the years progressed.

One day Mother and I were on our way to the bus to go into town, and one of my students and her father came toward us on the sidewalk. She said, "Hello Miss Lucile," but her father looked as though he was trying to place where he had seen me. Then his face lit up and he said, "Hello. I didn't recognize you with your clothes on." Then he stammered, "I mean outside of the studio." Before it got any worse, we said, "Goodbye," and hurried on to catch our bus. When we arrived at the bus stop Mother and I looked at each other and began to laugh. We agreed it was fortunate there had not been anyone close enough to hear his remark.

A small piano found a place in the studio. My guardian angel, who seemed to be sitting on my shoulder these days, led a wonderful girl to my sign in the window, which stated I needed an accompanist.

Madeline's husband was a Marine, and they had just come to San Diego and found an apartment in Ocean Beach. I not only found an accompanist but a wonderful friend. Madeline didn't need too much in the way of sheet music. Her fingers just danced over the keys with improvised melodies for ballet and popular music for tap. Her body moved with her music until she looked like she was dancing along with the pupils.

One day Mother said to us, "I have a surprise for you for lunch." Madeline and I were treated to tuna sandwiches, potato chips and Coca Colas, a rare luncheon, because all were seldom available. We did justice to her treat.

Madeline was furnishing their apartment, and when she told me she needed a bedspread, I volunteered to make one. I knew she was on a limited budget, and I wanted to do something for her. I was as happy as she was when it turned out well because I had never done anything like this before. I was so pleased I made matching pillowcases.

In 1942, I was asked to appear at the Orpheum Theater for a one night performance. There was to be a Bond Rally, and Ginger Rogers would make an appearance. She would relate how she had been involved in selling bonds and would conduct an auction to raise money. The advance notice in the newspaper said I would be performing tap and acrobatic dances for my part of the program. The newspaper sent a photographer, and he took my one and only cheesecake picture. The night was a success because admission was given by purchasing a war bond, and we had a full house.

Ginger Rogers was a gracious hostess for her ardent fans. She had won an Academy Award for her acting career, which was in full bloom. She became even more famous when she made the musicals with Fred Astaire.

The local USO was staging shows at the different camps and training stations. When I was asked to produce one, it was a challenge I enjoyed. I supplemented my line of teenage dancers with local acts and added professional acts from the nightclubs that were always happy to perform.

Annette Fabray was my M.C. She also played a guitar and sang western songs. The men loved her and enjoyed her stories. Annette was proud of her niece Nanette, who was just getting her start in motion pictures. I knew if she had even a small amount of her aunt's personality that she would become a star.

The men particularly liked one of the dances that was different. The three-part denim costume had a long circular skirt with a brassiere top to match. The girls sang "Paper Doll," a popular song at that time. After one chorus they bent down and picked up the skirts from the bottom edge and held the skirts up in front of their faces. I had found an artist who painted the likeness of pretty girls on light pink silk material that was sewn to the under side of the circular skirts. The paintings were of the face and down to the waist. Below the waist the material was tucked into the dancers ruffled trunks and matching bras. They did a kick routine.

We had a Hawaiian sequence where I did "Lovely Hula Hands" with the girls in abbreviated sarongs in the background. They joined me with "To You Sweetheart Aloha."

Two pretty blonde girl accordionists were popular entertainers. A retired ventriloquist gave spice and variety to the revue. Of course the traditional military tap dance closed the show. We did several performances a month in the camps in and around San Diego. The girls never tired of their ride in the back of the big trucks and flirting with the young men after they loaded the trucks with the costumes and accessories. Besides the costumes, two large lights on iron stands were stored on our ledge above the bathrooms. They were the hardest to load.

One of our acts was performing at the Shanghai, a local nightclub. The actor suggested Mother and I come and see the show. We went and our actor friend introduced me to the manager, who asked if I would work in the show starting the next week. Mother and I talked it over, and I later called and told him I would like to do it.

Opening night I went in early to rehearse and found a very embarrassed orchestra leader who had been given the chore of informing me I was canceled. The reason given was another dancer had become stranded, and they had put her in the show. I would not mind because I lived in San Diego. Later an agent told me what had really occurred. The dance teacher I had refused to work for was a regular customer, and told the manager she and her husband would boycott the club if I were to work there! Mother and I were not angry but were sorry she felt that way.

Some of my ballroom students were servicemen. Two were Marine buddies, and they became friends with Mother and me. Jan was recovering from a leg wound, and his doctor had recommended he take dance lessons. Mac was just going to accompany his friend, but he changed his mind when he saw me and said he would take lessons, too. Before long, he was asking me for a date. I told him I did not date my students, so he stopped the lessons. I still would not go out with him, so he made Mother his ally when Jan was having his lesson. To my surprise Mother asked me why I would not go out with Mac. I said it was because he was younger than I was. She said I could at least take walks with him. When I did, I found an interesting companion who also liked the rocky seashore with the tide pools. We would go there on Sundays. Mac was from Arkansas and had a southern drawl. He certainly was a southern gentleman and treated me with such respect I could not help liking him.

One night, I asked him to escort me to a nightclub where some older students were dancing in the floorshow. We had to walk a few blocks after we left the bus. My date and I were approaching another couple coming from the club. It was a

Navy officer with a young lady. She obviously had been drinking heavily, and as we neared them she was using profane language in a loud voice. Then a surprising thing occurred. Mac saluted the officer and said something about the language the girl was using, and that he did not like his friend being exposed to it. Then I was really surprised because the officer apologized.

My hours did not allow us to see each other often. When he began to talk about getting married, I didn't take him seriously. He and Jan left for overseas, and Mac wrote to me. His first letters spoke of his coming back to marry me and going to Arkansas. Then a letter came telling me I was to forget him because there was not any future for us. It was a real Dear John letter and Mother and I were puzzled and more or less relieved because his fantasizing about our future was worrying us. Then even more puzzling was a letter that came for me from his brother. He wrote I was to ignore the letter from Mac. He did not mean it at all but was afraid he would be badly wounded and did not want me to be tied to a cripple. I still did not hear from Mac again.

Occasionally, Mother and I would go to Long Beach on the bus to visit my brother, his wife Henrietta, and their son Douglas, who was just a tiny tot. While there one weekend, we went to Los Angeles to see Ed Wynn. After enjoying his show, we went back to my brother's home. As we walked, we talked about the dancing in the show. Suddenly, Mother fell, twisting her foot on a dog bone on the sidewalk. She fell sideways, landing on the purse she was carrying, and later complained about her side hurting. In a few weeks, she had an upset stomach and yellow jaundice, but she was reluctant to have medical attention. In desperation, I took her to my brother hoping he could persuade her to go to a doctor in Long Beach. I had tried to make an appointment with a doctor, but she would not let me.

Alton believed her when she told him, "It isn't anything. I'm all right. I will be better in a few days." Alton's friend, Fred, and his wife came to visit. Fred, who sold surgical instruments, and whose father was a doctor, took Alton aside and told him his mother was really sick. The next day Alton took her to a doctor's office. After an examination, Alton was told to take his mother to the hospital right away. After they had stabilized her, the doctor performed surgery. A closed duct had caused cirrhosis of the liver, and the liver had become too damaged to heal. I recalled she had complained of a pain in her side after she had fallen on her purse. She had probably injured the duct at that time.

When Mother was hospitalized, I made the trip to Long Beach as often as I could. When she went into a coma, I arranged for an advanced student who had been assisting me to take care of the studio. I stayed with Alton and was with Mother from morning to night even though she had a private room and her own nurses around the clock. Alton, Henrietta, and I were leaving for home one night when we met the doctor in the hallway. Alton said, "How can she live when she has such a bad heart?"

The Doctor said in a surprised voice, "Her strong heart is what is keeping her alive. There is nothing wrong with her heart."

Alton and I looked at each other in disbelief. She had controlled both of us all our lives with a fake heart attack whenever we tried to do anything she did not want us to do. Her coma lasted for two weeks, but her strong heart finally tired, and she died.

She was only sixty years old. I couldn't cry. I was hurting too much. At the service when the organist played "Lay My Head Beneath a Rose," one of my mother's favorite songs, I finally started to cry and could not stop. I couldn't believe she was gone. We had planned so much for the future. Now I would have to try and fulfill all the plans we had made by myself.

Annie, my mother's cousin, came to the funeral. After the service at the grave, she approached me and, after hugging me, said, "I am sorry Margaret is gone but now you can start to have a life of your own."

Everyone knew Mother had been my constant companion. I teased her once. "We are like a married couple. I earn the money like a husband, and you take care of me like a wife." Now I was on my own and what was I going to do?

I realized how unusual my life had been. I was 34 years old and had to start to make decisions for myself. Before, all I had to do was look into her face to see whether I was doing right or wrong. Even when we were apart, I had written to her daily to tell her what I was doing. She did have many friends, but for some reason she never approved of friendships I wanted to have.

Mother had suggested we should not become close friends with any of the children's mothers. She said she remembered my former years as a student and the attitudes and reactions of the mothers when I was favored. Now I was really alone with no one to turn to. Catherine was the only one I really knew, and she had her family to keep her busy. Madeline's husband had been transferred. I really missed her.

The USO wanted a second show, and because Mother had always made all the costumes, I needed a seamstress. One was recommended, and she came and measured the girls. When I did not hear from her for several days, I called and to my alarm she had changed her mind. She told me she had not started and had not even looked for material. I had to make the costumes in a hurry. Because of the wartime shortages, yardage was scarce. One of the girl's mothers offered to drive me to Tijuana where I hoped to find some cloth. My girls were to do a Russian folk dance before I did my Russian Cossack routine. Nothing I saw in materials suited me until some tablecloths caught my eye. When I could not find anything else that was suitable, I bought ten of them. They were for a small table and had floral designs in each corner. I purchased some white material for blouses and blue material for the skirts. After teaching all day, I spent nights making the costumes. The tablecloths were cut in half for the skirts, and I made the waistbands from the blue material. Then I made peasant blouses from the white material to complete the costume. They wore flowers in their hair. The rest of the costumes were made without any trouble.

I had decided to be my own M.C. and I enjoyed the new role. I did not try to be a comedian. I just introduced the acts.

Between classes one day, one of my students, Mary, came to me and said, "Do it, please, do it for me." I had no idea what she wanted me to do until she explained, "When you are with us all the time you are one person, but when you go on the stage you turn into someone else. I want to see how you do it. You seem to become sort of electrical!"

It was difficult to explain, but I tried. "When I am going to perform, a warm surge seems to go through me, and it helps me to perform."

A doctor once told me it was adrenalin going through the veins, and it happens with performers, athletes, and, I think, politicians, too. I am certain it is this wonderful feeling that accounts for the reluctance of actors and politicians to retire.

This young lady presented a problem. She was a beauty with long blonde braids and sparkling blue eyes. She had blossomed into womanhood early and the boys in the camps would surround her immediately. Joining the men I would say, "She is certainly a pretty girl." When they agreed I would say, "It is hard to realize she is only twelve years old." No more problem.... the group always dissolved.

The girls had been warned if I heard of anyone giving an address or phone number, they would be immediately dismissed. All of them were under 18 years of age, and I took my responsibility seriously.

One night, we went to a base that was opposite the airfield and was so well camouflaged no one knew it was there. I believe the men stationed there never had liberty unless they had a furlough.

I told the young officer in charge that the lights would have to be given separate extension cords, and he chose not to hear me. I warned him that they took a lot of power. He still did not pay any attention. Show time came, and I started my introductions. The lights came on, the lights went out! I was left with a dark room, without knowledge of when the lights would come on again. After a moment of hoping they would come right on, I told a joke. I knew it had to be above reproach because I had been warned to clean up some of Annette's stories. I had not thought they were so bad, but someone along the line had complained. Now I had to be careful. I told a story of the soldier who was climbing the fence to come back to camp after a night out. The guard on duty accosted him and told him to come back down and not try to go out again. My audiance laughed, the lights came back on, and the show began.

Our troubles were not over. "Tea for Two", a soft-shoe dance, was done by a trio of particularly pretty and well-endowed girls. The two part costumes of chiffon and satin bra and pants looked good on them. I had been lucky on their costumes. They were able to fit into three of my different colored acrobatic costumes. Their exit step was to bend over slightly, slap their thighs and slap their hands, 1234, 1234, and turn around and repeat. OOPS, one girl's bra came undone and almost exposed her. She tried hard to keep covered, which amused the fellows. I sympathized with her having been in the same predicament myself more than once.

The theater manager of the Orpheum called and asked me to work a week at the theater. The backstage doorman came to me one night and said there was a man who said he knew me and wanted to see me. It was Walter Cochrane, my former husband. As a war correspondent, he was stationed at Camp Pendleton with the marines until he was shipped out. My picture had been in the paper, and he had seen it and decided to see me. We needed a place to talk, so after the show we went to the corner bar, where else? I ordered a soft drink, and we started to reminisce. The time went quickly, and he asked if he could take me home after the show. It was good in a way to see him again, but the best part was when he actually apologized for his former suspicions of me and said he never realized what a good person I was and that I would never have been capable of cheating on him. I never found out what had changed his mind. That was the last time I saw or heard of him. Sometime later I asked a reporter if he had ever heard of Walter. He believed Walter had been killed in the South Seas. That is the way he would have liked to go.

The girls and I continued to do the USO shows for the duration of the war. The night of the Japanese surrender, I thought there would be signs of joy. On the contrary, the men were quieter than usual. There were too many unhappy memories of friends they would never see again.

An agent wanted to book me into the Bagdad again. I had enjoyed working there but I had decided I was happier teaching and told him that I did not want to work at any more nightclubs. Besides, my time was taken up teaching. I was glad to be busy. I was lonely without Mother.

Chapter 17

The war was over, and we began doing shows at the Army and Navy Y.M.C.A. and in the wards at the Navy Hospital. I was still riding on the bus or depending on friends for transportation. Mother's bills for the hospital had taken all my savings, so I had to start saving all over again.

A year later, I had saved eight hundred dollars, enough money for a second-hand car. A ballroom student who was stationed at one of the army bases offered to help me find a good car. He not only helped to find one but also would borrow it to take himself back to camp. When I finally had to ask him for the car because he had it all the time, I lost a student, but at least I had my car.

One night the telephone rang around ten o'clock. It was one of two sisters who were dance teachers. Margie was in tears, and I could hardly understand her. Finally she became coherent, and she told me she and her sister had been arguing and could she please come and spend the rest of the night with me? A taxi brought her after I said she could.

I knew her better than I knew her sister, because her husband, who taught tap dancing at their studio, had been on the same bill with me at the Shanghai club. When he went into the service, she had moved in with her sister, which evidently was not working out. Instead, she moved in with me. She needed help, and I was lonesome without Mother, so it was better for both of us.

It was easier getting around with my own transportation. I did more club dates. After a show one night, I offered two girls in the show a lift home. We stopped at a drive-in, and a sailor left other sailors in a group and came to the car. He said, "Could one of you girls recommend a good dentist?"

After discussing different dentists for a few minutes, he thanked us for our help, then asked for my telephone number so he could call me about my dentist. When we were driving away one of the girls said, "I wonder why he isn't going to the dentist at the base. He has found a new angle."

He called the next day, and told me his name was Harvey Young. He really didn't need a dentist, but needed an excuse to talk to me. He asked if he could come to see me. I told him I would be teaching until ten, thinking that would discourage him, but it didn't. When he came to the studio, he was polite, had a nice personality, and we laughed a lot. He had dark blond hair, blue eyes, and a trim figure that looked great in his sailor uniform. He told me he would be leaving the Navy soon and would go back to Springfield, Missouri. I thought a man his age would certainly be married. I asked him, and he said he wasn't. We continued seeing each other.

One afternoon the agent for San Diego's leading nightclub, the Paris Inn, phoned and asked for a favor. Would I please fill in that night for the girl soloist who was sick? He needed me for her spot in the revue. This was not the first time he had wanted me to work there, and I had always refused. This seemed to be an emergency, so I said I would fill in for the absent girl. It was a big place with tiers of seats and a larger than usual dance floor. The orchestra was excellent, and I enjoyed dancing there so much that night, that I stayed on. The absent girl had been a singer. I had been tricked, but I was glad he had done it. They needed a soloist lead dancer who was versatile, and I filled the order. The revues were more elaborate than we had done at the Embassy Club. The show's producer, who was known as Bunny, was thrilled to have someone with my background in his show. The chorus girls were talented, but they were just out of dancing school. He missed Hollywood and was happy to be able to talk about show business.

I began to choreograph the productions, and Bunny would transform the costumes he rented until they were beautiful. It seemed he was forever curling ostrich plumes after dying them and before attaching them to the costumes. He had boxes of jewels, which he sewed on the costumes, transforming them from ordinary costumes to exquisite garments. I was always starred in the production numbers and wore lovely costumes. The shows were well received, and every night the club was crowded.

It was difficult to teach every day, then dash downtown for the first show and work until two in the morning, but I did love it. I was glad I was not going to teach my night ballroom lessons for awhile, because teaching ballroom for three hours each night was hard on my feet.

My driving was adequate, but I needed more experience, which I found out on the way to the club one night. My road curved to the left, and a car was coming up from the direction I was going into. He turned late and forced me to make a wider turn than I should have. I ran up onto the curb, right into a telephone pole. The guy wire coming from the telephone pole was forced into my right front fender. My car came to rest on a mound of dirt. The combination of the guy wire and the mound of dirt was too much for the car, and it fell over onto the driver's side.

The sound of the crash brought neighbors out of their homes in a hurry. I turned off the ignition, reached up and rolled down the right window and put what I had been carrying on the front seat through the window onto the car door. I carefully stood, and prepared to exit from the window. I had to ask for help because the people standing by the car were in more shock than I was, and they were standing in my way. Finally, I was helped down from the window. As soon as I stood on the pavement, I asked. "Can I use somebody's telephone?"

A lady said, "You can use my phone," and she took me to her home. I called a garage for a tow, then the club to tell them I would miss the first show and why. I thanked the still excited lady and went out the door to go to my car.

A policeman approached me, and said, "Do you know who was driving this car?" I said, "I was, and I was phoning for a tow car."

"You are sure taking this calmly," he remarked. "I need to ask you some questions about what happened here." Then he led me to his squad car. Everything turned out all right, except that I hadn't obtained my driver's license and had only my learner's permit. I received my scolding and promised to take care of that right away. He and his partner not only did not give me a ticket, but they also drove me to the club. I thanked them for their courtesy.

I had trouble reassuring Bunny that I had not been hurt. He showed more concern for me than I had ever had. I did the remainder of the shows without any trouble. I was glad that I had insurance because the men from the garage righted the car too quickly and blew out my tires. Otherwise the car only needed a new window and a few repairs.

I had been in several revues when one night I came out of the stage door after the last performance expecting to see Harvey. He wasn't there, but someone else was. I was surprised to see my two Marine friends, Mac and Jan. Mac and I did not even have an opportunity to talk. Harvey came to take me home and was about to strike Mac because he thought he was annoying me. Jan and Harvey's friend Bill were able to step in and stop what was going to be a fight. The Navy boys and the Marines sometimes did not get along so well. I was relieved when the two buddies were able to stop the fight instead of joining in. When things calmed down, I told Mac I was surprised to see him after the letter he had written and that I was going steady with Harvey. We talked a little and he and Jan left.

After we did "American in Paris," one I enjoyed especially, I gave my notice to Bunny. I needed more rest. The added work was too much for me. Harvey and I didn't have much time to be together except for the weekends. It was late at night when I finished working, and I was usually tired. Margie, who didn't think much of him, tried to discourage the relationship. I had told her that Harvey had told me one night that not only was he married but had two children. He insisted the marriage had been over before he had joined the Navy. He thought his wife was planning to divorce him.

Margie's husband Freddie, was discharged from the service, and came to take Margie to Hollywood. They opened a dance studio there. Many times I wished she had not left me at this time. I needed her moral support.

I did try to break off the relationship with Harvey, but he couldn't see why. His pal persuaded me I was doing the wrong thing, Harvey needed me. I repeated the mistake I had made before with Walter, and began seeing Harvey again. When he left for Chicago to get his naval discharge, I thought he was out of my life for good. He told me that he was going back to Springfield.

A couple of weeks later on a Sunday morning, the phone awakened me. It was Western Union, and a girl was laughing. I could hardly understand her. She asked if she could read the message to me. It said, "No money, no clothes, no nothing. Meet me. Harvey."

A small voice said, "Be careful," but I didn't listen.

I met him and he told me he had been at the railway station in Chicago waiting for his train to Springfield. When the train for California was announced, he had boarded it. His belongings went on to Springfield. All he had was his shaving gear. His story of an unhappy marriage complicated with interfering in-laws was convincing. He said he would tell his wife to get a divorce. I financed him until one of his buddies told him of an opening at the icehouse, and he got a job delivering ice.

While I was giving lessons, Harvey would take my car and find entertainment for himself, coming back after I had finished teaching. He needed help one night because he had run the car off the road. When he telephoned me I was giving a ball-room lesson. It did not sound too bad until he told me he had gone down the embankment towards the flood channel of the San Diego River. My student drove me to where he had said he was, and there was not any sign of the car or Harvey.

We heard him calling, then I saw him pointing to where the car had come to rest halfway down the embankment. Trees had prevented me from seeing the car from the road. It was so out of sight that the tow truck men did not believe there was a car there. The police who questioned Harvey did not give him a ticket, believing it was just a failure to keep on the road in the darkness. Since no one else was involved, they left.

Perhaps he had gone to sleep. We both were grateful that he had not been injured. We were given a lift to the studio, and until the car was repaired, he spent his evenings in the cocktail lounge across the street. Then his divorce become final, and he asked me to marry him. He was five years younger but that didn't seem to bother him as much as did me. I said I would marry him.

I made the down payment on a house and furnished it. Bea came from San Francisco. We all drove to Yuma, Arizona, on June 25, 1946. For the second time, I was married in a city hall. After we had dinner, we drove back to San Diego to our new home. It was the second marriage for both of us, so we both hoped we would fare better this time. For awhile we did.

Bea left for San Francisco after buying us a stove for a wedding present. Harvey's buddy was able to take him to work because I needed the car to go to the studio. Mornings I worked hard putting in grass in the front and back of the house. I planted flowers and even planted a small vegetable garden. Harvey was always too tired to do anything around the house, but I was enjoying having a real home.

Another facet in my life had started on December 10, 1945, shortly after Mother had passed away. Catherine arranged for me to teach an acrobatic class for one of the meetings of the Associated Dance Teachers of Southern California. For years Catherine had wanted me to join the ADTSC, but Mother said I had always been capable of doing my own choreography. She had thought it would be a waste of time and money. She did not realize the other benefits that would have helped me with my studio. The association later became Chapter One of the Dance Masters of America. Besides the monthly Sunday meetings at the Hollywood Roosevelt Hotel, week-long conventions were held each summer, and expert teachers from all over the United States were on the faculty teaching performing arts and ballroom.

When I gave my presentation, I was nervous until I answered some of their questions and realized that I had knowledge that they did not have about teaching acrobatic work correctly. I had enjoyed the day and did not hesitate in saying "yes" when they asked me to become a member. There were examinations before a teacher could join, and I took them in ballet, tap, Spanish, and Hawaiian dancing. I passed all of them and was accepted that day when the members were called together to vote. There was not a test for acrobatic work, and later I was made chairman of the committee that developed that test.

The current president and vice-president were both from San Diego. The president was the teacher that I had not wanted to work for back when I was first interested in San Diego. She left when they were planning to accept me. Harry Hemphill, vice-president, was the owner of a large studio near Balboa Park in San Diego, and he welcomed me to the association.

Harvey was not even remotely interested in my dancing or the studio. Driving me to a meeting in Los Angeles was out of the question. Although Catherine would have driven me to the meetings every month, I did not attend regularly, but I enjoyed them when I did. One year when I started to sign a check for my dues, I hesitated. I had not been attending the meetings regularly I thought, why pay money for something I didn't participate in? I decided then to go faithfully every month and to see what would happen. Things did happen. I was elected to the board of directors, and then became vice-president.

One day Catherine phoned me and asked if I would be interested in helping Mr. Hemphill. His teacher for the baby classes was leaving, and he needed a replacement. He had called her for help because she had once taught the same classes. Her husband said, "Call Lucile."

She persuaded me to talk with Mr. Hemphill. When I went to the studio, I fell in love with the old place. It had quite a history, having started as the club house for the golf course near Balboa Park in the 1880's. For years, it was a music conservatory before Mr. Hemphill bought it for a dance studio. The large two-story, tan stucco building had porches in front and on the sides. It was an impressive building. The lawn had trees and rose bushes scattered around. I followed the walk around to the side entrance and opened the door. I didn't realize the building would be part of my future. I entered a room with a large desk and a bell displayed prominently. Tapping the bell brought Mr. Hemphill into the room. I barely knew Mr. Hemphill, an elderly man with graying hair and blue eyes, but I did know he was respected in the association. He remembered me and said he had admired the way I had taught at the meetings.

He explained his problem and said he hoped I could arrange some time to teach the classes. He understood I had my own studio but would appreciate my help if only temporarily. He gave me a tour of the building, beginning with an adjourning reception room with comfortable couches and chairs. It was used for the girl's dressing room and a waiting area for mothers.

The downstairs contained a large ballroom. On the opposite side there were several rooms including a room that had been a kitchen. One room had pictures on the wall that caught my eye. He told me they were of him when he was in vaudeville in the Twenties. He had been a female impersonator known as "The Huntress." He and his company had been a headline act and wore elaborate costumes heavily embroidered with jewels. They had been booked from the East Coast and had toured with the Orpheum Circuit, appearing in New York and other eastern cities. The reviews from the newspapers told of an illustrious career. We went upstairs to a door. It opened to a large sunny room with many windows and a view of Balboa Park and the canyon next to it. Beside the large mirror and good solid barres, there was a grand piano. The room was twice as large as my studio. One wall had two French doors that he explained led to the living quarters, a complete apartment.

We continued our tour of the studio, which was old but in good condition. Before leaving I promised I would try to rearrange my classes in Ocean Beach because I would love to take care of the children's classes. Two classes were in the morning and the other two were after lunch. I would have to change my own schedule. When I got home, I found that Harvey didn't mind my taking on extra work. This was to be the pattern in our married life, I discovered.

Besides the baby classes at the Hemphill Studio, I soon realized I could be teaching more students if I had the time. Mr. Hemphill wanted me to close my studio and work every day at his. I was not ready to close the studio in which I had invested so much work. I was still proud of it and how much I had accomplished there.

Mrs. Hemphill had a room in a building in the heart of San Diego where she taught ballroom lessons, mostly to young sailors from the fleet in San Diego Harbor. She was petite, like a tiny doll. The only time I saw her was when she paid me. I knew she had control of the purse strings, and there was not much doled out except for necessities.

One day after I had finished my lunch, I went though my past receipts. I found she was making errors, always in her favor! She apologized and made up the difference. The errors stopped, but I checked my pay from then on.

An adult student was performing at the YMCA. She was breaking in the new comedy routine I had given her. It was a familiar place; I had put on shows there often.

We exchanged a big bear hug backstage after the performance, and I told her, "The audience loved your dance. I'm proud of you."

To my amazement she started to cry. I asked what I had said to make her cry. She told me. "You have never given anyone a compliment unless it is earned. You just complimented me and I'm so happy."

Realizing then that I was doing the same thing my Mother had done to me, I became more generous with compliments.

My Uncle Joe phoned from Hollywood and said he and Aunt Mildred were coming to see us for a few days. It turned into a long visit because he was out of work. Worse still, he was out of money. It was a repeat of the time when I had stayed with them in Chicago for a week. He still gambled too much, and she had not cut down on her drinking. For awhile, Harvey was happy to have a drinking partner, but that didn't last long. Every day Uncle Joe went to Caliente to the race-track after spending long hours the night before consulting the race forms. He would figure the forms until early mornings, then bet on a hot tip and lose, instead of betting on the horses he had picked.

They had been with us for several weeks when he said, "My family in Hollywood has sent money. I can be with them until I get on my feet again. Can you take care of Mildred until I send for her? I will send what I can to help with her expenses."

Of course I said, "Yes."

Mildred did little to help around the house. She had lived in apartments and hotels too long. In the South she had always had a maid, so it was easy for her to lounge around, do her nails, and read the magazines she purchased when she went out to buy more liquor. The money went to her. My work kept me away from home all day and some evenings. Saturday afternoon and Sunday I worked alone on the yard. Harvey did not like yard work, and Mildred would not have known how to even sprinkle the lawn. I wasn't happy with the situation but did not know how to change it.

Harvey began to talk about having a place in the country where we would raise chickens. A friend told him all he needed to do was buy chicken feed from this company, and they would buy his chickens. I did not pay any attention at first, but when he made many promises about changing his ways, I finally said we could try it. After several Sunday drives, we found a couple who would trade their three-and-a-quarter acres for our home. When I saw the neglected yard in contrast to my well-kept lawns and garden, I groaned. The house was old, and through the years rooms had been added at different levels. We felt certain that Mildred would go to Joe, but she came with us, and that really worried me because of her smoking and drinking. I told Mr. Hemphill I would work full time for him and reluctantly closed my Ocean Beach school. There were so many memories connected with the school, among them the ocean.

In the beginning, before my schedule was so full, there was time to go down to the beach. I'd lay in the sun and then try to swim between the waves. I remembered on Sundays when I had taken my portable radio, a book, and a blanket to spread on the rocks further south below the high cliffs. The view from there was always wonderful, and I loved the sound of the waves breaking against the rocks. The spray would fall on me gently, and it would feel especially good on a hot afternoon. I would take walks to look in the crevices and watch the sea anemones open and close with the tide. The small crabs scrambling around always amused me. I would miss the sea gulls, watching them and hearing their noisy screeching. It all seemed eons ago.

When we moved inland to the ranch, Harvey's boss gave him twenty baby chickens that were installed in a small coop outside our back door. The big hen house that could have kept hundreds of chickens was never cleaned. I kept up a small garden in the back of the house, which furnished us with tasty tomatoes and vegetables. Two times a week I was up at dawn moving the troughs the water that were hosed into the rows of trees on one of the acres. It was a hard job because it was on a slight hillside. The ripe peaches and apricots were delicious. Harvey took most of them to his fellow workers. I would have loved to have canned them, but I did not have enough time nor the energy after I came home.

We were greatly relieved when, at last, Mildred went to Hollywood to join Joe. She had given me a bad time more than once when she was high. Harvey said she resented me because I had done so much more with my dancing than she had. I wanted to give her my love, but she didn't want it.

When the twenty chicks became hens, we enjoyed the eggs they laid, but Harvey never mentioned anything about going into the business. He had found out about the work involved after we bought the ranch, and he had lost all interest.

We had to rise early in the morning because Harvey had to be at work at seven, an hour's drive away. My late afternoon classes caused us to come home after dark, and I would have to start dinner then.

To my relief, Harvey decided we should return to San Diego after a year of country life. Again he would not go to a realtor. We found a house through the classified ads. We traded for a small house and I hated to think of the money that had been wasted. For the third time I worked without help to make the yards presentable with grass and flowers. Harvey's money went for his cigarettes and liquor, and sometimes he bought gas for the car when he was using it. All my life, it seemed I had worked hard with nothing to show for it. More students than I expected had made the move to the Hemphill studio with me. I was making money, but it was disappearing fast.

I thought of divorce, but this was my second marriage, and I kept on trying to make a go of it. It seemed, though, the harder I tried, the harder it became. At that point, I was not sure what to do. I only knew that somehow things had to get better for me.

Florence, my new pianist, became my friend and helped me with the recitals and the yearly show at the San Diego Fair. I had two lineups of girls for shows for senior citizens. Eight girls were from eight to twelve years of age. The teenagers were on the senior shows and also performed at the Navy Hospital and the YMCA. Our large recital every year was in a school auditorium. Florence and two musicians helped to make our performance more professional. Just as I had done when I was dancing professionally, I used mostly standard music. Each year I would receive several telephone calls from strangers wanting to know when I would be having my recital. They did not want to miss it.

Costumes were not ready made like they are now. Instead, I would receive catalogs showing swatches of material. After first designing all the costumes, I would figure the yardage needed and send for it. When it arrived, Louise, one of the mothers, would help me. All the material had to be measured, cut, and given to the mothers with directions for sewing. Some would arrange with another mother to make her child's costumes. I knew the costumes were almost done when the phone didn't ring so often, and I no longer had to tell someone how to do this or that.

When it came to choosing a few mothers to help backstage, I had to be a real diplomat. Everyone wanted to help. There were problems, and some I remember. After the show started, I would have the next dancer in the wings ready to go on stage. One time the small child who was waiting to go on next suddenly started to cry and said, "I can't do it," and clung to her mother. It was so unlike her I was really puzzled. Her mother took her away, and the next dancer was brought backstage. The next day, the mother called and informed me the little girl had the measles! She wanted to do her dance so much she had not told her mother she didn't feel well.

One of the favorite numbers in the show was the five year olds doing their tumbling. My big mat was on the floor with each girl alongside it waiting her turn. Starting with somersaults, front and backward, the tricks progressed in difficulty. When they could not do the trick they sat still.

Only a few were left to do the front overs. Sherry, one of the tiniest, had showed me the day before that she could do the front over. So she was allowed to join the others. She was so tiny she did not have a waist, and the little trunks she wore did not stay up too well. When it was her turn she went up onto her hands, stayed there a brief moment and then came down again without going over. She tried again and again. Each time she would give those tiny pants a hitch up. The audience was starting to laugh quietly. Everyone was fascinated by this diminutive figure with such determination, who would not give up. She must have tried a dozen times until at last she did a nice front over. Some in the audience cheered along with the applause. That night she was the star of the show.

One time my tiny Cuban dancers were led by Yvonne, a talented student, who later became Snow White in one of the traveling Disney productions. She went across the stage with the line up of little ones shaking their maracas and following their leader. Yvonne never turned to face the audience! The group did the entire dance facing right stage. What does the dance teacher do on these occasions? She laughs, too.

One year the students insisted I perform in the recital. They wanted to see me do a toe dance. I waited in the wings. I was alarmed. I felt so flat! The orchestra played my musical introduction, and suddenly from my toes to the top of my head I felt a rush of energy. Then my routine just flowed from me and I danced on air! I was sorry when the dance ended. The bonus came when the audience gave me their hearty applause. I had forgotten the wonderful sound of applause and felt a little sad those years were over.

For years, my life never seemed to change. My love for dancing and teaching kept me going. When I realized I was never going to have the child I had dreamed of, my baby classes became even more precious. Our love was mutual, and I basked in the love I could see in their eyes. They did give me a problem I could have lived without. They would give me their colds.

I would not enroll any students until they were four and a half years old. One day, a young mother came with her baby still in diapers and wanted to know if there was a class for her child. Parents thought because the children moved their feet in time to music on the radio they had talent. I would explain that if they started dancing too early it might even hurt their young bodies.

One day during a baby class I heard footsteps coming up to the top of the stairs and stop outside the door. I wondered who it was and why they did not come in. I opened the door to see a lady, who said, "I thought you had a baby class. I wanted to watch it."

I asked her to come in. When she saw my dozen cherubs sitting by the acrobatic mat patiently waiting for my return she said, "How do you keep them so quiet?"

I told her. "They are told to be quiet, and they know they will not have any lessons if they don't obey."

They did not have ballet but we interpreted classical music. I joined them in picking imaginary flowers, or we flew like birds. Tap was more like an arithmetic lesson, they learned how to count. A mother told me what happened when her child went to kindergarten and was asked if she could count. She proceeded to count, one and a two, and a three, and a four, etc.

Mrs. Hemphill became ill and went to the hospital where she was diagnosed with terminal cancer. She kept her husband busy going to stores and getting delicacies and feminine lingerie she had refrained from buying before. Now she wanted everything when it was too late. This taught me a lesson I never forgot. I began to treat myself to some of the things I wanted instead of waiting for sometime in the future that might never come.

Mr. Hemphill realized he had more money than he had thought, and he decided he wanted to have a nice home away from the studio. He needed to have a place for all the things he had started to buy, including a new car. He asked me if I would like to take over the studio. I was overjoyed. He kept a few students but stopped teaching when he started to travel. At that time I had at least a hundred and twenty five students, which I personally taught without an assistant. For once, I began to have a bank account that grew instead of shrinking.

Part of my dream came true when we moved into the living quarters of the studio. I had a dining room with French doors leading to a porch, besides a living room and two bedrooms. Also, I had the wonderful dance studio.

We should have sold the house, but instead I made it presentable for renters. After a year they moved, and we did sell it. Making it look good again was a lot of hard work, and we made a profit of only two hundred dollars. Harvey invested it in some mining stock which we later sold at a loss.

If there was anything Harvey and I shared it was a love for dogs, and we eventually had four of them. He had given me a small collie when I was still in the studio at Ocean Beach. She was so fastidious that I called her Lady. When we had the Ocean Beach home, a neighbor's cocker spaniel had a litter and we were given a jet-black pooch. His father was not a spaniel, so his hair was as short as a bulldog's which gave him an unusual appearance. He ate so much we named him Hungry!

On Valentines Day, we had tried to keep them apart, but evidently we failed. Later, I became a midwife, because Lady was having a hard time giving birth. After a frantic call to a friend for help, I followed instructions and helped Lady give birth with a Turkish towel. Over Harvey's objections, we gave all the puppies away.

The two dogs went with us to the new home. One day when I was teaching in the upstairs studio, I could see a small black dog across the street. It roamed around the trees all day. When I went down to fetch Lady and Hungry to come up to the living quarters from their outside fenced in yard, I found three dogs. The black cocker spaniel was so emaciated it was able to squeeze into the yard between the picket fence slats. We fed her and advertised in the papers, but no one claimed her. She was so grateful and happy, that she wiggled what was left of her tail. The effect on her rear provided her with the name Wiggles.

She and Hungry gifted us with another litter of pups conceived on Christmas. Hungry was a sentimental lover! Harvey insisted if there was a black and white puppy we would keep it. There was, so now we had Bubba, our fourth dog. We found good homes for the rest of the puppies.

Bubba was a darling dog. If I allowed him to go into the studio with a ball he would play polo all by himself. It was fun to watch him skid around the big floor, batting the ball. In the living room, we had a footstool that was large and had legs, so there was space underneath. Bubba would place the ball on one side and hit it so it would come out the other side, and then he would quickly run around and catch it. He taught himself these tricks while the other dogs would just watch him play.

Hungry was a sweet dog even if he looked mean. I was in back of the studio building cleaning the immense fishpond that had huge goldfish in it. It had been there a long, long time. To my surprise, Harvey came out to help me. We finished and put things in the garage facing the alley and went upstairs.

"Where's Hungry?" I asked.

Harvey said, "He was outside with us. Didn't he come in?"

I went outside and called "Hungry, Hungry," down the alley. Returning home, I passed our garage and heard a plaintive whine. We had closed the garage door with Hungry inside. A happy pooch was released. I had thought nothing of this until I told my friend Louise about it. She asked, "You went down the alley calling out 'Hungry?' What did your neighbors think?" I replied, "I hope they were all in their homes eating their Sunday dinner."

Bubba was a calamity dog. One Sunday Harvey took him hunting for rabbits when he was just six months old. When Harvey first shot the gun, Bubba stood still, but on the next shot, Bubba ran away. Harvey looked for him for a long time. Then he came home for me to help search. Each day we looked but without success. Harvey was able to go out and look for him on Thursday and took his gun with him. Aiming at what he thought was a rabbit behind a rock, just in time, he saw it was Bubba. He was thirsty and thin from hunger, but there was not a mark on him. Not even a sticker from the weeds. We were relieved he had come out of the experience so well. He was still a happy puppy until Christmas when I noticed he was passing blood. I found part of a Christmas ball on the floor. I rushed him to a veterinarian who promised to do all he could to save him.

In a few days he called for me to come for Bubba and told me to feed him soft food for awhile. He asked me if I had noticed Bubba was different from my other dogs. When I said he was more playful, he said, "He still acts like a puppy, doesn't he?"

"Well, yes." I answered.

The veterinarian asked, "Has he had any trauma that you know of?"

I told him he had been lost in the hills for five days. He explained, "Bubba is mentally retarded." He was right. Bubba remained a dear, happy puppy for the remainder of his life.

A few years later, when I was living in a different house, I lost him when someone left the gate open, and he ran into the busy street and was killed. I mourned his loss for weeks. He was retarded in some ways, but he never messed, growled, or snapped at anyone. He just gave his puppy love to everyone.

When I had my 40th birthday I made many resolutions. I decided my life was going to begin at forty. Things were going to get better. Unfortunately, it did not work out that way. My birthday was on the 22nd of March. On the 10th of April, which had been my mother's birthday, I broke my foot! The accident happened when Dodie, one of my advanced students, had just gone through the Russian dance I had done for so many years. She danced it, but without any verve, so I said, "I'll show you what I mean."

I had been sitting and watching her dance. I started the dance without warming up. After going around the room with the first step, I started the first of the squat steps. I felt a snap in the side of my right foot as I went down. Louise, my friend who took care of the desk sometimes, had come upstairs and had been watching. I told her, "Quick, go fill the bucket under the sink with cold water. I think I just broke something."

I called my doctor telling him what happened and he said, "Come to the office right away." Louise helped me to her car, and we drove to my doctor who confirmed my fear after an X ray. Clutching the X ray, we drove downtown to the orthopedic doctor he had called. He told me to hold my foot up, and instructed the nurse to hold it with the toes held so my foot was flat. He put on a cast that reached to my knee. My break, which resembled a snapped twig in the X ray, was in the metatarsal area below my little toe. He said it could not be set because it was too shattered.

Three mornings later, on a Sunday, I was awakened with a dreadful muscle spasm in my calf. I could not walk on that leg or massage the muscle so it just kept the cramp. I called his office daily, morning and afternoon, and was told he would call me but he didn't. I took all of the accumulated pain pills from my dentist. They helped some.

On Thursday, Louise took me to his office. He did not take my pain seriously and warned me that I could not have a heel put on the cast if he cut it down. I told him to go ahead anyway. When he finished, it looked like a Dutch wooden shoe. He drilled holes on each side alongside my arch so I could tie a ribbon through them and keep the cast in place. I was on crutches for several weeks and had to teach mostly sitting down.

Going down the stairs was what aggravated me the most. I had been advised to sit down and lower myself, one step at a time down the steep steps. Instead, I used the crutches successfully until, about six steps up, I lost my balance, and I flew down the rest of the way. The landing was picturesque. I was on my left foot with my injured right foot out in back in a perfect arabesque. I did what I had been told from then on. One step at a time while sitting on my rear end.

Before the accident, I had been doing the choreography for a benefit show. The producer, Mrs. Kimball, owned an Arabian horse that was really handsome. She also had numerous expensive Oriental rugs and tapestries. She had written a story, and my friend Catherine suggested I should help with the production. Everyone donated his or her talent. I was "The Goddess of the Sun," the featured dancer. I also did some of the directing. The production showed off all the elaborate Oriental trappings, a throne, and huge pillows used by the cast to lounge on.

The dancers were all young. Fortunately all their dances had been choreographed before I was injured. Using my crutches, I continued rehearsing the show. Mrs. Kimball insisted I go to her husband for X rays (he was an X ray specialist). He told her he doubted if I would ever dance again. I did not know this when she called and said she had just realized that all the dancers were of school age, so she was replacing me with a student from San Diego State College. I told her that was a nice idea using all students, and I would help the new girl with a dance. I was happy to do whatever I could to help.

One night after I shed my crutches, I was timing the dances. I went through most of them myself because there were so many absent. Mrs. Kimball came in while I was dancing. Next day she asked me to be the soloist again!

Catherine was sitting in the audience alongside Dr. Kimball opening night and could hardly wait to tell me how astonished he was at my performance. We performed our production a few times, and it was fun, but I was happy when it was over.

Did my husband help me at the studio? Not at all. I realized my marriage was not working at all. We had few friends, and in all the time we were married, we never went to a movie. With him it was a bar or nothing. I gave up and told him he would have to leave. He left after saying he didn't know I was unhappy. I took time to help him with the apartment he rented. A few days later, he came to me and told me he had rejoined the Navy.

I decided I did not need four dogs. Some mothers had complained about Hungry, who looked so vicious. He was really a sweetheart, but I decided I should not take the risk of a lawsuit. Lady I did not trust because she was unpredictable. It was too difficult to find a home for two adult dogs. One day, I put Lady and Hungry in the car, took them to the veterinarian and had them put to sleep. Strangely, I wept for them more than I did for my failed marriage.

Before a week had gone by, I had a telephone call one morning from Aunt Bea in San Francisco. She was crying and told me she had lost her job and asked me what she was going to do? Poof! There went my dream of having a life of my own and some freedom. Instead, I told her to come to me. She moved in.

Harvey managed a transfer to the Air Force (a neat trick; he did have a winning personality). He was sent to Biloxi, Mississippi. When he was transferred to the state of Washington, he came by on New Year's Eve. A month later, he phoned and wanted me to close the studio, join him living in a mobile home, and party all the time. Instead, I asked for a divorce and a year later I was a free woman.

He wrote me two letters from England during the next year. One asked for cotton handkerchiefs. He did not like the linen ones. Also he asked for a phonograph record for his girlfriend, who was a Wren in the English Air Force. I should have ignored the letter but I sent them. He did not even send me a thank you letter. Later I did get another letter stating his girlfriend was pregnant, and he needed some money so they could get married. I could imagine him telling her, "It's worth a try." I tore that letter in pieces so I would not weaken. I never heard from him again, which was all right with me.

My ballroom classes were becoming more popular. I had benefited from the expertise of the best ballroom teachers in the United States when the association had their conventions. Tom Sheehy who taught the movie stars in Hollywood told me to take all the classes because there would be a day when I would want to teach ballroom instead of all the other hard work. When our association gave their week-long conventions, I started at nine in the morning with ballet and would finish at ten in the evening with ballroom classes. Afterwards, Catherine and I would fall in bed exhausted.

I liked to lead, figuring I'd be more experienced in telling the men what it took to lead their partner. It was convenient because there were always more women than men in the classes. I needed to instruct wives how to follow. They had a tendency to lead if their husbands didn't.

I was asked to teach ballroom classes with groups outside of the studio. I did well but even though I was in my forties, I was thought to be a young girl still. I felt I needed more respect! Instead of wearing my hair in an unsophisticated manner, I pulled it back into a bun in the back of my head, and in my opinion, I looked older. It worked, and when I changed it to a softer look later, I looked young again. Some asked if I had had a face-lift!

I received a telephone call from Babs Gordon, a ballet teacher in La Jolla. She wanted me to instruct a cotillion she was starting. The work was familiar because of the classes I had participated in with the association, but I did not have the time it took to take care of all the business that went along with it. She explained she only taught ballet and knew little ballroom, so if would I teach the dancing, she would take care of the business part. For two days a month she offered me a hundred dollars, one day for practice and the other for social dancing. I accepted. The La Jolla Jewel Cotillion was a success for several years. La Jolla was called the Jewel of California because of its location by the sea. The natives called it a village. Its shore curved inward with a charming bay that was green as an emerald. In the winter there were many snow birds from the east. The language you heard was so English in town, you would think you had been transported to England or Canada.

The young people were so unaccustomed to being told what to do, it was a difficult task to teach them. A cotillion was not only for the purpose of learning how to dance, but it was an opportunity for them to learn the social graces. On more than one occasion I would almost cry from frustration, but I would not give up on them.

The spring dance each year was a pleasure as I watched them enjoying themselves with their newly acquired knowledge. The parents, who attended this formal affair, were more than pleased with the results. It was a busy night for me, playing the requests for favorite tapes besides entering the music for the mixers in order for everyone to dance. I took pictures when the awards were given for the year and also a few candid shots.

The American Band Stand influenced the young students' style of dancing. I taught them all types of ballroom dancing. Swing was their favorite. They could elaborate on it with their own dance styles. It took me awhile to realize when they asked for a waltz, they really wanted a "slow dance." Then the favorite partners would get as close as possible, with the girl's head nestled in the crook of the boy's neck. I often wondered why they never complained of neck pain.

Years later, former students came to me, apologized for their behavior, and thanked me for having given them confidence in themselves and in their social life. They also said they could master any of the fad dances because of their dance background. Maybe it was worthwhile after all.

320

Chapter 18

I lost a good friend when Mr. Hemphill died, although he had not been around the studio very much before his death. He had never told me who he was leaving the studio to. After his death, I found out that he had left it to a friend who had been like a son to him. I knew him from his frequent visits.

For some time I had wanted a fire escape from the second floor, and I asked the young man who had inherited the studio if I could have one. He suggested that I call the bank and talk to the executors of the will. They agreed it was a good idea, but they suggested an inspection before anything was done. The inspection resulted in the building being condemned. I guess someone thought it was humorous. They told me termites had eaten most of the wood frame, and all that was holding the building up was the stucco! I was given notice to vacate. When I talked to the person in the bank, he told me to take my time relocating to a studio and a new home.

One man offered to build a studio for me in the La Mesa suburb because he thought a dance studio was needed in the community. We found the building code for a dance studio had so many safety features that it would have been too costly for me to lease it. Finally, I found a place where my classes could be held, but I had to conduct them differently. The space was good but was divided into two rooms. The rear room I used for the ballet barre and acrobatic work on the mat I still had. The front room became the space for my ballet floor-work and the tap and modern jazz classes. Being on a busy street and near a school, I thought it was a good location.

While I taught at the new location, we lived in the old studio until we found a new home. The old building was quiet, except for mysterious creaks, and we were glad for Bubba and Wiggles who were sensitive for any unusual sound.

The new house I found had everything we all needed, Bea had her own bedroom, I had mine, and a small room became my office. It was a split-level house. The living room was level with the street, but because of being constructed on a hill, the rear part of the house was on a second level. The rooms downstairs were rented to boys from the nearby college. They could go to their own entrance by going down steps alongside the house. I thought having renters would help on my payments. For some reason that I never was to know, they gave notice they were leaving almost immediately. Fortunately, I replaced them within the month. I had counted on the income.

Two men signed up for private ballroom lessons in the evening. They just gave me their first names. One was obviously an employee of the other. One day the local paper showed the picture of a new furniture store that had just opened. It was part of a chain and the owner's picture was shown. The owner was my mysterious student. I didn't let on I had seen the article. When he decided to reveal his identity, I told him I already knew who he was. We had a good laugh when he realized he had not been a mystery man after all.

One evening we discussed hobbies, and he showed an interest when I told him of my photography. He suggested I might be interested in doing a newsletter for his several stores. Next lesson, he showed me copies of the previously published newsletter. When I told him I had never done this type of work. He told me, "You are capable of doing much more than teaching dance; you could handle this. Your classes start over every fall when school starts. Why not try something less seasonal?"

Mr. Jack told me the newsletter had been published every other month. After some thought, I decided I would like to do it. Each issue covered two stores. I was told which two stores would be first. Following his instructions, I took pictures and interviewed the managers and employees. Mr. Jack wrote his editorial about policy and future inventory. To fill in spaces in my columns, I added articles pertaining to the business and even a few appropriate jokes.

When it was dark, after teaching, I took pictures of the store windows. In the daytime, the camera would capture the reflection of the street rather than the window display. I was given a Polaroid camera without any directions, but I learned how to cope with it.

I presented my first dummy copy to the district office where the printing of the circulars was done. I found they had only expected photos and copy for them to set up. Instead they received a completed newsletter that only needed to be printed. They just had to copy my work. Mr. Jack was satisfied and I continued the newsletter for two years. I found the best time to work on this project was after Bea had gone to bed and it was quiet. I usually worked until two in the morning.

The dance association was demanding more and more of my time. When I was vice-president, I suggested we might change the format for the banquet, which was always held the last night of our weeklong convention. In consequence, I was made chairman of the next year's banquet at the Statler Hotel in Los Angeles. Instead of the big cold room with a stage, I asked for the hotel's spacious ballroom. There was room for dancing in the center of the tables set for dining.

Several weeks before the banquet, I asked a modern dance teacher to choreograph a dance to the Lord's Prayer. The big night came, and instead of the customary invocation, a dozen young ladies dressed in flowing white costumes interpreted the song. Derral Call, the husband of one of our members, sang the song. He had an excellent voice, and the room became silent as he sang the inspirational Lord's Prayer.

The officers at the head table were introduced, and we were served the first portion of our dinner before the first half of the show. I had changed the format of the entertainment. Instead of the usual students performing, the teachers, who had been professionals before opening their studios, gave us lively entertainment. They were a great success. Following the dessert, I asked the teenage girl students, who were in their lovely evening gowns, to form a line beside the entrance to the room. I had called the El Toro Marine Base and had arranged for two busloads of Marines from the base to come in their dress uniform to join us. They were waiting in the hall, and as they entered single file, they offered their right arm to the astonished young ladies. We had a few Marines left over, so they joined the teachers, and they enjoyed each other's company, too. When everyone had settled down, the second half of the floorshow went on followed by dance music. The evening was a great success and established a new format for the succeeding conventions.

The next election, I was elected president with a unanimous vote. I was teased about my having called in the Marines to insure my winning the office. My two years as president were busy, because there was a need to build up the membership and the treasury, which the board and I managed to do. I was flattered when they said they should change the rules and keep me on as president, but I said, "Maybe later."

In 1955, the first year I was president, Ginger Rogers was the honored guest at our convention banquet, and I presented her with a pair of small tap shoes that had been gilded. While sitting with her during the evening, I had an opportunity to chat with Ginger, whom I had always admired. She remembered the night in San Diego and said that she wished she had seen me dance.

The next year, Donald O'Conner was the recipient of the gilded tap shoes. I went to the studio where he was filming to give him his award, and we had a short time to talk. I reminded him of the time when we both had appeared at the Warner Brothers Theater in Hollywood when he was a small boy in the family act. I told him, "You were a noisy boy when you and your pals ran up and down the halls between the dressing rooms."

"I've heard this before," he said, and gave me his wonderful smile.

Our monthly meetings started early with the board meeting, and the general meeting. Performing arts classes took the rest of the morning. Eleanor Powell was our luncheon guest several times, and we found time to talk about our shared love, dancing. We enjoyed her tales about some of her experiences in her films. Elly was a friend of Mr. Morgan, the Capezio district manager, and his charming wife Trini Goni. After our luncheons, the afternoon was devoted to ballroom dancing. Our members or a guest teacher gave the classes.

One of our teachers, Agnes Ward, introduced us to one of her former students, Mary Tyler Moore, at one of the luncheons at the Statler hotel. We were given a view of what happens behind the scenes at a T.V. production. She was just as pretty in person as she was on the screen, and we all enjoyed her witty remarks.
Bobby and Cissie, from the Laurence Welk television show, taught ballroom steps

several times. Bobby was a former dance student of Charlie Baker, one of our members, and we were all proud of him. When Bobby started his ballroom dancing, one of his teachers was Chloe Call, who had numerous successful cotillions in the Long Beach area. Bobby and Cissie were always popular attractions, and were favorites of students of all ages.

During one election, the teacher who had been secretary-treasurer moved up to be president. I agreed to be secretary-treasurer when she pledged she would help me. A few weeks later, she moved away without warning, and I was left with a lot of work. I inherited a carload of boxes and had to figure everything out for myself. I was secretary-treasurer for several years. One of my major duties was arranging for hotels for the meetings. Our own yearly convention was always held in a major hotel and involved planning for the whole week. When the national convention was held in our district, it meant planning for hundreds of people, again for a week. Arranging for them in Los Angeles meant more traveling for me. Aunt Bea had retired from her work, and I kept her busy helping me at the meetings and conventions.

I was obligated to go as a delegate to Miami Beach to the Fountainbleu Hotel for the national convention. I came home holding the office of "Area One, Vice-President." This meant attending the next year's convention in Boston. I was thrilled to be in Boston again. My days, however, were spent in meetings and the evenings in classes, so I was inside the hotel all week. I had arranged to leave late the next day after the convention closed. Before taking my plane home, I did some exploring, and I managed to see the Metropolitan Theater, where I had danced so many years before.

I still had my bread and butter teaching to do. The student shows had been replaced by teaching ballroom at different military installations. Judy and Patti, who had been with me for several years, assisted me. I demonstrated, with the girls facing me, and then we three would dance with the sailors who were in a long line. We progressed down the line with each phonograph record change. It was amazing how much the men learned. I was told that they would practice on board ship.

My three-year lease expired in my two-room studio. I stopped having renters and took my students to the remodeled room. I learned how to wallpaper and actually became pretty good at it. I had smaller classes and still grossed more income, because there was less overhead.

I had been teaching at home for several months when I received a call from Mr. Richardson, owner of the Silverado Ballroom. The teacher who had taught ballet and tap in the daytime and ballroom classes on Tuesday and Wednesday nights had left. I had known and liked Mr. and Mrs. Richardson for years, so I consented to teach there. Unlike starting afresh in a new studio, all I had to do was bring my music with me. The students that I had been teaching at home came to the ballroom. Others came to me from the neighborhood.

I taught the ballroom classes that had been meeting for years. They were a joy because the adult men and women really wanted to learn, and many were good dancers who wanted to keep up with the new dances. They were at ease changing partners, so the beginners learned quickly. I always taught my dancers in a big circle, so changing partners was a matter of the men moving forward and introducing themselves. The extra women would join the circle when they changed, and the other extras would drop out.

On Tuesday nights I taught either rumba or tango from nine to ten. Then until eleven I taught cha cha, or samba. Mambo was a favorite for awhile. I devoted time to fad dances, too. Wednesday nights, I taught waltz and fox trot from seven to nine. Some of the new steps came from the Dance Master ballroom classes but most were steps that I developed. When I was asked to teach at the association workshops, I would give them my original steps.

The Silverado ballroom was the meeting place for the Dancer's Guild, a club I had been a member of for several years. The special parties the dance club held were fun, one in particular. It was Halloween and another teacher and I did an imitation of Edgar Bergen and Charlie McCarthy. I was the dummy, Charlie, and we had fun developing our comedy act. We received hearty laughter from our audience.

I also staged a ballet composed of some of the male members. Not wanting to worry about those muscular arms, I gave them balloons to cavort with, and cavort they did, with hilarious results in their various colored tutus. They also did the hula I taught them with added embellishments and had the party in an uproar.

Two ballroom students, Dr. Roemick and his wife had been taking lessons in the Latin class for several months. One night they said they wanted to talk to me. He explained he was a professor at San Diego State College, and he wanted to know if I would be interested in teaching the Faculty Wives Club. The former dance teacher had stopped teaching the class two years before, and they wanted a new instructor. Would I consider teaching the group? I wondered how would I get along with a room full of professors, all with degrees, when I had not even graduated from high school. I thought I would like to try it. I told them, "Yes."

The fall semester and the first night arrived, and I was nervous. I explained my method of instruction. They were a bit reluctant to change partners at first, but during the intermission, I was told they thought it was a good idea. Some remembered the lessons they had taken before, and they helped the newer members when they changed partners. While driving home after the class was over, I gave a big sigh of relief and said to myself, "They have just as many left feet as anyone else."

When we had our semester break, two of the professors told me they were learning new teaching psychology beside learning new steps. That surprised and pleased me.

During my second year, Dr. Roemick asked if I would be interested in teaching at the college. The chairperson of the Women's Physical Education Department, Dr. Florence Shannon, had seen my name in the faculty newsletter and had called him. The current ballroom instructor was taking a maternity leave of absence. If I said yes he would give my telephone number to Dr. Shannon. I was interested, and a few days later, I received her call. I met Dr. Florence Shannon in her office, and she told me about the position.

Classes were held two days a week. They needed a replacement for the spring semester. If I were interested, I would receive some papers from Sacramento. I said I was. The papers arrived, and when I began to answer the questions, I thought my chances of teaching at SDSC were slim. I had to leave so many spaces blank. What high school had I graduated from? Where had I received my college or university degree? What degrees did I possess? I began to think the situation was hopeless. I had nothing to enter, so I wrote, "Please read the following page." Then I filled a page with my dance history. When it was finished, I was surprised. I had done all of that! There were many paragraphs, starting with dancing professionally at eleven and my experience in theaters, movies, and the choreography for night clubs. I followed with my nineteen years of teaching in my own studios in San Diego. I wrote about my presidency of the dance association and that I was currently chairperson of the ballroom dance committee.

I returned the papers. A week later I received a phone call requesting I see Dr. Shannon. I went to the school immediately to hear whether or not I had been accepted. I had not realized how much I wanted the position. Dr. Shannon told me I had been accepted and that they were giving me a higher status than she had expected, which meant more money. That surprised both of us. My very extensive background with the many years of experience made up for my lack of formal education. We worked out a schedule for two hours, Tuesday and Thursday mornings, that would not interfere with my studio work.

At the start of the semester, the department secretary, Geneva took me to the office I would share with a tennis instructor. The desk was big, but it was soon filled with papers, and I was at a loss to know what to do with all of them. Geneva patiently answered all my questions because some of the material was foreign to me. I followed her suggestions, and a few of the pages went into the circular file.

The women's gym ceiling of skylights was so high that I wondered if I would be heard. I hoped the singing lessons that had taught me how to project my voice would help me. Luckily, I never had to resort to a microphone.

The registration office had closed my classes when they had reached thirty students. The list I received had more girls' names than boys. I met my first class and the bleachers were filled with crashers. I explained to them I would enroll boys until the classes were even. When they were, I added one more couple at a time until I had sixty in the beginner's class.

My dance expertise was never questioned, but at first I had trouble answering the questions the new students would ask about procedures. I had never gone through the process of entering a university or college. When I found that rules were changed from semester to semester, and I was no more at sea than the other teachers, I relaxed. There were many occasions to recall the saying; "The right hand does not know what the left hand is doing."

Several weeks passed, and I was asked to return for the fall semester. That was to be the pattern for the years to follow. Every semester they asked me to stay on, adding classes until I had six, giving me half-time status. I said I did not want any more because, if I were to become a full-time teacher, I would have more responsibilities and committees to chair. With my present position, the only meetings I had to attend were at the beginning of the school year, leaving time for my other work. Also, I realized my lack of higher education would really surface if I were a full time teacher. The little antagonisms I had ignored from a few other teachers would increase. I knew that it was natural that some would resent a person without degrees.

My schooling came from the "school of hard knocks." Because of my experience, I was allowed to teach at college level without a degree. I would not have been allowed to teach in elementary schools. I had been given a lucky break when I had been asked to teach the faculty class. I realized it would have been wasted if I had not been experienced. You can be at the right place at the right time, but it does not do you any good unless you have adequate knowledge and experience.

I never asked registration to stop the practice of closing my classes at thirty. I always had more crashers than I could handle, and I was able to have as many boys as I needed in a class of sixty. When I started intermediate classes, I did limit the size to thirty students, and I taught ballroom choreography, something we all enjoyed.

The girls never lacked for boy partners. Some of the former boy students became so interested, they returned semester after semester. The girls were really happy to have the more advanced dancers. I would tease the fellows, telling them, "I would like to think it's just dancing you want, but I think the girls are the big attraction."

Cupid attended the classes, too. Several wedding invitations were mailed to me at different times. I still receive letters, thanking me for being instrumental in a happy couple meeting. They say they are still dancing.

Before long I had students coming to my office for advice just as they had come to me in my studio. My policy, as it always had been, was to allow them to talk out their problems. They needed a listener who would not say, "Why did you do it in the first place?" When they talked, they realized why certain events had changed their relationship, and usually figured out the answers for themselves. If it were a situation I had been in, sometimes I would tell them what I had done. This was not to tell them which way to go, but just to let them know others had the same problems and had lived through it. So would they.

I had to get accustomed to couples living together instead of just dating. Usually it was the girl who had trouble understanding why the arrangements did not last or result in marriage. Sometimes it was the man who was bewildered, "Why did she leave me?"

No one ever commented on my method of instruction, with one exception. One day I met Dr. Shannon in the hallway after a class. I told her, "We were just doing the twist." She looked at me with dismay.

"They are doing it anyway," I said, "and not all are doing it right. I showed them how to do it so they would not injure their knees and backs."

"You're right," she said. " Keep up the good work."

The next day Florence suggested I teach each fad dance that came along, and soon, some of my advanced pupils went into dance studios to teach the latest dance craze. From there, some of them opened their own studios and taught ballroom and charged prices I would never have dared to ask! I don't know what happened to what they majored in because they continued with their successful dance studios. They thanked me for the background I had given them.

Each semester before finals, I would have a dance party. The class before the dance, I would give them instructions in the social graces. They certainly needed it, and many of them thanked me for the advice. After I was given the advanced class, they performed at the dances. When I heard that LSD was sometimes added to punch bowls when no one was watching, I asked Bea to come and sit by the refreshments so that we would not have that problem. She enjoyed watching the dancing, and the students liked to talk to her.

The faculty dance club asked me to start a cotillion for their children. I said I would only teach and they would have to do all the other work a cotillion entailed. They agreed to this plan. I met with some of the mothers, and we had our cotillion. It lasted several years until the young people became too much to handle. I wondered what had happened to parents raising their children to have good manners. I would not condone ill manners but could not start from the beginning. There had to be a foundation to work with.

Florence Shannon and I became friends. She and Geneva pushed for my advancement. I did not realize the importance of being elevated to halftime. If I had not achieved that status, I would not have been eligible for insurance and retirement.

Bea and I included Florence in our activities after she retired. We had been worried about Florence living alone, and, with her approval, we made arrangements with a neighbor. We called Florence each morning, and one morning when there was no answer, we alerted the neighbor. She looked into a window of the apartment and could see Florence unconscious on her couch and called the police.

When I arrived the firemen were forcing a window open next to the door so that they could open it. The television was on, and there was an open book by her hands. They could not revive her. They took her to the hospital here she partially recovered. She never returned to her apartment but lived in a nursing facility for a few months until she passed away. She had been a good friend, and I missed her.

I gave up teaching my daytime classes at the Silverado after I hired another teacher to help me. It did not appear to be working when I lost pupils every first of the month. After letting the teacher go, I returned to teaching some of the students at home. They were the pupils that had stayed with me when I had made all my changes and had worked so hard. They were fun too.

The college became a university and enrollment increased every year. Most of the time I enjoyed teaching at the university until the "Hippie" era, when I did not enjoy it as much. Some students began to have an attitude of, "I dare you to teach me." When I crossed the campus to the offices, I would hide my mouth with my hand because I could not help but smile at some of the outfits they wore. They could have gone to a Halloween party and won first prize.

One day I saw a person walking by the gym. It looked like a girl. No, it was a boy. After checking out the different parts of attire, I still didn't know, and I recalled what my brother had told me. "If you can't tell, it does not make any difference anyhow."

My faith in the public education system diminished. Notes left in my letterbox to tell me of an absence were barely legible. Words were misspelled and used incorrectly. One day after class, a young man asked me if I would use simpler words. Some did not recognize words of over two syllables! In the years that I instructed at the university, only one student came to my office to say that my method was not to his liking. That was all right. I didn't like his reasoning.

There was a large percentage of students in their late twenties who were still relying on their parents to support them. Majors were changed. Far too many were undeclared. I thought, what a waste! I reflected on my early years, which I had taken so seriously. What had happened to make things change so drastically?

Rain would not keep the young people away from classes, but warm weather did. One evening was especially inviting. Midway through the lesson I noticed half of my dancers had disappeared. So I called roll again, checking the names of the absentees. I told the remainder of the students that they could leave, so that they might enjoy the evening also. I would have to repeat the lesson anyway.

The next time the class met, instead of calling out the names, I went to each person. When someone showed interest in what I had written in my roll book, I would let him or her see they had been marked absent. Before starting the class I reminded them that perfect attendance was required for an A grade. Groans could be heard. I informed them I would call roll at any time during the next classes instead of at the beginning. No one slipped out of the room again, to my knowledge.

Another ballroom teacher (who also taught folk dancing) and I agreed on the type of clothing to be worn to the classes. The girls were asked to wear a dress or blouse and skirt. The boys were to come up to the same standards. When the other teacher was calling roll for her first class, a young lady challenged her on the attire. She said she and her boyfriend only had unisex clothing. She was told to obtain a locker and to change into a dress or a skirt and blouse for the class. The girl came to the next class in a blouse and skirt, except the blouse was a see-through, and she wore nothing under it. She was told if she could not obey the rules, that there were many who would. The girl and her boyfriend were out of the class.

The skirts became shorter and shorter until I began to think it might be better if the girls wore slacks. When their arms went up, so did the skirt. I was relieved when I that saw most of the boys seemed so absorbed in the steps that they did not appear to notice anything. Then, one of the boys told me after the class that one of the girls wore pantyhose without any other clothing in that area. Now I had something else to watch for.

With sixty in a class, it was hard to identify everyone. I had stopped trying to remember names. There were too many to remember. I took pictures with a number held at their shoulder. The number corresponded to the number by their name in my roll book. I had made charts for the tests, and they would be graded while I watched them dance. One or two complaints occurred through the years, but I could show them where they had been graded. I had it down in black and white.

The first thing I did each semester was to demand their full attention and I was strict. If they were talkative, I just stood and waited until they were quiet. Only once did I become impatient and raise my voice. I do not know who was the most startled. It really did not take long before they knew what I wanted, and we all relaxed. Then the classes became more fun.

I loved my students and dancing, and they knew it. When a book was published by the students, grading the teachers, my critique said, "Miss Iverson loves dancing and makes every effort to show her students how to enjoy it also."

I decided the classes that came for a double session were doing better than the twice-a-week classes, so I asked for double classes for all my students. In this way, I could revue previous work before teaching the new work. My students were good dancers because they remembered their steps. In ballroom, I also numbered the steps as they learned them and that was how they were to practice them. Each type of dance-waltz, fox trot, swing, rumba, cha cha, tango, samba-had their order of numbers, and the system worked well.

The work I had been doing for the furniture stores changed. I was to do an audio-visual program instead of the newsletter. I taught myself how to use an old reel-to-reel tape recorder, cutting the tape with a razor and splicing it together with scotch tape. The instruction book had been lost years before. I must have been doing a good job because one manager said, "I did not know I talked so well." There were stifled snickers because the others knew he talked with many aah's, creating spaces. The cut out aah's had fallen on the floor at my home.

Using my personal camera, I took slide pictures of the employees and the store's windows. Every other month I prepared for the new program.

Stores were located in San Pedro, Torrance, Oceanside, Vista and in other towns that were miles away. I would go to them after my classes at the university for my night pictures, and I would be taking pictures at eleven o'clock at night. My brother would leave a side door unlocked for me at his home in Long Beach. Going to bed at two in the morning became a regular occurrence. Now, instead of their receiving the newsletters, I went to the stores before they opened. This was easy when I went to the local stores, but when I did the northern stores, I had to go to my brother's the night before. Then after the slide show, I would hurry to San Diego to teach my classes at the university.

Besides working for the stores, for a few months I also taught interior design at the seventh grade-level at schools. This was for the Home Furnishing Institute. (I had taken a night class, and I had also learned from the work I was doing for the stores.) It was different, and I enjoyed the young girls' questions.

When I was told the program for the stores would be discontinued, I was relieved. It was a lot of work for the sum of two hundred dollars a month without an expense account! I was happy not to be traveling so much.

Since San Diego State had become a university, more classes of modern dance were added. Also, I was told we were to have a ballet class. My happiness was short lived when one of the modern dance teachers was given the class. The next semester I was asked to replace her, and I taught two ballet classes. At last!

Thirty in a class was more than I really wanted, but there was a large demand. Fortunately, the dance room was large. The portable barres I designed were stored across the hall in the large gym under the bleachers.

The first fifteen minutes were spent in warming up exercises. Late students could not join the class until they had warmed up their bodies. Early on, I had explained that their muscles were like wax and had to be warm to be flexible. Also, I was adamant about their clothing when they came and left. I told them even horses wore blankets after workouts. The girls had to wear a skirt or dress over their tights and leotards. I have not become accustomed to the girls and women wearing what used to be dance apparel on the streets with no cover-ups!

Because of their age, I was lenient about the "turnout," the five positions required. Their bones and tendons had "set" and forcing them into the artificial position could injure them. I did not want them to have bad knees or hips. They were above the age to begin a career of ballet dancing. Again, I was strict about attendance. They were told, "If you are not in class I cannot teach you. Every lesson, there is something to be learned." If they were unable to dance, they were to come to the class and watch and take notes.

Evidently I had a different personality for the ballet and ballroom classes. One student, Caroline, who was to become one of my best friends, told me later that

I played many roles. After she had taken the ballet class, she enrolled in a ballroom class. She hardly recognized me. I showed stern discipline for ballet, was friendly for the ballroom, and again was a new person entirely when we became friends.

I heard some complaints and questions frequently. "How can you hold your leg up so high in the air?" "How can you turn so easily?" "How can you give us a hard lesson, change your clothes, and teach a two hour ballroom class? After my ballet class I just want to go home and rest."

I never gave up dancing with my students and never sat down, but worked as hard as they did. My body was still trim, and I enjoyed my classes as much as I did when I first started teaching.

There were boys who came into the ballet class, and they soon found it required strength to be a dancer. When I demonstrated how important it was to pull the muscles of the legs really tight to achieve a really pointed toe, I would point my toe and ask a boy to try to turn my ankle to one side. At first they tried tentatively. Then they really tried to make my ankle move. No one ever was able to do so. I was in my sixties at this time. My body was trimmer than most of theirs. I did not smoke, go out night after night, drink, or heaven knows what else!

A good percentage of the students took their schoolwork seriously and would just study harder at finals time. Others would party, and when the final test was to be given, they were bleary-eyed from all night studying, with pills and multiple cups of coffee to keep them awake. I wondered if they could have passed the same exams six weeks later.

One day, I got a telephone call from another San Diego university. Would I be interested in teaching ballet classes for them? I told them I did not have the time, but I had a girl who would be capable of teaching ballet. She was hired, and she is still there. It must be around twenty-seven years now. I hear from her every Christmas, and she is steadily doing more important work. I cannot take full credit for her ability because she had been dancing for years, but I do think I was some-what responsible.

There were requests from some of my ballet girls for more work. So, I started classes in my home for them. They were not interested in a dance career. They just wanted the exercise. I was asked to start tap and jazz classes too. Many of them told me they wished they had continued the lessons they had taken when they were younger. These young women were a pleasure to teach, and some are still in touch with me.

Once I had a dream the night before school started. The bleachers the students usually sat in for first roll call were overflowing. As I walked through the gym, I could hardly make my way through, there were so many crashers. The dream continued with the ballet class. Most of the dance room floor was completely covered with crashers. The next day, when I went in for my first classes, it was weird because my dream had become a reality. There were almost as many as I had dreamed about. I continued the practice of adding the crashers to fill in my classes, and I took them in by grade, graduating seniors first, seniors second, and, if there was space, juniors. It would have been nice to think it was just my reputation, but the students were obligated to have a semester of athletics to graduate. They thought the ballroom class would be an easy course. Some did drop the class when they found it was harder to learn to dance than they had thought. Someone who really wanted to learn took their place.

When we had the last ballet class of the semester, I asked everyone to sit on the floor, and we had a question and answer period.

"How many of you will want your children to take dance lessons?" I asked.

Almost everyone did. They then listened to my advice about what to look for in a teacher because the wrong one could cause damage to the small body. I informed them that, in some cities, to receive a license to teach dance, instructors had to have the city building department's approval for their studio. There were no tests to become a teacher, and the privilege was badly abused. I advised them to watch classes before they enrolled their child.

I still enjoyed my evening ballroom classes at the Silverado Ballroom. I taught new steps for several years and never duplicated a step unless someone asked for a review. Al, a young man who demonstrated the steps with me, would be waiting for me in my private lesson room. I would hurry from my class at the university, and often on the way I would make up what I was going to teach. When I showed him the step, it would be the first time I had actually done it. We had a good laugh many times when we named the steps.

One married couple loved to dance and did so at every opportunity. They attended every class and practiced faithfully. One of the nights when I was a judge for dance competitions, they were at the same dance. They danced all the cha cha steps and never repeated a step, and I was reminded of many I had forgotten.

Catherine called to tell me she had promised to bring me to an interview with some teenagers who were very serious about learning to dance and wanted a cotillion. I said, "No! No! No!" She insisted until I went to see these unusual boys and girls. They were so sincere that I said I would teach them one class. I was amazed when they really worked hard. The class had some wonderful girls and boys. After four years, they outgrew the class, and I discontinued teaching the cotillion the next year. The new students were too hard to handle and not at all like the original group.

One Saturday night before I had left the cotillion, I took my music equipment back to my private room at the Silverado Ballroom. The dance competition that Mr. and Mrs. Richardson were conducting was having the last tango contest before the overall competition. It was a competition open to professionals, and they wanted me to go into it because there were few contestants for this final event.

"I don't have a partner," I said.

"Yes you do. Gary doesn't have a partner, and he wants to enter. So, you can dance together."

I was tired after a hard day and was reluctant to dance with Gary. He was much younger. We had not danced together often, and we had never done the difficult tango together. He had asked the Richardsons to persuade me to be his dance partner. As a favor to them, I consented, and we won first place!

The overall competition would be next. We would have to compete in it. Waltz, fox trot, rumba. mambo, and tango were to be judged. Gary and I would be competing against dancers who could have done exhibition dancing professionally. They had spent thousands of dollars on lessons and had practiced together for years. I had judged them in former competitions, so I was aware of their capabilities. I did not think it wise for me to enter in the final competition. Gary and I found time to practice, but all he wanted to do was the tango. That night I had mixed emotions. I had never before danced in a ballroom competition, and I wished we had practiced more. But it did give me an opportunity to dance for pleasure, a rarity for me.

We did not intend to, but we added a few laughs for the audience. Gary's lead was so strong that he threw me away from him in a rumba step and I landed on my derriere. Of course I laughed and went back to him, even if we were disqualified. Partners were not to stop contact in the rumba, and we had certainly done that.

Mambo was one of my favorites, and Gary hardly knew how to do it. I flavored the few steps we did have with flirtatious movements, and he stopped dancing and went to a chair on the side of the floor. I followed him, and danced in front of him, miming my desire for him to continue dancing. He reluctantly got up and danced with me again. The audience laughed and applauded us. Some people told me later that they thought it was planned. No one was more surprised than I was when we won the tango final. He liked the dance, and I could follow him because of his strong lead.

I was to remember it for a long time because the strong lead had aggravated the arthritis which had started in my neck and shoulders. There were X rays taken of my back and neck. The R.N. in the doctor's office told me I would have to stop dancing. I took my pills faithfully, went in for traction, and tried not to feel sorry for myself. My advanced student, Judy, taught for me when I was unable to take all of my classes at the studio. When I had concluded judging a ballroom competition one evening, instead of going home, I decided to stay and dance. Voila! I felt so good I went home and threw away all the pills. The next day I called the therapist and told her I wouldn't need her again.

My schedule was too heavy. There was a period when I was exhausted every night. I had my university classes, besides classes and private lessons at home. I enjoyed my ballroom classes at the Silverado Ballroom, but I would not get home until midnight. I generally had one or two outside adult classes as well. Besides the several years working for the furniture stores, I was still active in the dance association.

Why did I work so hard? There were two reasons. Challenges were something I loved. If I did not know how to do something, I taught myself. I never learned to say "No" when it came to work. I worked on whatever it was until I was satisfied. The second reason was the house. Mr. Jack had given me a loan when I had found the house I wanted, so I had four trust deeds. The owners had two mortgages besides the first loan. They were not able to handle their debts and were selling the house. I took the trust deeds in order, starting with the smallest, the fourth. When that had been taken care of, that money was applied to the third. That was paid off and both amounts went into the second until I only had the first one the bank held. It received the money that I had been accustomed to doing without. I kept my own set of books and gave a cheer when my interest was lower than the principle.

The day came when I did not owe any money to anyone, and I have kept it that way ever since. A new car would be paid for in cash. If I wanted something, I put the money aside until it could be bought. Otherwise, the money was banked for my future.

The Temple Dancers from the Masonic Lodge had been together for a long time. They were of all ages, and loved to dance. Some had taken lessons as children, but most had very little experience. They performed their dances at the temple for certain occasions, and yearly they would perform at a national gathering. They needed new dances. I had been recommended, so they came to me.

Because of the Egyptian motif, I decided to teach them parts of the two dances from "Aida," the opera I had done in Los Angeles and San Francisco. Arms are a problem with novice students, so I had them use scarves for one dance. They danced both dances at the National and made a hit.

Viola, one of the girls, was a neighbor, who had asked me several times to join her on a cruise. I felt I should not leave Bea, and I could not afford two fares. Then fate stepped in when my Ford Torina was hit on the freeway in the Los Angeles area. When the traffic slowed for an accident, I had stopped. The driver of a Cadillac crossed over lanes to avoid hitting another car and crashed into my car. A considerate onlooker drove me to Long Beach, and the car was towed there, also. The dealer who had sold me the car said it was a total loss.

I had called my brother, and Alton helped me choose a new car, a blue Ford LTD, one just like his, only a 1978 model. It looks like new inside and out, and I am still driving it. It is safe, comfortable and it has been well cared for.

The insurance company insisted I have X rays with an orthopedic doctor to ascertain if I had a whip lash, or some other injury. When we viewed the X rays, he said, "I don't understand it. You can do all the positions I ask you to do, but the X rays say you should not be able to do any of them." I explained I was a dancer, and we just did not conform to the usual pattern. He dismissed me with a clean slate.

One day shortly afterwards, I received a telephone call from the insurance agent asking to see me. She had a check for me! It was a settlement in case I should have trouble in the future. I had some extra money!

Bea insisted I take the cruise with Viola. Bea didn't want to go. Viola loved dancing as much as I did. In one of my other adult class, she was my dance partner when I demonstrated new steps. My first question after we had boarded the ship was, "Will there be any men to dance with?"

When the third couple danced, Viola was on her feet ready to dance. Before long we were receiving compliments. Wives asked me to help their husbands and no one ever made a negative remark about us, at least I never heard one. Later, we took cruises to Alaska, the Caribbean, and Mexico. There never were partners, but the fact that we were dancing was good enough for us.

342

Rider and Myself on Our Wedding Day, October 26, 1980

Rider's Favorite Picture of Me

Rider and Lucile in 2003

I am 91 years old in 2003

Alton and Myself as Babies
in a Frame Made By Our Daddy

Chapter 19

In 1977 I had my sixty-fifth birthday, and I continued teaching at the university. During the 1978 spring semester I gave my notice to the department chairman that I would like to retire. I just wanted to teach the students who were coming to my home studio and my adult ballroom class, and I wanted to have some time for myself. Then I heard the other ballroom teacher was also leaving because her husband had been transferred, and they were moving away. I asked the chairman if it would be better if I stayed another semester. He thanked me for staying and was relieved that he did not have to look for two ballroom dance teachers at the same time.

He found another teacher who could do both ballroom and folk dancing. I kept on with my classes until the end of the year. The department gave me a farewell dinner, and one of the modern dance teachers gave me a splendid tribute. He said I was the only dancer he had known who had made her living and had supported her mother and aunt solely as a dancer. Usually dancers have help from their families or other sources.

In January 1979, I went to the Social Security office and was given a form to complete. When I returned it to the lady she asked, "Were you born in 1912?"

"Yes," I said.

"Why didn't you come in before your 65th birthday in 1977?"

"Because I was still working."

"When did you retire?"

"Last year, in 1978, at the end of the semester at San Diego State." I wondered why she was asking me all these questions.

"You didn't know you were supposed to come in before your sixty-fifth birthday?"

"No," I said, and her attitude of disbelief made me feel like a little kid who had been caught robbing the cookie jar, or, perhaps she thought I was from another planet.

She explained, "First, you were supposed to sign up for Social Security before your sixty-fifth birthday. After your birthday you would start to collect Social Security. If you continued to work, you would be deducted a certain amount until you reached the age of 70. After that, you would not have to fill out the forms stating how much you earned and you would not have any further deductions."

She seemed to be doing mental arithmetic then said, "I hope you haven't messed up your Medicare. I'll see what can be done about it. Come back tomorrow morning and we will try and get this straightened out."

I promised to return early in the morning.

Bea and I talked that night about my tardiness, and she was in the dark as much as I was. We wondered why someone hadn't told me. She had retired as soon as she was sixty-five, no problem. Viola wasn't entitled to Social Security because, when she was a teacher in elementary school, they had voted against it. She was my only confidant and I guess everyone else thought I knew what to do.

I was too busy making my own retirement money to be concerned about Social Security. I read the papers but never read anything about Social Security. I had thought I'd do that when I was ready to retire.

The next day I was told I was lucky. I would be receiving Medicare without any restrictions. I told her how much I appreciated her efforts. Then I told her I was teaching a ballroom class every week and a few lessons at home, and she gave me the instructions on how to report it.

It was awhile before I realized that I would be receiving a check each month and I did not have to do anything for it! My friends reminded me I had been taxed for Social Security since the thirties, so I deserved everything I received.

Without classes at the university, my schedule was light. There was so much to do, and now I had the time to do things. Most of my life I had worked days and evenings without much time for myself. My evening hours started when most were having their leisure time. It was like I had disappeared when I started the long time stretch at the university. For the first time in my life, I would have time for activities that did not pertain to work.

I started to do some of the things I had wanted to do for a long time. I even laid a brick path to the house. My roses, gardenias, fuchsia plants, and fruit trees looked better. We enjoyed our own figs, lemons, avocados, and strawberries. I started a garden of vegetables and we enjoyed them during spring and the summer months. Bea and I were able to go often to Las Vegas to see the wonderful dancers at the casinos. This was something we really enjoyed.

The kitchen needed to be painted so I tackled the job. I knew it would take time, so I asked Bea to visit my brother Alton in Long Beach. It would be easier for both of us, because she always thought it would only take a day or so to paint a room. I knew kitchens took longer than other rooms, and I didn't need any problems.

After she left, I removed all the cupboard doors and stacked them into the garage, where I had decided to paint them. I was interrupted when I had a call from the gymnasium secretary at the university. She wanted to know if she could give my telephone number to a young man who was in town briefly and wanted to brush up on his ballroom dancing. I told her she could give him my telephone number.

He came to see me, and we made arrangements for his lessons. Tom was in San Diego to practice optometry at the naval bases before he graduated and received his degree. He thought it would be a good time to have dance lessons.

In the first week of lessons, I learned he had worked off part of his scholarship at New Mexico State University doing carpentry and painting, so I suggested he paint for me in return for his lessons. He agreed. After he was finished at the bases he would paint until dark, then we would dance. Afterwards it seemed natural to ask him to have dinner with me before we started the lesson. One night we tried to convince each other whose state had the best Mexican food. I did not change his mind when I took him to my favorite Mexican restaurant. Once we had gone out to dinner, we began to do some of the things he was unacquainted with. We went to his first professional baseball game, dined at a dinner theater, and we both enjoyed the famous San Diego Zoo. I had not been there often, and it was nice to have an escort who was a courteous, good looking young man. We both had a crazy sense of humor. He made me laugh more than I had ever done before.

One day Tom asked me, "Why don't you ever go out with your friend Rider? You talk about him often."

"He is too young" I said. "I've known him since I gave him lessons years ago and he asked me for a date. He was twenty years old then, and I was forty-two. I refused and told him people would think I was his mother. Besides, I never dated a pupil."

With a quizzical look, Tom said, "So he is in his forties now. And he is still too young? Yet you go out with me and I am just twenty eight?"

I didn't know what to say. He was grinning at me, and I didn't have an answer. I found myself wondering about my friend Rider. I had just talked to Rider on the telephone.

Tom went back to his home up the coast, but he did come to visit me several times later. One Friday I drove to my nephew's home in Huntington Beach to spend the weekend. Sunday morning I thought of Tom and called him at his apartment. He suggested I come by on my way home, and we would go out to dinner.

After our Chinese dinner at his favorite place, we went to his apartment, and he made a cup of tea for me before I left for home. Bea and I had not purchased a microwave yet, and I was fascinated when he boiled the water in his. I had never seen one before. What happened a few minutes later really gave us a good laugh.

He would be leaving for home in Las Cruces, New Mexico, after he graduated. This would be a final good-bye. Just before I got into my car, we kissed goodbye, and all the streetlights went out! It was darker than the inside of a coat pocket!

He said, "Wow, I never had a kiss before that made all the lights go out!"

And I was old enough to be his grandmother! We parted laughing.

Bea became ill and refused to go to a doctor (a family trait). I told a doctor her symptoms, and he told me to take her to the hospital. The examination told them she had a bleeding ulcer.

She could have applied for Medicaid, but she never did. The doctor told me I should attend to it for her. I went to the offices without much hope. I explained the situation, and the man I talked to really took care of it. He had everything ready for me the next day! The belated surgery, though successful, could not help her. She also had lung cancer. Smoking two packs a day since she was a young girl had taken its toll. After she had a week of intensive care, I was awakened one morning with a phone call from the hospital. It was the doctor who told me Bea had passed away in her sleep.

Now, my brother, his wife and his son were all the family I had left. Bea had never been one to collect anything and generally gave away frivolous gifts, so I did not have much to do. I found myself wandering around the house like a lost person.

The person who called me daily to see how I was getting along was Rider. He asked how he could help me. I thanked him but told him there was just paper work and that I would be busy doing that for several days.

My girl friend Viola insisted I attend a dance at a lounge in a local hotel where her dance club was meeting. She danced with members, but I didn't know any of the members of her dance club. I made the mistake of dancing with a stranger who then asked to sit with us. We only danced the one dance because he certainly did not belong to any dance club and had been sitting at the bar.

We were left at the table alone when Viola went to talk to a friend. After a spell of small talk with this boring fellow, he asked, "Your place or mine?"

I said, "No" so emphatically he left.

Because of this type of situation and my aunt's attitude about men, I had hardly dated for years. Two days later, when I was washing dishes, I said to myself, "Why can't I find a man who would love me and want me as a friend and not for other reasons."

For the second time in my life a voice spoke to me! It seemed to be right there in the room with me: "You have Rider." Like the time when I was so unhappy with Walter, and the same voice had said, "You don't have to stay with him."

After I recovered from my surprise, I began to think about my long friendship with my former student, starting with how we had met years before. His brother was taking private dance lessons to please his girl friend. He had liked the lessons and persuaded his older brother Rider to take lessons, also.

My new student, Rider, was a serious redhead, six foot two, who dwarfed me because I taught ballroom in my ballet slippers. That made me five feet four and a half. I taught him the basic steps, and even though he memorized everything, he was taking a long time to dance with confidence. He was my last appointment for the day, so he would stay, and we would talk awhile. When I felt he was not interested in learning how to dance but was just coming to see me, I told him he was spending a lot of time and money on his lessons, and I did not think he was advancing enough. I thought we were saying good bye, but he thought differently.

A few days later he telephoned and said, "Now that I am no longer taking lessons, may I take you out to dinner?"

I thanked him, but refused, and thought that was that. How wrong I was. He was persistent and kept in touch with me often.

He continued to telephone when he knew I would not be teaching and would ask if he could come and see me. Then he would bring small gifts for Bea and me. Finally I attended a concert with him at the high school auditorium where cultural events were held. Parking was always difficult at the school. I had told him I didn't like to walk in that area of town late at night. He wouldn't take that for an excuse. That night he came for me in a taxi. When the concert was over, we walked across the street to his car. Earlier, a friend had picked him up when he had parked it there in the afternoon. He had planned it so I would not have to walk any distance.

When he was drafted and sent to Germany I thought, "This will end this one-sided romance."

Instead he sent gifts to Bea and me, in addition to almost daily postcards. Rider came to see me after he returned from Germany. Bea had convinced me I should discontinue our friendship, so I made up a story about a jealous boyfriend. I told him I'd better not see him anymore. He left, and I did not hear from him for years, until Bea and I received a wedding invitation. The event was on a Saturday, and because of my classes, I could not attend and sent our regrets.

A few years passed, and Rider called and asked me if I would give his older son acrobatic lessons. I found his boy, Steven, a delight, but he was only four years old. I taught him until he was ready to start cartwheels and I could not get him to do them because he said he was tired. In the next lesson, he got on my lap and, putting his chubby arm around my shoulder, lisped, "Let's talk." I told Geri, his mother, that he was not ready for lessons.

Bea and I were invited to have dinner with the family. I thought Geri and Rider were doing just great, and we had a pleasant evening. Years later I had a telephone call from Rider, and he told me that he and Geri had separated.

"Are you getting a divorce?" I asked.

"Not for awhile," he said.

A few weeks later, he asked for a date, and I said I did not think I should go out with him until he was single. After Rider and his wife finalized their divorce, I went each year with him to the county fair and also had dinner and attended the theater at Christmas time These were our only meetings for a few years. We remained just friends.

There were infrequent phone calls, and when he learned my gardener was unable to work for me any longer, Rider offered to come over once a week to cut my lawn and help me with my gardening. He was working nights, so I began fixing a lunch for him before he went to work. This was not too easy because he was a vegetarian, and I knew nothing about that type of diet.

I enjoyed having Rider help me with my gardening and we got to know each other better. The day after I heard the voice, when Rider telephoned me, I said, "Would you like to take me to a movie?"

The answer was immediate: "Tomorrow night?" Rider, who never took a day off even when he was ill, wanted a date the next night!

I said, "How about Saturday night?"

I was like a teenager getting ready for a boyfriend. I did not have to worry about what I was wearing, how to act, or what time I was to get home. I was finally going out for a lovely evening without anyone to criticize me.

We started to date, and after two months something happened to me. I realized I was in love! Never had anyone been so thoughtful or tried to make me so happy. We never had enough time for all we wanted to talk about. It was wonderful. It was as though we could be together forever and still feel we needed more time.

On Memorial Day weekend, I decided to make believe he was my husband. He helped me cook, insisted on washing the dishes, and only wanted to do the things I preferred. I liked it.

The next day I surprised him by asking, "Do you still want to marry me?"

After he recovered from his surprise, he said, "You said you never wanted to be married again. But if you've changed your mind, the answer is, Yes!"

There was a twenty-two year difference in our ages, of which my friends were quick to remind me, besides the different kind of life we each had led. He had never left San Diego except for short trips and was still doing the same work he had started with. There were those who thought he would be bored having my peers for friends. But most of my friends were younger than he was because they were former students.

We went together through the summer. I began to make a list of guests for the formal wedding and reception. The list was over a hundred, and I was still counting. We decided to limit it to our families, and agreed we would each invite a special couple.

One of my students from my adult dance class was a retired Navy chaplain, and he offered to perform the ceremony. In October 1980, we were married in my colorful yard in front of a gardenia bush in full bloom. My brother gave me away, and his wife was my maid of honor. Their son was the rest of my family. Rider had his mother, brother, sister, and his nieces and nephews. We had a wonderful group. Our wedding was perfect. The reception was in my studio, which I had decorated for the occasion. We spent our honeymoon in British Columbia. Now, more than twenty years later, I have a wonderful husband, and we are told we act like newly-weds. Only twice has anyone thought I was his mother.

I continued my adult ballroom class until my knees began to say "enough." I gave the class to our two friends, Carl and Caroline, who had met in one of my dance classes. They have had wonderful success with it and still instruct it every week.

When I had my left knee transplant in 1989, it became the first of many hospital experiences. Two days after my surgery, I was to have lunch in a chair by my window, after I had been washed by a nurse's aide. I was to walk to my chair using my walker. When I turned at the foot of my bed, I suddenly collapsed over the walker. My elderly nurse and I managed to get me to my bed before the room was filled nurses.

A technician reached for the oxygen mask on the wall. With a loud hiss, a spray rushed out and hit the nurses, who screamed. He replaced it and started over again. The same thing happened. I was still conscious, and I started to laugh. It was just like a comic episode in a movie.

He said, "I'll try once more."

Several female voices said in unison, "No you won't." I felt my bed being pushed towards the door. Then all went black.

I awoke in a dark room. From behind a curtain I heard a man's voice asking, "Have you called her husband?"

Another voice replied, "He was on the telephone, and the operator interrupted the call. I told him to come to the hospital, because, we had put his wife into a different room."

Then my world went dark again,

When I became aware I was trying hard to breath. Opening my eyes I realized Rider was holding my hand and was distraught. Each breath I took was an effort, and I was tired. When I saw how frightened Rider looked, I decided I'd keep on trying to breath. I really wanted to have a longer life with Rider.

I closed my eyes again.

Later, when I opened them, I found I had been transported to intensive care, and was connected to two bottles. Besides the intravenous in my right arm, there was something else in my left.

A voice informed me I was going for a ride. There was discussion about changing me to a gurney, then they decided they could manage my bed even though it was larger. That decision was to cause a lot of trouble.

Two female nurses pulled the bed while a male nurse held the bottles hanging over my head. Loading the bed into the passenger elevator was the first problem. It was not meant to transport a bed and three people. Later I heard, because it was Saturday, they had been called in and were not the regular team.

We were going to another building, which meant opening and shutting heavy doors. I guess I was supposed to be unconcious because I was ignored and my crew laughed all the way. Later the girls must have had bruises because they had bumped into every door and door knob on the way. I was not unconcious and was again feeling as though I was in a comedy movie. When they noticed my eyes were open they told me I was on my way to have a test.

The first one was interesting. I had a screen inserted in my side to prevent any more blood clots going to my lungs or to my heart. I watched the whole procedure on a TV monitor. The operator of the machine would say, "This is going to hurt." I would wait for the pain, which occurred several times. When I was leaving the room, I said to the young man, "Did you ever have a bad muscle spasm? That's pain."

When I was back in intensive care, a tall man came to the foot of my bed. He said, "Mrs. South, I am Dr. Saronoff, your doctor. You have had a lung embolism and we almost lost you. Blood clots went to your lungs. You are on Heparin now and we think you are going to be all right."

The result of the next text was shown to me later, when it was shown to Rider. It was a different type of x-ray of my lungs which showed the blood clots. When Dr. Saronoff said it looked like a Christmas tree decorated with red lights, he was right.

I was so grateful for everything that was being done for me, I asked Rider to go to Sees, a wonderful candy store, and buy a ten-pound box of candy for everyone.

When he came back, he told me he had purchased two five pound boxes. One for the emergency staff and one for the intensive care staff. Then I relaxed.

Dr Saronoff, who was was taller then my six-foot-two husband, came to talk to me again. He said I was doing very well for a seventy year old lady. I was improving. Everything was under control. He held up a piece of paper to show me. It was a diploma.

GOOD SPORT OF THE DAY
♡ AWARD ♡
GOES TO LUCILLE SOUTH
FOR HER PATIENCE +
SENSE OF HUMOR WITH
THE ICU STAFF ON May
13th, 1989

He said, "I have been in this hospital for a long time and this is the first time I have seen anything like this."

I still have my award. Rider had it framed and it is in my studio.

I had therapy at the hospital and at home. The young man said he had never been so bored because I had memorized all the exercises and did them without his prompting. Instead of telling me to push harder he had to tell me to take it easier.

I had started to write to Tom's mother in Las Cruces, New Mexico, after she had written to thank me for being a surrogate mother to Tom. We had visited his mother and father on one of our vacation trips. She sent us a clipping about Silver City, New Mexico, being a good retirement town. We visited there three times in different seasons, and, when Rider retired in 1989, we moved to Silver City.

Our home is wonderful, and we keep busy doing volunteer work. At last the two fortune teller's prophecies came true. My happiness did come to me when I was in my later years.

We have been asked why we bought such a large home. We had to. Both of us are pack rats. When I was convalescing from my first knee implant, we moved here. By himself, Rider packed every single thing in the house. This book could not have been written if Mother and I had not kept so many of my clippings and the many, many photos. I never had time to "go through" things to throw them out.

One of the first things we did after we were settled in our new home was to attend the clubs we both were associated with. We were each installed into offices. At first, I was a secretary to two different senior clubs.

Then I bought a computer because Rider thought I should write about all the experiences he was hearing from me. I had fun learning how to use a computer and how to write a book. It has been a joy and a challenge to compress my life into these few pages, digging up the wonderful memories and writing them down. Rider's eldest son, Steven, is still in San Diego with his wife Tracy, their four-year-old boy Trevor, and their lovely daughter Abigal. Matthew, Rider's younger son, is currently studying at the university in Wilmington, North Carolina. Tanya, Rider's mother, passed away just before her hundredth birthday, a few years ago.

My brother Alton died of a heart attack while caring for Henrietta, who had Alzheimer's disease. Now she is gone, and my family is composed of my nephew Douglas and his very talented wife Diane. They live in Prescott, Arizona. She is an artist and author of children's books. He is an excellent photographer, and his photos enable her to draw and paint lifelike images for her paintings and books. They both enjoy traveling and they make motor trips all over the country. I enjoy hearing about their backpacking experiences.

Because of arthritis and two knee implants, plus a right hip implant, dancing is not so important to me anymore. I enjoy seeing others dance and bask in the reassurance Rider gives me. He tells me, "You have passed the knowledge of dance to thousands, and they all thank you for it." In fact, just recently, I was asked to teach dance to two teenagers preparing for the upcoming Miss America contest. I enjoyed working with them in spite of my handicaps. They were both good students. One of the students was Miss Grant County Teen-ager and went on to become Miss New Mexico Teen-ager. She interpreted the soft shoe eccentric dance I had taught her in just the way I had wanted it done. She is an intelligent, beautiful girl and I understand she is on her way to a career in modeling, though she is still in her senior year at school.

When I hear the song, "Somewhere Over the Rainbow," which was one of my Mother's favorite songs, I like to think of her, somewhere, giving me her smile of approval once again and saying, "You have done a good job, Lucile, in giving our love of dancing to so many people."

I thank my Mother for raising me with a snug rein and for teaching me the golden rule, "Do unto others as you would have them do unto you." She also taught me that when I gave someone something, I should not have the other hand out waiting for something in return. Mother and I had good and bad experiences, and I believe the old saying, "This too shall pass away" helped us to keep faith in the future.

I added several more rules to live by. When something is lost or broken, I tell myself, "It belonged to me; it did not own me." This saves me a guilt trip.

I was not young when I read, "Love people for what they are, not for what you wish them to be." I wish I had heard that very good advice earlier. I've been so lucky to have had so much love given to me by pupils and friends throughout the years.

Religion has played a large part in my life. Perhaps I have not attended church as frequently as I might have, but I have always felt I had my own church in my heart. As a small child I began to say my prayers every night. I say a prayer at other times, too, when I am troubled. I ask Him for help. If my prayers are not answered, I know there is a reason, and I try to accept what I have been given.

When I did something that turned out to be wrong, I did not allow myself to brood over it. In my mind, I examined the reason for having done whatever I had done. Then I resolved never to do it again. So I would not agonize with a guilty conscience. I would visualize "it," put "it" in a box, and put "it" into a closet. Then I did what usually happens when you put something in a closet, I'd forget about "it."

I have this in three places in my home.

MAY GOD GRANT ME THE SERENITY
TO ACCEPT THINGS I CANNOT CHANGE,
THE COURAGE TO CHANGE THE THINGS I CAN,
AND THE WISDOM TO KNOW THE DIFFERENCE

Two times in my life I heard a voice and felt my Guardian Angel watching over me. I am thankful to Him for giving me joy and happiness in my life. From the time I became conscious of the world around me, the world has become an entirely different place. The inventions that would have been thought of as wild dreams have become real. It has been a fantastic time to be alive. As for my dance career, instead of fame and money, I have had my love for dancing, and it has given me a full and wonderful life.

356

Dancebag Publications
3420 Royal Drive
Silver City, New Mexico 88061